A Grandson's Inh

A Grandson's Inheritance

admirals, farmers, merchants and a gun-runner

Max Peberdy
Felicity Evers
Alyson Peberdy

2011

First published in Great Britain 2011 by
Max Peberdy, 5 Lowther Hill, London SE23 1PZ

British Library Cataloguing in Publication Data.
A catalogue record for this book is available from the British Library
ISBN 978 0 9567837 0 7

Cover photographs from top left clockwise:
Ethel Betteley Garnett (née Billing); Lady Violetta Ingleby-Mackenzie and
Surgeon Vice-Admiral Sir Alexander Ingleby-Mackenzie at the Queen's
Coronation, 1953; Thomas George Evers at the Calcutta Races circa 1924;
William and Emily Wall on the Packington Hall Estate circa 1914.
Centre: Farman biplane, the type of plane used by John Longstaffe to
carry guns from Texas to the revolutionaries in Mexico, 1911.
*Back cover photograph of the authors and grandchildren
by Neil Palmer, John Palmer studio, Early, Berkshire.*

Copy editor: Robin Haig

Typeset in 11.5/13 pt Garamond
by Anne Joshua, Oxford
Printed in Great Britain by Information Press Ltd, Oxford

for

Alexander and Felix Evers

CONTENTS

ACKNOWLEDGEMENTS

Many people have helped us to research our ancestors and write this book. Family members recalled their memories and provided photographs and we give very special thanks to Angus Mackenzie-Charrington, Bruce and Marie-Ann Evers, Hilary Evers, Elizabeth Pearce, Carol Shuter and Roger Burrows.

We drew upon accounts that some family members had already written: Robert Peberdy's research into the early Peberdy families in Saddington; Angus Mackenzie-Charrington's paper on his father's naval career; Violetta Ingleby-Mackenzie's family tree of the Mackenzie line back to the seventeenth century; Freda Owen's recollections of her Welsh childhood in Caernarfon, and Tim Evers's description of school days at prep school and Winchester.

There were occasions when our research *got stuck*. Either we couldn't get further back with a family line, or were faced by a puzzle we could not solve. When this happened we called upon the help of professional genealogists: Sara Scargill worked on the Inglebys; Ruth Simpson on the Yorkshire Evers and the Bradford Unnas; Vanessa Morgan on the Warwickshire ancestors; and Geoff Dewing on the army and navy records held at the National Archives.

Thanks must also go to the staff at libraries and record offices, specifically at the Society of Genealogists; the India Room at the British Library; the Leicestershire County Records Office; and the Framework Knitters Museum. A special mention needs to be made of Malcolm Tovey for sharing his encyclopaedic knowledge of the Leicestershire Fire Service and archive materials.

Four people gallantly read early drafts and gave valuable comments on content, accuracy and style, though any errors persisting remain entirely the responsibility of the authors. In this context we acknowledge the help of Morag Peberdy, Leisl Osman and Robert Peberdy, and the copy-editor Robin Haig. Anne Joshua exhibited huge patience and skill guiding the production of the book through the design, typesetting and printing.

The greatest acknowledgement goes to Morag and Angus Evers who provided us with grandsons and thus the reason for writing the book, and finally to Alexander and Felix for accepting the gift.

INTRODUCTION

This book is a gift for two grandsons, Alexander and Felix Evers. It describes their *inheritance,* but not an inheritance of land, property or money, all of which they might well prefer, but an inheritance of biology and culture. It is a book that attempts to describe the people who have contributed to their genetic makeup, and the social and historical events that shaped their ancestors. The story is much broader than an account of the dozen or so people in the last few centuries who have shared their surname. It gives an account of the 80 to 90 family lines that have contributed to the genetic network that eventually manifests itself in two small boys living in London.

Most children have four grandparents. Of course the identity of a grandparent may not be known, and for many children one or more of their parents' parents may have died even before they were born. But with only a few exceptions, such as Egyptian Pharaohs, it is almost universal that we have parents who in turn had parents, with the result that each of us has four people who are our grandfathers and grandmothers.

For Alexander and Felix their four grandparents are Kenneth, Felicity, Max and Alyson. For better or worse their genes are derived from their mother and father, Morag and Angus, who in turn inherited their own biological roadmap from these four people. The aim of this book is to go back seven generations – about two to three hundred years – and identify the names of these genetic forebears and to discover something about their lives. Seven generations takes us from parents to grandparents; and then to great grandparents; great, great grandparents; great, great, great grandparents, great, great, great, great grandparents; and finally to great, great, great, great, great grandparents and to the mid to late eighteenth century. The number of these ancestors doubles each generation, and at the seventh generation back there are 128 great[5] grandparents who have contributed to Alexander and Felix's genetic profile, and 252 ancestors in total over the seven generations. Well, in theory that is the case, but real life is messier. In the 1870s a set of first cousins in Alyson's family married, and as first cousins they shared a common grandmother and grandfather, the consequence of which is to reduce the potential number by two, to a mere 250 ancestors (our boys were robbed!).

Figure 1: Back seven generations

When we started the research we knew very little about any of these people, even the ones who had lived in the previous 50 years, so it has been exciting for us to learn about our forebears, and to understand the derivation of some of our attitudes and behaviours. To research 250 people was ambitious and eventually we had to settle for the identification of 203. Though official records in the UK are very good, and it is relatively easy to find out quite a lot about people born after the 1830s, some of the grandparents were born elsewhere in Europe or worked in India, and it was these two categories who make up the majority of the missing 47. But such problems are also potential opportunities and the shortfall may provide Alexander and Felix with hours of occupation to identify unknown ancestors and so demonstrate that they can beat us even on our home ground of family research.

Identifying such a large group of people has enabled us to do two things: firstly, write about some interesting characters (it would have been very unlucky if the 203 had all proved to be deadly dull), and secondly, to see how the big historical events and social forces affected their lives and impacted on the material well-being of the different families. There are no prime ministers, national heroes or notorious criminals among the 203, but there are two admirals, one of whom was present as a naval captain when Napoleon surrendered in 1815; merchants who established businesses in India; sportsmen who broke records on the racecourse and cricket field; a gun-runner who was one of the first to use the newly invented aeroplane to smuggle weapons into Latin America; and men who, though less colourful, contributed to the world as judges, farmers, doctors, firemen, police officers, hosiery workers and vicars. Of course half of the ancestors are women, and though few had careers outside the home their lives are also interesting and the book attempts to tell some of their stories.

But identifying a relatively large group of ancestors over almost three centuries has also enabled us to see some of the historical processes at work and how societal change affected the fortunes of the different family lines. The world of the seventh generation back ancestor was very different from the world of the grandparents writing this book: the agricultural revolution and the Enclosures; the coming of the railways and the opportunity to travel; industrialisation and the movement of rural families into the towns; the growth of Empire and the trade that followed the flag; the social and educational legislation that gave universal access to health services and schooling; and the upheaval of two world wars with the terrible consequences for individual families and the challenge to the old order of things – these things can all be seen working themselves out in the lives of the 203. It makes history real, as these events are not just accounts in books about long-gone people we cannot identify with but changes that led to who we are today. Some of these big historical happenings were very good for our ancestors and it is interesting to see how social mobility carried some of them upwards, and others down.

It is obvious, but it needs to be said, that a history of previous generations can only recount the things that have been recorded, survived and then revealed. To write outside this is speculation and guesswork. The history of the forebears is thus the history of what we have been able to find out about them, their names, dates of birth, marriage and death, occupations, where they lived, and some glimpses of events in their lives. Far more difficult to discover, and for many of the ancestors impossible, is to know what they were like as people. Where they clever or dull? Witty or boring? Adventurous or cautious? Friendly or prickly? Just sometimes their personality does appear, like the young man in 1819 (a great, great, great, great grandfather) who was asked in his application to join the Honourable East India Company whether he had bribed anybody, and replied *'Certainly not!'*.

The main sources of information for those who lived before the great grandparents are the official records of birth, marriage and death, church baptisms, and the ten yearly household census returns that began in 1841. In addition we have been able to draw on registers of professions (for the grandfathers who were doctors, dentists, lawyers and clergy); old school records (not only the famous public schools year books but also village school attendance records); trade directories, military records, newspaper accounts, personal diaries, and the final documents of all, wills and inventories (the methodology is outlined in Appendix A).

For two of the family lines – the Peberdys and Garnetts – it is only the recent generations that moved away from quite specific geographical locations: the Peberdys in south Leicestershire, and the Garnetts in Northamptonshire. This has made it very easy to trace back the family trees to the early parts of the 1700s. With the Mackenzie line a great grandmother very thoughtfully wrote down the family lineage from the 1650s. However the Everses have proved more difficult, as their family network consists of a web of Scottish and English merchants in India who had the mobility to marry, give birth and die in either England or far away in distant places. We know what some of the ancestors looked like as some portraits and miniatures exist for the early Victorians, while from the 1890s there are family photographs. For more recent generations we have been able to use oral history, that is the anecdotes and stories that the older members of the families have related. In the last part of the book each grandparent has told the story of their life (or at least those bits they are willing to share with two grandchildren!) and these give a much more personal picture of what it was like growing up before the Second World War, and during the years immediately after.

Seen as a whole the seven generations are like a complex river system, where small brooks join streams that feed into rivers that eventually reach the delta and the open sea. The four main rivers have the family names of the four grandparents: Evers, Ingleby-Mackenzie, Peberdy and Garnett. Each of these river courses and the grandfathers that carried the surname has been traced back seven generations, but of course each married and the wife moved from her family to join this new river. So in addition to the four main families it has been possible to identify more than 80 family lines that have also contributed to Alexander and Felix's genetic makeup. These are the rivers that flow into the four main watercourses – this is shown in Figure 2 (with all the family names listed by generation in Appendix B).

The chapters of the book are structured around the four genetic rivers – Angus's parents Kenneth Evers and Felicity (née Ingleby-Mackenzie) and Morag's parents Max Peberdy and Alyson (née Garnett). Though the analogy of a river system is easy to understand, it is an inaccurate explanation for why Alexander and Felix have particular genes because unlike streams that feed into rivers and thus increase the volume of water, each generation does not acquire more and more genes; instead the newly created life recombines its parents' genes to produce a set unique to each child. The exceptions are the y-chromosomes inherited from the father and the mitochondrial DNA that is passed down from mother to child. So following the river upstream from Alexander and Felix to their father Angus, and then back to John Evers born in 1745, gives us the route that the x-chromosome has followed but of equal interest is the maternal line from Morag Peberdy to Ann Holmes, a little girl in 1815, the year of the Battle of Waterloo, who, skipping over the Derbyshire Hills, was the holder of the mitochondria that now enables each of the two grandsons' millions of body cells to work.

In writing this family history we became aware of how lucky we were to be able to identify so many of the ancestors. In talking to others about our project a frequent response was *I wouldn't be able to do that because . . .* and then a range of reasons emerged from a parent or grandparent being found as a baby abandoned on London Bridge; coming from a country where the records have been destroyed or never existed, to key family members killed in the Blitz with nothing known about their past. The Everses, Ingleby-Mackenzies, Peberdys and Garnetts have been relatively easy to research as all followed convention and got married before they had children (well, almost all), they infrequently divorced or separated, never ran off, stayed most of their lives in one occupation, and kept going until a decent age. They could almost be described as boring but fortunately two things have mitigated this description; firstly, that though they were respectable they often had brothers, sisters or children who did foolish, but interesting things. And secondly, the two World Wars thrust ordinary men and women into some extraordinary situations.

Though the four families lived through many of the same historical events and social changes, these forces impacted in different ways. The Everses had lived for many generations in the isolated Yorkshire Dales, but with industrialisation and the arrival of the railway, they moved across the Pennines to Manchester. Two generations later they lived in Essex and had jobs with overseas trading companies in London. The eldest son took ship to Calcutta, returning 25 years later, a rich man who bought a country manor house in Wiltshire and rode to hounds. The Inglebys and Mackenzies became one in 1832 and three generations of doctors followed. The last in line became a Surgeon Vice Admiral and accompanied the young Queen Elizabeth from her Coronation in Westminster Abbey. For at least five centuries the Peberdy family lived in the rolling grassland county of Leicestershire. They were reasonably well off yeoman farmers until they lost their land at the time of the Enclosures. Two generations of shepherds and livestock men followed until the 1880s

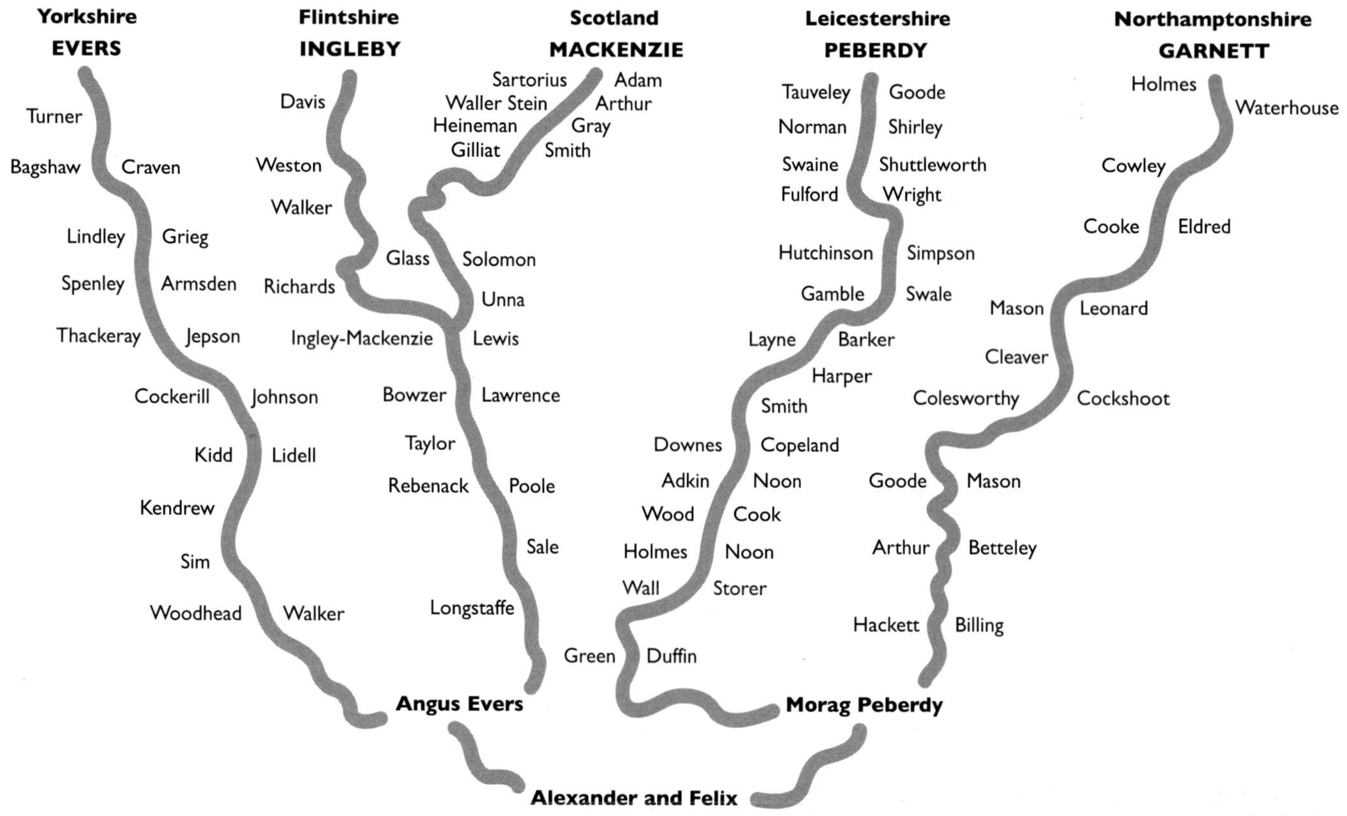

Figure 2: The Four Family Rivers

Yorkshire EVERS
Turner, Bagshaw, Craven, Lindley, Grieg, Spenley, Armsden, Thackeray, Jepson, Cockerill, Johnson, Kidd, Lidell, Kendrew, Sim, Woodhead, Walker, Longstaffe

Flintshire INGLEBY
Davis, Weston, Walker, Richards, Glass, Ingley-Mackenzie, Bowzer, Taylor, Rebenack, Poole, Sale, Lawrence, Lewis, Unna, Solomon

Scotland MACKENZIE
Sartorius, Waller Stein, Heineman, Gilliat, Smith, Gray, Arthur, Adam

Leicestershire PEBERDY
Tauveley, Goode, Norman, Shirley, Swaine, Shuttleworth, Fulford, Wright, Hutchinson, Simpson, Gamble, Swale, Layne, Barker, Harper, Smith, Copeland, Downes, Adkin, Noon, Wood, Cook, Holmes, Noon, Wall, Storer, Green, Duffin, Goode, Mason, Arthur, Betteley, Hackett, Billing

Northamptonshire GARNETT
Holmes, Waterhouse, Cowley, Eldred, Cooke, Leonard, Cockshoot, Mason, Cleaver, Colesworthy

Angus Evers
Morag Peberdy
Alexander and Felix

Figure 2: The Four Family Rivers

when they moved into the city. The Garnetts followed a similar course, from cottage industry workers in Northamptonshire in the early 1800s to a move by the end of the century to an industrialised village on the edge of Leicester.

One of the interesting things that exploring a large number of grand-parents has enabled us to do is answer some of the questions that start – *how old were they when . . .?* How old were they when they got married, had children, retired and of course, died.

They were a respectable lot; they did things in the proper order – they got married, and within a year or less had their first child. Comparing the date of marriage to the date on the child's birth certificate shows that sometimes it was a close run thing. Of course it is difficult to discover what people don't want others to find and the Victorians and Edwardians were clever at disguising things they wanted kept secret. For at least one great, great, great grandfather and mother it has taken hours of research to fathom out exactly who had married who and when. But in the Alexander and Felix ancestry the vast majority of children were born a suitable interval after the wedding day.

Until quite recently marriage has been the basis of family life and an important determinant of material well-being. It is difficult for us today to appreciate just how dependent a woman was on her husband; her social and economic standing was the mirror image of her husband's position. Virtually none of the grandmothers had a paid occupation after they married and it was not until the 1950s that a few trailblazers combined marriage with a career. Grandmothers from a middle-class background remained at home up to the time of marriage and acquired the skills needed to manage the running of the house and servants. In contrast if she were from a poor background living in the country she would help bring up her younger siblings and then go into domestic service. Or if living on the edge of an industrial town like Leicester, they worked as framework knitters or in a hosiery factory until marriage but after that cooking, washing and child rearing was their life.

For women therefore, marriage came early – the average age among the grandmothers was 23 (see Appendix C, Table 1). Interestingly, this average is consistent across all four family lines, with just a slightly higher age of 25 for the Everses. This average also held true across the generations, with a grandmother born in the 1700s being as likely to marry about this age as a women born in the 1800s and first part of the 1900s; it wasn't till the 1960s and the universal availability of contraceptives that the age of marriage starts to rise. Generally the poorer the grandmother's background the earlier her marriage, but even among the rural Peberdys and Garnetts less than a fifth married younger than twenty.

The grandfathers' picture is more complex. The average age at marriage was 28 but for the Peberdys it was 25 and for the globetrotting Everses it was 30. Among small farmers and agricultural workers the choice of partner was quite limited, but they did have access to a tied cottage and so could marry relatively young. For the Everses out in India they needed to establish their careers or business before it was possible to set up home. For example seven of the men on the Evers family line in India did not marry till their mid to late thirties. It was also the case for some of these merchants that this was a second marriage, their first wife having died.

How old were the grandparents when they left the river course leading to Alexander and Felix and became part of the ancestral records? Well, surprisingly old. A child born today in the UK can expect to live to 79 but the average child born a century ago would not have made it past 50. Yet these statistics are misleading because most of this difference is due to the changing rate of mortality among children. Even in the 1700s and 1800s if you survived to your fifth year, and certainly if you got into the teenage years, you could well live into your eighties and even nineties. By definition Alexander and Felix's grandparents made it to adulthood, married and reared surviving children. On average death came to the men at 68, and to the women at 71 (see Appendix C, Table 2), but very many lived into their eighties. Perhaps surprisingly, the grandfathers born in the eighteenth century lived longer on average (77) than those born in the nineteenth century and first part of the twentieth century (65) though for grandmothers there is a slight difference in favour of the later centuries. The explanation may be that the oldest grandparents were living in the rural areas and during a period of relative prosperity, whereas the later generations of men were employed in unhealthy work environments and during a time when it was socially acceptable to be a heavy smoker.

For many ancestors it has been difficult to find the date when they died, especially in the later part of the nineteenth century when there was greater mobility within Britain and to and from India. Thus the average length of life figures for our ancestors are based on quite small numbers and so firm conclusions cannot be drawn. But having said that it is still interesting to compare the four family lines to see who comes out on top! It is the Evers grandfathers and grandmothers at an average age of 76, followed by the Garnetts at 71, Peberdys at 69 and Ingleby-Mackenzies at 67.

It is time to read the book. There are nine chapters. The first four take each of the family lines and describe what the research discovered. Then in the next chapters the grandparents tell their story; Kenneth died before this project got underway and so we have tried to write the story that he might have recounted. The final chapter brings it all together – an impossible task, but we have attempted to identify the themes and events that led to where we are today. This book is primarily for the next generations. Alexander and Felix are young and may have little interest in reading about the old men and women who came before. But perhaps when they reach our age, in about the year 2060 they will pick up a dusty copy (a book by then may be a curious form of communication) and wonder at the lives their forebears led.

PART ONE

The Four Families

To give the mundane its beautiful due.
John Updike

CHAPTER 1

Evers: Seven Generations

Alexander and Felix have the family name *Evers,* and of all the ancestral lines it is this one that probably holds the most interest to them. There is a family belief that the Everses may have descended from Huguenots, but going back seven generations to the mid eighteenth century does not give any support to this idea. The early Everses came from North Yorkshire, and lived in the village of Thornton in the North Riding, about three miles west of Pickering. The derivation of the family name is confused. As with the name Peberdy the records give many different spellings (depending on how the vicar or curate thought it should be spelt). Thus the surname is written as Evers, Evor, Eure and even Evans. The first record of the surname is found in 1221 as Euers and it probably derived from the Anglo-Saxon Efer or Eofor, meaning either a wild boar or a dweller at the edge of a hill.

The name was present in the area for many centuries. In 1330 a William Eure (Evers) was a bailiff of Sir Ralph Hastings while in the next century there is an account in 1498 of medieval violence involving the Everses (*Thornton le Dale,* Reginald W. Jeffrey, West Yorkshire Printing, 1931, p. 119). Sir Roger Hastings was an unpopular landowner in Thornton. He was attacked by 'his enemies' as he and his wife were riding through the village. All the villagers came out to watch in the hope that he would get his just desserts but he escaped and fled home. The following month a second incident happened, this time led by Sir Raif Ivers (Sir Ralph Evers), who:

having ascertained the date of his return, waited for him at Brompton to murder him. But Sir Roger had sent his servants in advance. Coming out from concealment Sir Raif cried 'ye false hirson . . . I shall learn ye curstesy and to know a gentleman' and thereupon set an arrow to his bow saying 'And ye master were here I would stoppe hym this way'.

This account of the intended murder was denied by Sir Raif, who in turn accused Sir Roger of going 'beyond the common law and pretending that his actions were according to ancient custom'. One accusation was that Sir

Roger had 'enclosed the fields of Thornton . . . to the great hurt of the King's tenants'. The outcome was a happy one for the Everses as the unpopular Hastings family, as in all good children's stories, left Thornton, never to return! The Everses were landlords themselves, and there is a record dating from 1542 of the family living in Dereham Grange in the Thornton Marishes, an estate partly in Thornton and partly in Pickering.

By the mid 1700s our line of Everses were more humble folk. Going back seven generations brings us to **John Evers**. He was born in 1745 in Thornton. When tourism began in the nineteenth century, Thornton won the title of 'most beautiful village in Yorkshire'. To distinguish it from other Thorntons it became known in the late 1800s as *Thornton Dale* and then a *'le'* was added in the early twentieth century (to give it a more upmarket image). It is a big farming parish with moorland and limestone. By the time John was an adult the village had a population of about a thousand.

John Evers was an agricultural labourer. In 1767, when he was 22, he married Ann Spenley. Neither could read or write and they signed the marriage register with an 'x'. Ann lived in the adjacent village of Ellerburn and was eight years older than her husband.

The Spenleys were also a well-established local family, who had been farmers in the area from at least the start of the 1600s. By the standard of the time the Everses had quite a small family, probably because Ann was already 30 when she married. They had four children – Ann, John, David and George. The first son, John, died when he was just seven. The family remained in the village and both parents lived into a good old age, Ann dying first in 1823 aged 86, and John in 1827 aged 82.

George Evers, the third son, was born in 1778, and it was George who entered the trade that he and then his son, were to follow for the next 80 years – carpentry and joinery. In the village there were four joiners: William Allanson, Thomas Moody, Robert Simpson and George Evers. We can only guess as to why George became a carpenter rather then staying on the land, but one reason may be that Thornton's fields were enclosed as a result of the local Enclosures in 1789 and again in 1795. This would have resulted in many small farmers losing their land and a reduction in the need for agricultural labourers. George married late – he was 35 – but unlike his father he married a woman much younger than himself – Eleanor Cockerill. Eleanor was just 21 and together they had 10 children: William, Jane, Mary, Ann, Thomas, John, Eleanor, Henry, Robert, and Benjamin (Alexander and Felix have

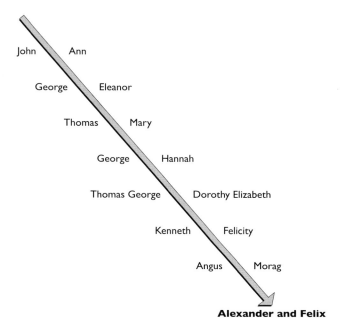

John   Ann

George   Eleanor

Thomas   Mary

George   Hannah

Thomas George   Dorothy Elizabeth

Kenneth   Felicity

Angus   Morag

Alexander and Felix

Figure 3: The Seven Generations of Evers

a lot of distantly related Evers cousins out there!). Eleanor was a local girl and her family also had a long ancestry in the area. Henry Cockerill, for example, had been fined four pence in the fourteenth century for cutting down an oak tree in the village and carrying it away. Thornton was growing. By 1831 the population was 1,368. Besides the parish church there was a Methodist chapel and a free grammar school. The school had been built by Lady Lumley to give 'free instruction in grammar to all children in Thornton when they can read the English Testament'. And it may have been here that George, unlike his father, learned to read and write. There were also twelve almshouses for poor aged villagers.

Eleanor died in 1854 (aged 62) and George in 1864 (aged 86). They both left wills, though the amounts of money were small even by the values of the time; less than £50 when Eleanor died and less than £100 for George. By the time of their deaths two of their children had also died. Robert at the age of 13 and Eleanor at 24, and it was their daughter Mary who had to sort out the probate. By this time Mary had married a local farmer and was Mary Weetman.

To Manchester

Thomas Evers was the eldest son of George and Eleanor. He was born in Thornton in 1824 and followed his father's trade, but he did not stay in the village. It wasn't just Thomas who moved away, because in the 1840s and 1850s the population of Thornton declined. It was improved transport and communications that led many younger people to leave. The village had been quite isolated up to this time; for example in very bad winters the roads would be blocked with snow from November to March. Even in the early years of the nineteenth century there was only one stagecoach a week. But things changed in the 1840s with the arrival of the railway and this gave easy access for the first time to York and Scarborough. Some time about 1850 Thomas left to take a job in York. At 27 he was still unmarried and lodging in Soothill. But he was soon to meet the young Mary Kendrew who was working as a servant. She was a Yorkshire woman, born at Cowthorpe, a village a few miles west of York. Her father William and her mother Ann Thackeray were both Yorkshire people, her father being a farmer cum agricultural labourer and then a joiner. Perhaps it was through joinery that Thomas came to know the Kendrew family. Thomas and Mary married in 1853 and moved across the Pennines to Manchester. It is likely they moved because Thomas had found joinery work in the city. They did well. Thomas's youngest brother Benjamin (who was 15 years younger) lived with them and Thomas had set up his own business.

They soon had a son, George, and then eight more children, all born in Manchester: Agnes, Eleanor, Edith, Mary Ann, Thomas Cockerill, Grace, Alice Jane and William (yet more distant Evers cousins!). The business thrived and by 1871 Thomas was employing two men, and they had servants to help in the house. By the turn of the century he and Mary had retired to Chorlton in Manchester. Thomas is described on the census as a retired builder. Living with them was their youngest son William, who was unmarried and working as a merchant clerk. Thomas died in 1907 at the age of 83. He had made his will in 1885 some 22 years before his death so he was obviously a man who had concern for his family and planned ahead. He left £3327 13 shillings and 4 pence – a sizeable sum in the nineteenth century. His main instruction was that Mary should have an adequate pension and he directed that sufficient money be placed in Government bonds to give her a weekly pension of £3 10 shillings. After her death the estate was to be divided equally between their children.

The Evers family line leading to Alexander and Felix was taken forward by their eldest son **George Evers.** He was born in 1854 and didn't go into the family business. Instead he became a shipper's clerk, and by so doing prepared the way for his son and grandson to go off to India and do very well (but that is still some years away in our story). In the mid nineteenth century Manchester and its not too distant neighbour, Liverpool were centres of industrial production and the gateways to the markets all over the world. Thus there were plenty of jobs going in the administration of overseas trade. In 1875 George married Hannah Woodhead. Hannah was working as a servant in Manchester. Her father, George Woodhead had originally come from Whitwell in Derbyshire but like thousands of other rural people had moved into the big city to find work. At the time of his daughter's wedding he was a glasscutter. Hannah's mother was Sarah Kidd, born in 1817 in Chorlton cum Hardy in Lancashire

It is likely that by this time the Everses were Methodists. Hannah's parents were members of a Wesleyan chapel and so Hannah was brought up in this tradition (her second son William Evers eventually being ordained as a Methodist minister). The Woodheads can trace their line back many centuries in Whitwell (till at least the 1650s) and its possible that George Woodhead left Derbyshire, not simply to find work in Manchester but because he was illegitimate – a stigma that probably made it quite difficult to marry a Whitwell girl. His father – John Jepson – did eventually marry George's mother Clarissa Woodhead but as George was originally baptised with his mother's maiden name he obviously decided to remain as a Woodhead.

A lost opportunity – George Evers lived in Manchester in the early part of his life and as a young shipper's clerk would have worked either in the city itself or in Liverpool. Also living in the area and just four years younger was Elizabeth Cockshoot, an ancestor who enters our story a little later. Elizabeth's father was a coachbuilder and driver and, given that the Everses were joiners, it's even possible that the Everses may have done work for the Cockshoots. The family history could have been very different if instead of marrying Hannah, the 21-year-old George had met, perhaps at the Manchester or Liverpool Chamber of Commerce Christmas Ball, and fallen in love, with the (possibly) stunningly beautiful Elizabeth. But this didn't happen and so it was George's great grandson Angus Evers who eventually courted and married Elizabeth's great, great granddaughter Morag Peberdy thus bringing together the 'y' and 'x' chromosomes that make up Alexander and Felix. If things had worked out differently then these two sets of genes could have been united 128 years earlier!

George and Hannah had two sons and two daughters: Thomas George was born in Beswisk in Lancashire in 1877; William was born next in 1883, Grace in 1884 and Nellie in 1886. There is a four-year gap between the first child and the second and this may be because George and Hannah took an important decision; they moved south to Essex.

Essex

They lived first in Leyton, and this is where William, Grace and Nellie were born. It seems likely that George made the move from Manchester to take up a more senior job. By 1891 he is described as a 'clerk to a coffee merchant'. The family is reasonably well off and can afford to have at least one live-in servant and Thomas George attended Salway School in Leyton.

By 1901 the family had moved further east to Prittleswell (just to the north of Southend on Sea). George is still with the coffee merchant, but Thomas George has left home, and William is a sorting clerk and telegraph worker. It seems likely that father and his younger son William commuted up to London each day by train. George and Hannah remained in Essex until after their retirement, and George, like his father, grandfather and great grandfather, lived to an old age – George dying in East Finchley (47 Park Hall Road) in 1947 when he was 93. His will had been made eleven years earlier in 1936. He left £6119 7 shillings and 4 pence, and like his father his main concern was to ensure that his wife would be financially secure. Interestingly, in his will he instructed that after Hannah's death the estate be equally shared between their youngest son William and their daughter Grace. There is no mention of Thomas George – he may have felt that his elder son had become so wealthy he didn't need any further provision. Thomas George had become rich, but sadly as things turned out he was to die five years before his father.

To India

In each of the four grandparent family lines there is a *character* that stands out as somebody who has taken a different course from their own parents and grandparents. **Thomas George Evers** was a man of drive and talent. Even with the limited amount of biographical detail that exists, the things that we discovered show him to be an exceptional person.

T. G. Evers, or *Tom* as he was known to his parents and siblings, and *Timothy* Evers as he liked to be known later in his life, went out to Calcutta as an assistant in one of the many British owned 'agency houses'. It's not known exactly what year he arrived in India but his name appears on the list of residents for the first time in 1899 (when he was 22). He stayed for a quarter of a century, had tremendous sporting success and settled back in England in the 1920s as a very rich man. He was the right sort of person in the right place at the right time.

During the 80 years or so before the young Evers set sail for the East huge changes in world trade had come about. The 'old markets' of Europe and North America were overtaken by the emerging markets of Africa and the Far East. In India the Honourable East India Company (EIC) had lost its monopoly of trade after the 1857 Mutiny and it was the merchants of Glasgow, Liverpool and Manchester who were to develop the evolution of the agency houses. Thomas George worked for a number of these companies, the first being Shaw, Wallace and Co.

The term *agency house* originally implied nothing more than a company that did business on behalf of another company, and most firms in British India started as representatives of local manufacturers or merchants. But gradually during the nineteenth century a core of richer firms used their capital to develop into much larger companies with many different interests, and 'agency house' came to refer to these bigger mercantile organisations. At the start of the nineteenth century manufacturers in Manchester and Glasgow began to see the potential market in India for selling the goods that the factories in these two cities were producing at rates never achieved before. When trade was freed from the control of the EIC it was Scottish and northern England businesses that sent out agents to manage the sales in India.

Thomas George married into one of the Scottish merchant families – the Walkers. Much of the expansion of Far Eastern trade was the work of Scottish family groups, the reason being that most of the early exports to the east were textiles and it was Glasgow, and Scottish merchants in Liverpool, rather than Manchester, that led the trade. Initially the ships returning to Britain brought back indigo, silk and jute. In the 1860s tea came onto the scene. This was the period of the 'tea mania' when almost every retiring British official in India (army officers, civil servants, engineers etc) set up and ran a tea plantation. The demand for agencies to sell the tea also increased. After the opening of the Suez Canal in 1869 and the extension of the telegraph to India, the old style of merchant companies began to change. Business became faster and more competitive, and the agencies started to specialise – in jute, tea, cotton, wheat, rice, teak, coal, ships, distilleries, and in the building and running of railways.

By the time that Thomas George arrived in the late 1890s the biggest houses had become successful because they had discovered 'good management'. They recruited talented young men who could run a business. Entrepreneurship and management were the principal ingredients for growth but not the only ones. Another was the flow of capital from London and the trading houses became major investors in jute mills and collieries. But that brought risk and two of the biggest agencies went bankrupt in 1906 but fortunately not the one that employed TG. After a period with Shaw and Wallace, Thomas George worked for Thomas Cumberledge and Inskip and then J. Thomas and Co. This company was an agent for indigo, tea, jute, and jute fabric. There was a marvellous directory produced each year that listed everything a British person living in India would ever want to know. It was called *Thackeray's India Directory* and ran to more than a thousand pages. It listed all British residents and TG is recorded as living in the heart of Calcutta.

Work was only part of his life; he also threw himself into the sporting and social activities of the city. Almost as soon as he arrived he joined the Calcutta Light Horse as a trooper, and served on a part time basis, from August 1899 to 1916 when he left for England to take part in the Great War. He was a good rower (and won a cup in June 1901) but he excelled at riding. Many of the surviving photographs are of him on horseback either riding out with friends, or more impressively winning races at the Calcutta Race Course.

The world of the British in India was a very distinctive culture and Thomas George, leaving England that first time in the late 1890s, would have had to learn very quickly how a European in late Victorian society needed to behave. Precedence and knowing one's place were important, and the rules were all clearly laid down. The *Thackeray's Directory* devoted many, many pages to listing orders of precedence, and everyone from the Governor General and Viceroy at the top, through the 21 mahajaras, senior civil servants, army officers, bankers, merchants and those in trade, knew just where they fitted and what protocol demanded in terms of who sat next to whom at dinner.

If you wanted to know whether an Inspector of Smoke Nuisance was higher than a Junior Settlement Officer you had only to look it up. (Charles Allen, *Plain Tales from the British Empire*, 2008.)

The days of quick fortunes had gone but the agency houses offered adventure and prospects to the right sort of young man who was ready to take responsibility and could survive the harsh baptism of a 'first tour' of four or even five years without home leave. Accounts at the time give a picture of what it may have been like for TG:

The majority of the British in India . . . were businessmen, some contracted to the old-established trading companies or to newer industrialised concerns, some working in the large city emporia, others working as managers or engineers in tea or coffee or jute. It was often said that theirs was not the 'real' India, but in terms of numbers they were in fact the most representative of the British in India; young men who came out as junior assistants. Until the air-conditioner turned the office into a refuge from the hot weather it was more often a shuttered, silent and somnolent place, where the only sounds were the creak or the whir of the punkahs, the fluttering of papers under large quantities of paper weights, the scratching of pens of the babus and the soft padding of the chaprais's bare feet as they circulated files or cups of sweet, milky tea. (ibid pp. 227–228.)

Calcutta was already a very big city. When T. G. Evers arrived there were more than a million people. In 1912 the political power shifted to Delhi but Calcutta remained the pre-eminent business centre of the country. As the 'most horrible city' in Asia it had no serious rivals with poverty and huge overcrowding as more and more rural Indians came to the city seeking work. For the Europeans it was also a 'city of gulfs' where nobody knew anybody outside their own particular sphere. On one side of the Hoogly River was British Calcutta, a world apart from the areas where Indians lived. Here were the government buildings, the cathedral and the racecourse. The residential areas reflected the social divisions – there was the old parts of Central Calcutta where palatial house had been built and around them the new buildings and blocks of flats where the young men from Britain, like TG, lived when they first came out. As you got more senior and you wanted a tennis court and rooms for more servants, you moved further out to the suburbs. In the early years TG lived in a chummery – a household shared by three or four people and a cook.

Thomas George was good at sport and that is the key to understanding the great success he had out in India. Sport was more than just a pleasant pastime:

Sport was the great thing in the old India, an obsession that had its roots in the dread that unless one kept fit one would catch 'some dreadful disease or other'. It thus became a credo of British India that to indulge in some sort of physical exercise was essential – particularly in hot weather – and the result was a generation or two of enormously fit people who went in for every sort of game and every sort of sport . . . (ibid p. 120).

TG had a gift for riding and training horses. He had joined the Calcutta Light Horse when he first arrived. It was a volunteer force consisting of about 300 men and in terms of sport provided an alternative to hunting, the mounted paper chase. Specially designed courses and jumps were prepared, a paper trail was laid and riders went out in competing teams very early in the cool of the morning to get to the finish in first position. But the place where TG had his real success was the Calcutta Race Course. There were many clubs in the city but membership was very strictly controlled. As a member of the Calcutta Light Horse he was eligible to join the United Services Club, and working for an agency house gave him entry to the Bengal Club. Most newly arrived young men joined the Saturday Club which was the social club for dancing, squash, swimming and generally an active social life. Next there was the Tollygunge Club on the outskirts of Calcutta, a very select club with a six-year waiting list, which had a golf club and a racecourse. The first record of him winning a race is in 1907 on *Geebung,* then more winners in 1910, 1911 (*Highland Fling, Pathfinder*) and two in 1915 (*Larkspur* and *Archie Hall*).

Marriage and the Scottish Merchants

Not all his time was spent working and riding – in 1914, just at the outbreak of the War, he married. He was 37. Today that seems quite old for a first marriage but it was not at all unusual in India during that period because most young men could not afford to keep a family on the low salaries that they got early in their careers. A second reason was the scarcity of young European women. Most British families sent their children back home for their education, so eligible young girls were far and few. Many would come out to visit their parents at Christmas and stay for two or three months. They came out by boat, usually in the late English autumn and the young unmarried men referred to these P&O liners from Southampton as the *Fishing Fleet.* The ideal catch was a beautiful daughter of a wealthy family. For the young women who returned without finding a husband the boat back was known as the *Returning Empties.*

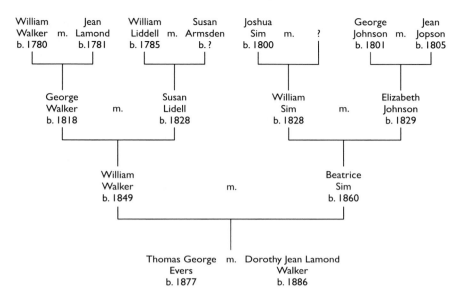

Figure 4: The Scottish Merchants in India

Thomas George married well. Dorothy Jean Lamond Walker was 28 and from a wealthy Scottish family; W. Walker and Company were merchants and bankers in Madras. It was Dorothy's grandfather, George Walker, who built up the business in India. He was born in Glasgow in 1818 and from the 1840s to the end of the century travelled back and forth from Madras. His father, William Walker, had been a manufacturer in Glasgow and it seems likely that George had originally gone to India to act as an agent to sell Scottish-made goods. His mother, also Scottish, was Jean Lamond and this is obviously where Dorothy got her middle names. George Walker married Susan Liddell in 1847 in Madras. Susan's father William Liddell was another Scottish merchant, having worked in India from early in the nineteenth century (thus giving Alexander and Felix many Scottish ancestors down this genetic line and not just through the Ingleby-Mackenzie family line). Susan's mother, Susan Armsden, was from a Lincolnshire family; her parents had married in Boston in 1815.

Thomas George married into this large extended Walker family. Dorothy's grandparents, George and Susan, had ten children, some born in Scotland, some in Madras and some in London: Susan in 1848, then William, George, James Lamond, Lamond, Annie, Alice Lamond, Robert, Alfred and Gertrude. By the 1860s they had a big house in Wimbledon (246 Woodslea, Cottenham Road) with five servants and

Plate 1.1 Madras 1914: the marriage of Thomas George Evers and
Dorothy Jean Lamond Walker.

many gardeners. Dorothy's father was the first son, William, who had
been born on the beautiful Scottish Isle of Bute in 1849. He married
Beatrice Sim, who was from another long established merchant family
based in Madras and Bombay. Beatrice had been born in Ambleside in
Westmoreland (1860) and it seems likely that her father died when she
was quite young as she and her mother, Elizabeth Jane Johnson, lived with
her Johnson relatives in Westmoreland and then Liverpool. Refreshingly
her mother's family were not merchants! Her father had been a Scottish
physician with a practice in Cockermouth in the 1840s and 50s, but both
Elizabeth's parents had also died when she was quite young.

The War

Thomas George and Dorothy were married in December 1914 at the
Cathedral in Madras. For a short period TG resumed work in Calcutta,
and their first child, Elizabeth Jean was born in September, but it must
soon have become obvious that the War that many believed would be over
within months was going to need all the resources of the Empire to defeat
Germany. He and Dorothy took the ship back to England and TG
volunteered for the Army.

By January 1916 he had joined the 2/1 Essex Yeomanry and applied for
a commission. He was appointed as a second lieutenant. His application
helps us to picture him. In terms of physique he was created to be a jockey

Plate 1.2 Dorothy presented at Court – about 1905.

– just under 5 feet 6 inches tall, weight a little over 8 stone (115 pounds) and chest 34 inches. He had 'not suffered from any serious illness . . . had no mental or bodily infirmity, or physical imperfection . . . was of pure European descent . . . had good vision without glasses . . .' and the only distinctive mark on his body was a 'small scar on top of head'. He was passed as 'fit for military service'.

   Some of his initial training was on Salisbury Plain and he was based for four months at Netheravon. Dorothy and their baby daughter were living with her family in Wimbledon but she was able to spend some time with him in Wiltshire and on one visit she stayed at the Dog and Gun Inn at Netheravon, which by coincidence, ninety years later, became the local pub of the Peberdy family when visiting their cottage in the adjacent village.

   The Essex Yeomanry was on home defence. In September 1916 they were based at Leybourne Camp in Maidstone, and by 1917 had become a cyclist unit. We can imagine that with TG's love of horses this was not likely to meet with his approval. Early in 1918 he joined the 38th Central India Horse in France. They were not involved in any major action at this time and in February they were sent to Egypt to become part of the 4th Cavalry Division, and for the remainder of the war the Division fought in Palestine. They were engaged in a number of battles: in April and May the

Plate 1.3 Thomas George and Dorothy riding out in the early morning
before the Indian sun becomes too hot.

Second Trans-Jordan Raid, and then in September in the final offensive –
the Battle of Megiddo and the Capture of Damascus. After the war the
Division was selected to remain in Palestine as an occupation force.
However, demobilisation started before the end of 1918 and by May
1919 most units had left. The entry on TG's war record states '1st
February 1919 Embarked at Port Said for UK'.

   He had travelled all the way from the security of India to help defend his
home country, and had played his part to the full. We can imagine the
wrench of being apart from his wife and daughter and not knowing
whether he would ever see them again. Throughout this time he carried a
small piece of paper in his wallet on which was written a sentiment that
guided many of his generation. It is a line from the prayer of St Ignatius: *To
fight and not to heed the wounds* . . . a piece of paper that his third son,
Timothy, still treasured more than 80 years later.

Plate 1.4 Thomas George returns to England to enlist in the
2/1 Essex Yeomanry, 1916.

Return to India

When he got back to England he saw for the first time his son – Kenneth
Austin Evers – who had been born in Wimbledon in September 1918.
The family took the boat to Calcutta and Thomas George continued
work as a tea broker, with even more success at the race course. In 1920 he
had major wins on *Cracksman, Way of an Eagle, Cinnamon* and *Linton*.
More wins followed in 1921, 1923, 1924 and 1926, and the *India
Planter's Gazette* duly recorded his wins, seconds and thirds. His record
was quite remarkable. He rode more than 150 winners and set a record at
one meeting of winning five of the six events on the card. As a national
paper reported in 1926 when he was about to return to England:

Mr Tim Evers was beyond all question the hero of the Monsoons. He rode
ten winners, trained three and captured R's 5,150 in stakes. I doubt if this
record has ever been approached by any amateur in Calcutta. It is delightful
to be able to say that the guerdon in every case was thoroughly deserved. If

Plate 1.5 Back in India after the war, Thomas George continues
his success at the Calcutta Races.

Mr Evers was the darling of the gods, he was also the pet of the public. The latter backed his mounts with confidence, for he was always out to win and he aimed at the goal with all the skill he possessed. I think his best performance were his own horses, trained by himself, namely Yusylas and Craigendorrie, but whenever he secured the verdict it was by dint of accomplished horsemanship. He is one of the best amateurs I have known in this country, his form in the saddle recalling the early glory of Captain Conran. He goes home shortly and is offering Yusylas, Craigendorrie and Reha for sale at prices which seem to offer a great chance of remunerative investment. I cordially wish him godspeed . . .

In 1922 Dorothy had her third child, another son, Thomas Hugh. It's not known why they decided to move back permanently but it may well have been because they had three young children and didn't want to be separated. All European families faced this dilemma:

For the first years of childhood there were few shadows . . . But the real threat to happiness was something that no English parent with children born in

India could ever forget. 'When my first son arrived . . . I looked at him and thought – Oh dear you'll soon be five or six and then I will have to take you home and leave you there and be separated from you' . . . The regular exchange of weekly mail provided a frail link between parents and children that weakened as every month and year went by. (ibid pp. 17–18.)

TG retired from J. Thomas and Company in March 1926. The Indian staff presented him with a scroll inside a silver container. Their words are moving while at the same time capturing something of the relationships between the two nationalities: 'We repeat no conventional language when we say that your going away will create a great gap in our midst as your proverbial magnamity, your genial sympathy for the poor struggling Indian Assistants, your interest in their welfare, your constant efforts to ameliorate the conditions under which they exist have won for you the hearts of all.'

Making a Home in England

The family bought a large, but dilapidated house, Hill House, in the Wiltshire village of Little Somerford. They had it renovated and Thomas George became a country gentleman. He continued his passion for horses

Plate 1.6 Hill House, Little Somerford, Wiltshire.

Plate 1.7 TG out hunting with the Beaufort.

and hunted with the Beaufort. He was active in the local church and was a churchwarden. The boys went off to Abberley Hall School in Worcestershire, as the headmaster was a family friend, and then on to Winchester. Jean went to Finishing School. But then tragedy struck. Dorothy was diagnosed with cancer and died, aged just 52, in 1938.

That family tragedy was terrible but in the world outside the walls of Hill House things were also looking very grim. It was obvious to most that war with Germany was probably inevitable. TG's eldest son, Kenneth, was just finishing at Oxford and volunteered for the Army. Jean had returned from Finishing School and invited Elisabeth, one of the mistresses, to stay with the family in Wiltshire. Elisabeth was half French and half German. She and Thomas George fell in love and married. The war broke out in September 1939 and the fourth Evers child, Timothy, was born.

In February 1942 Thomas George was taken ill with cerebro-spinal meningitis and died. He was 65. It must have been a huge shock to all the family, and his youngest son was still just a baby. It is appropriate that the final words about this quite remarkable man should come from his younger brother. William Evers was ordained in 1907 as a Methodist minister. He, like his brother, had left England, but to be a missionary, first in Kingston, Jamaica, then on the Turks Islands and finally in Panama. He

Plate 1.8 Thomas George shortly before his death in 1942.

had returned in the 1930s to be a minister in Huddersfield and in a
number of towns in eastern England (retiring in 1950). On hearing of his
brother's death he wrote the following letter to Elisabeth:

Rev W. H. Evers
18 Grange Road
Bishop's Stortford   February 24th 1942

My dear Elisabeth
    Grace phoned us the grievous news of Tom's passing yesterday at midday.
We went immediately to Finchley and saw the parents. They were very sad
but their extreme age has left them less acutely sensitive to such an
overwhelming sorrow. He was a loving son and all through his life was
entirely faithful to both Father and Mother. He was a wonderful brother to
me. Being five years my senior I always looked up to him with awe: he has
helped me far more than he ever realised I think. I admired his strength of
character. His directness of purpose, his brave spirit, & all those qualities of
mind & heart that made him the man he was.

But we think of you and his family. We are glad to remember that you had these last years together. They were supremely happy years for him and they certainly centred in yourself. Yours is the greatest loss & I wish I could comfort your heart. I believe that these days of bitterest sorrow will bring the assurance that your mutual love still binds your lives together: that the grief will be assuaged in the consciousness that the earthly presence though unseen is still real and truly living & helpful; that the strong gracious life which you have shared is not out of reach.

May God himself comfort your hearts.

Marie sends her loving sympathy with mine in this dark hour.

Yours sincerely

Will

Elisabeth and young Timothy left Hill House but remained in the village for a few years. Timothy grew up and went off to Winchester and Elisabeth retired eventually to Bath. The Evers line that leads to Alexander and Felix continued with **Kenneth Austin.** His story comes later.

CHAPTER 2

Ingleby-Mackenzie:
the Coming Together

Alexander and Felix's paternal grandmother is Felicity Evers, but before she married Kenneth her maiden name was Felicity Ingleby-Mackenzie. Alexander has inherited at least one thing from his paternal great grandfather, and probably many others, but we can be sure of one as among his Christian names is *Mackenzie*.

The Mackenzie line and the Ingleby line came together in 1832 when John Andrew Mackenzie married Ellen Ingleby in Walthamstow Parish Church. The Inglebys were wealthy and the Mackenzies were descended from a distinguished Scottish family.

The Mackenzies

In the 1950s Felicity's mother, Violetta, drew a family tree that named the Mackenzie ancestors back to seventeenth century Scotland. Looking at census data and births, deaths and marriage records it has been possible to confirm that the things she recorded are accurate.

Scottish history is complicated – very complicated, especially for a non-Scot. There are arguments and counter arguments as to the origins of the Mackenzie clan. Some claim that the family are descended from an Irish aristocrat, Colin (Cailean) Fitzgerald whose ancestor was a certain Otho and a member of the retinue of William the Conqueror. Many discount this and claim that it was a Highland leader called Kenneth in the 1460s, whose son John was the first to be known as Mackenzie; in Gaelic he was known as *Ian Mac Choinnich,* 'John son of Kenneth', but this name could not be pronounced by those not speaking native Gaelic. The closest foreigners could get was Mac Coinni or Mac Kenny which when written became Mackenzie (the z having the same sound as a y in the fifteenth century).

Violetta's family tree takes us back to the mid seventeenth century. This was a period of great upheavals. Charles I attempted to impose the

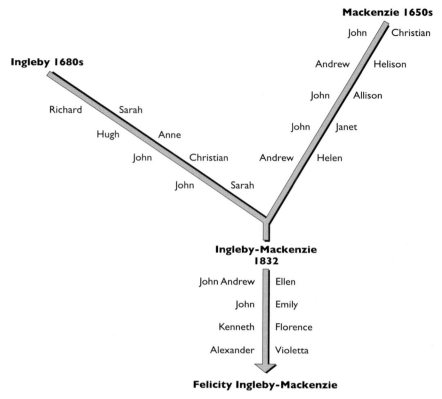

Figure 5: The Ingleby Mackenzie Line

English form of worship into Scottish Calvinist and Presbyterian churches. Not surprisingly the Scots didn't think much of this and resisted. The third Lord Mackenzie of Kintail (a certain George Mackenzie) had always been loyal to the King but even he joined those who opposed what Charles was foolishly attempting. There were many prominent and titled Mackenzies at this time.

A distinguished Mackenzie was Sir George of Rosehaugh (b. 1636, died 1691). He was born in Dundee and became a lawyer and politician. His uncle, another George, was the second Earl of Seaforth. As a lawyer, he was involved in 1661 and 1662 with the 'witch-hunt' trials, when more than 600 people were accused of practising witchcraft. Though George didn't deny the existence of witches he believed that popular superstition and hysteria should not lead to unfair trials. In 1666 he was chosen as advocate for Dundee and was knighted. He rose rapidly in his career and in 1677 became Lord Advocate. He was very loyal to the Crown, and as unrest in Scotland became widespread his strong resolution to maintain the law led to his unenviable nickname of 'Bluidy Mackenzie'. He published many books and papers, not just on legal subjects but also political theory; he insisted, for example, that the authority of the Scottish monarchy was 'divinely ordained, absolute and irresistible'. His books were very influential, and Oxford University praised him for the service he had done to the King by his writings. In 1678 Charles II publicly thanked him. However he fell out of favour with the next King (James II), and in 1689 he was forced to move to England, eventually settling in Oxford. But he was not to live long, and in 1691 he suffered a haemorrhage, and died.

This is where it gets complicated. George Mackenzie had married twice and after his death his surviving son from his second marriage, another George, succeeded to his father's estate but he died shortly after without any children. The estates then went to his second daughter from his first marriage – Elizabeth, who by then was married to Sir James Mackenzie of Royston. So it seems unlikely that the Ingleby-Mackenzies are directly descended from 'Bluidy Mackenzie' but it is possible that the line is related to his uncle, the Earl of Seaforth. The evidence for this comes from Violetta's family tree. Her earliest reference to a direct ancestor is to **John Mackenzie** (who would have been born about 1650):

John Mackenzie came down from the North with Lady Mary Mackenzie of Seaforth. Not known who his wife was. He had a son, Andrew Mackenzie.

John is said to have been a shipowner. Research into the old marriage records reveals that he married Christian Adam about 1674 and they had seven children (Christian, Andrew, Alexander, Katherine, George, John, and William). It is **Andrew Mackenzie** who takes forward our family line. The only things we know about Andrew was that he was born on 1st April 1676 at Torryburn, on the north bank of the Forth river, and that he married twice; first to Alison Arthur on 27th January 1703 and then to Elizabeth Seller in 1720. Andrew had a son from the first marriage, and this son, **John Mackenzie**, married Alison Stein, the daughter of a rich Scottish distiller, on 14th March 1742 at Alloa near Clackmannan. They had a son also called John. This **John Mackenzie** married Janet Glas in Stirling on Christmas Day 1764. She was the daughter of the Provost of Stirling and five years later they had a son called **Andrew Mackenzie**. This Andrew married Helen Gray on 15th July 1801 in Dundee, where he worked as a merchant. Helen's father was deceased and she gave the place of her birth as Ballygaray.

They left Scotland for London. It seems probable that Andrew had his business in the heart of the city. At the turn of the nineteenth century there were six London merchants with the name Mackenzie but only one Andrew and he was described as a 'distiller', living in Darby Street off Drury Lane. A few years later he had moved to South Street, Finsbury Square. The child who was to begin the Ingleby-Mackenzie dynasty, **John Andrew Mackenzie**, was born on 14th July 1804, and baptised a few weeks later at St Luke's Church, Old Street, Finsbury. His brother William was born the following year and a sister, Catherine, in 1808. John became a merchant like his father and when he was 28, he and Ellen Ingleby, applied to the Archbishop of Canterbury for a special licence to marry (usually this happens when the couple are marrying in a parish where neither of them is residing). On 10th April 1832 they were married at Walthamstow, in Essex. Today it is part of Greater London but in the early nineteenth century it would have been a quiet rural community, ideal for taking the stagecoach into London for a weekend ball.

Plate 2.1 St Mary's Church, Walthamstow where John Andrew Mackenzie married Ellen Ingleby on 10th April 1832.

The Inglebys

Researching the Inglebys has been challenging, partly because they were a large family with many business interests across both England and Wales, but also because cousins, sharing the same surname, married (a Miss Ingleby married a Mr Ingleby to become a Mrs Ingleby).

Oral family history has a belief that the Inglebys came from Yorkshire and that there was a connection with a *Lowkland Hall*. The surname is a North Riding name, most commonly found around Ripon. Lawkland is near to Austwick and has been the home of Inglebys for many centuries. The most famous Ingleby was Sir Thomas, one of the Justices of the Common Pleas in the reign of Edward III. He founded Ripley Church and there is an Ingleby connection to Ripley Castle. He died in 1415. The Inglebys were a strong Roman Catholic family up to the seventeenth century, and in fact a Frances Ingleby was hung, drawn and quartered in York in 1586 for his Catholic faith. He was beatified by Pope John Paul in 1987 so if this Ingleby is *one of ours,* then we have a saint in the family!

However research back to the late seventeenth century doesn't find any direct connection between the Yorkshire Ingleby line and the one that joined with the Mackenzies, though it is possible that before the mid 1600s the family had come from Yorkshire. Ellen Ingleby's father John Ingleby (born in 1781) was a silk manufacturer in London, while her mother, Sarah Richards (b. 1790) was quite a wealthy women in her own right, as she had inherited income from her mother's family, the Walkers, who owned property in the Dorsetshire town of Poole. Like many children at that time the young Ellen experienced tragedy as both parents died when she was still young. Her mother died, probably in childbirth, when Ellen was eight. The family were living quite close to St Paul's Cathedral, in the parish of St Matthew in Friday Street (the street name still exists but not the church). Father and daughter were alone, but within a year John had remarried and with his new wife moved out of London to Walthamstow. But when Ellen was 14 (in 1825) her father died.

This is where it gets complicated. Ellen went to live with her father's younger sister Mary Ingleby. The Inglebys were a large extended family. Ellen's father John had been the son of a John (born in 1749 and married to Christian Weston in Coventry in 1779); this John's father, Hugh Ingleby, was born in 1723 in Halkyn in Flintshire, and his father, Richard Ingleby, born about 1685, had a mining business in North Wales. Richard and his wife had many sons and daughters but one of them, Thomas Ingleby (b. 1711) had moved to Cheadle in Staffordshire, and his son William Ingleby (b. 1747) had married Ann Tomlinson and was part owner of a copper mining business in the county.

When Ellen was orphaned she moved into her Aunt Mary's home. Mary Ingleby had married William Ingleby's son Rupert in 1815, and hence Miss Mary Ingleby became Mrs. Mary Ingleby. Rupert Ingleby was also a silk manufacturer in London, so we can guess that the families had been very close – possibly even in partnership. But when Rupert's father died he inherited parts of the copper business in Staffordshire, and it seems likely that the family moved from London to Cheadle. Rupert, like his father, was one of the early industrialists who provided some of the essential materials needed to power the revolution that was taking place in the heart of England. The industrial revolution was pioneered by men like Rupert Ingleby. He was a 'smelter of oar' at the time Ellen married John Andrew Mackenzie, and a few years later is described as a 'copper and brass merchant'. Rupert and Mary had eight children and by the late 1850s had retired to Billericay in Essex where the 1861 and 1871 Censuses describe him as 'a gentleman with income from a joint stock company'.

It is interesting to understand how the Inglebys built up these business interests. Rupert's father William Ingleby was born in 1748 in Cheadle and his wife Ann Tomlinson was from a Cheadle family. Ann's father William was an innkeeper while her mother, Jane Waller, was from Biddulph, to the north of Cheadle. William and Ann Ingleby had nine children, including four sons of whom Rupert was the second. The family owned both land and shares in brass and copper works. Cheadle has a long tradition of iron ore smelting, certainly dating back to the fourteenth century and probably well before. Furnaces became commonplace during the sixteenth and seventeenth centuries, and the industrial revolution provided the incentive to search for more ore. Water mills and then coke replaced charcoal as the source of energy to drive the smelting process. By the nineteenth century there was a huge expansion of coal mining in the area, with hundreds of merchants and lease agents organising the production and sale of the different commodities needed by factories all over the country.

The Ingleby family of William, his brothers and uncle and his own sons, had shares in several brass and copper works in Staffordshire, Lancashire and Flint. They were also farmers and owned Spout Farm (New Spout being an area close to Cheadle) as well as being partners in one of the largest brass works in the country. The original company was called the Old Spout Company before modernising its name in 1788 to the Cheadle Brass Wire Company. The Cheadle business had been established by Thomas Patten in 1734. Patten was an innovator, with the wealth to develop new technologies. Brass was a much needed commodity and Cheadle had extensive coal of the good quality that was needed in the making of brass. Patten employed experienced brass smelters from Germany and Holland and soon the business thrived and became extremely profitable. Some of the brass was made into ingots and sent chiefly to Birmingham brass foundries, while the brass that was to go

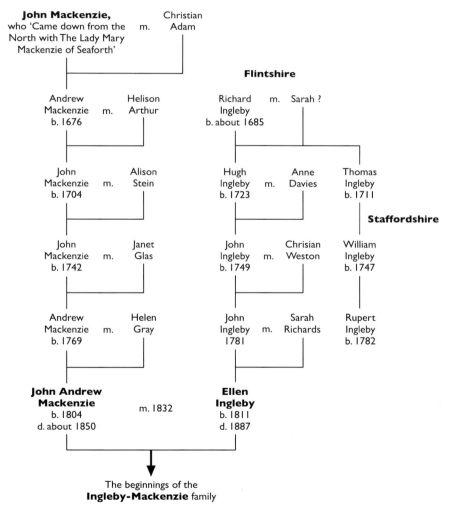

Figure 6: The early Mackenzie and Ingleby family lines

into wire was produced in sheets and sent to wire mills. The wills of the different Ingleby family members are full of details about the share proportions they held with Thomas Patten in many different companies. The companies flourished, though in the 1820s there was a difficult period when the records show that wages had to be cut (and probably dividends to the shareholders). The Cheadle works struggled on until the company was eventually dissolved in 1852. The works were then bought by Thomas Bolton of Birmingham who saw the potential in copper telegraph wire, and set up a new business, the Channel Submarine Telegraph Company, that subsequently thrived on the site for more than a 100 years.

Rupert Ingleby entered the family business and like his father and uncles had interests in a number of smelting works. When Ellen left his home to marry they were wealthy. He and Mary had a large family, and once they became rich and could live comfortably from their shares they did not stay in Cheadle but moved back south to Essex. It's not surprising that they preferred Essex to Staffordshire, because as the smelting industry expanded the pollution to the area became intense. As one of the Inglebys wrote in her diary:

It was dreadfully noisy from the foundry, the air was gritty, and everywhere there was an acrid, metallic, sulphurous smell which mingled with the gassy fumes from the coke they used for smelting. It burnt my nostrils and coated the back of my throat. And it was so dirty . . . The grass and hedges around the works were black with it, all the buildings around were blackened, it came into the house – you could even taste it in the food. (*Finding Susanna*, p. 148.)

The Ingleby-Mackenzie family: Three generations of doctors

At the age of 21, when she had *come of age* Ellen married; she chose as her church Walthamstow, the place where her father had died seven years before. She was well off. She had inherited money and income, not only from her mother and grandmother but also from her great aunt, the wonderfully named Fasby Walker, a spinster of Peckham Rye, who left her income from the Walker properties in Poole. So John Andrew Mackenzie had made a very good marriage. Two years and two weeks after their marriage John and Ellen Ingleby had a son – **John Ingleby**

Mackenzie. John was the first to have the new Ingleby family name, and the first in a profession that sons were to follow for almost a hundred years. John was baptised in the City of London at St Peter Le Poer on 21st April 1834. His father's occupation was given as 'merchant' and they were living at Providence Row in Finsbury Square. The father died when John was still young; the date is not certain but by the time he was 15 his mother was described as a widow and John was a private pupil in Kent, living in the house of Marshall H. Vine, Widower, and Perpetual Curate, Sholden'. John's mother and younger sister (another Ellen), were living close by in Ramsgate. Being a widow would have drastically changed Ellen's life. For a start, in respectable middle-class society even the way she dressed was prescribed. There were four stages: *first mourning* immediately after her husband's death when she would have worn lots of crepe on matt black; *second mourning* meant she could wear less crepe, and jewellery so long as it was jet; *third mourning* meant black without crepe, while the fourth stage was known as *half mourning*, and Ellen could wear white, grey or purple (but with black trimmings). So when John Andrew Mackenzie died Ellen had a year and a day in full mourning, nine months in second, three in black and six months in half mourning. That was the minimum but it was thought proper to linger over each stage.

John went on to study medicine, and became a Member of the Royal College of Surgeons when he was 22 (in 1858). He registered as a doctor the following year and then went up to Cambridge University to read for a MB, eventually being licensed with the Society of Apothecaries in 1863. It is not known why John decided to become a doctor but a possible explanation may be that it was through his mother's influence. Rupert Ingleby's younger brother (his mother's distant cousin) John Tomlinson Ingleby did not follow the rest of the male family into the copper and brass industry but instead became a doctor in Birmingham. 'Uncle' John Ingleby had been an assistant to the local surgeon in the Cheadle area but when he married (to a daughter of another partner in the Cheadle Brass Works) he moved to a practice in Birmingham, and he soon had a good reputation for specialising in 'women's complaints'. So it may have been his example that led Ellen to guide her only son into this profession.

It seems likely that when Ellen was widowed she looked to family members like 'Uncle' John for support. But Dr John died and this side of the family became embroiled in scandal. 'Uncle' John's only child was Charles Ingleby. He was a student at Oxford and was then ordained, becoming a curate of a parish not far from Cheadle. After a very short courtship he proposed to the daughter of a wealthy Staffordshire family,

Susanna Sneyd. They married, but within a few weeks Susanna had returned to live with her parents; in effect it was the end of the marriage. This was scandalous in itself, but it became known throughout the district that Charles had been violent to his wife after she had pointed out to him at the end of their honeymoon that he had not consummated the marriage. Terrible rumours circulated about the Reverend Ingleby, that he was not a 'complete man', and eventually he lost his parish and was dismissed from the local Clerical Society. The shame must have been almost intolerable. But Charles was wealthy and settled £100 a year on Susanna, rising to £150 after his mother's death. All the horrific details of the scandal are related in *Finding Susanna,* the excellent family history of Mrs Susanna Ingleby.

Once John Ingleby Mackenzie had qualified as a doctor in 1859, he obviously decided it was time to marry, because in September 1859 he proposed to the 19 year old Emily Eliza Rebenack. Her father like John's, had also died young; she had been a baby in Bombay when Captain Rebenack had died in the service of the Honourable East India Company.

The first Ingleby Mackenzie doctor

John was of the first generation of doctors that today we would just about recognise as being a doctor. Doctors at the start of the nineteenth century had an understanding of health and sickness not much altered from the beliefs held by Hippocrates two thousand years before. Pain was part of life and there were few, if any known methods of pain relief other than opium-based drugs or alcohol. A staggering statistic is that two thirds of children born in London at the turn of the century died before the age of five! The inquests on dead infants in 1837–8 shows that almost a third died primarily from being given opium as a way to stop them crying.

In order that surgeons could get training in anatomy the practice of digging up newly buried bodies and selling them to medical students was prevalent right up to the 1830s. However, the year that John was born the Anatomy Act was passed, which ensured that only properly qualified doctors and students could legally dissect bodies. The development of modern medicine was just beginning as John was studying at Cambridge. The first anaesthetics were being used (ether in America in 1846, and chloroform in England in 1847). By the time John qualified even Queen Victoria's doctors were giving anaesthetic at the royal births. Lister was pioneering antiseptics and was the first to use carbolic acid when amputating limbs. He also developed many new techniques in surgery, such as the use of catgut for sewing up incisions, while in France Pasteur was experimenting with the first vaccinations to prevent diseases like smallpox. It must have been an exciting time to be a young medical student, science was actually providing the tools and knowledge to do more good than harm!

Once John finished at Cambridge he and Emily moved to Sidmouth in Devon, where he took up a post of general practioner and surgeon. Why Sidmouth? It seems likely that his mother had relatives living in the town. The notorious Rev Charles Ingleby had once visited his wife's relatives the Sneyds in Sidmouth, and in fact Charles had proposed to Susanna when she was staying with them. Whatever the reason, it was in Sidmouth that the newly married John and Emily set up home. They had their first child within the year, Helen Ingleby Mackenzie, and then five sons, John, Kenneth, Colin, Rupert and Donald, and another daughter, Emily. They stayed in Sidmouth for 17 years. John's widowed mother and sister also moved to Devon and lived in Torquay. Mother and daughter entertained many of the Ingleby relatives in Devon. They were well off, but there is sadness here as John's mother Ellen died in Newton Abbot in 1887 leaving a sizeable inheritance to her daughter (more than £10,000). Ellen did not marry and lived all her life with her mother but died less than six months after her death.

John and Emily moved from Devon in 1880 to Rugby and another general practice. It's possible that for a few years before the move John was working at both Sidmouth and Rugby. This would explain why his two youngest children (Donald and Emily) are recorded as being born in Rugby well before 1880 and why Emily's widowed mother (Mrs Rebenack) died in Rugby in 1875. The final family move came in 1887 when John started working in a practice at Powis Square in London; then three years later he moved to another practice in Cavendish Square. But he was not to have long in this new practice as he died in 1892, aged 58.

Before moving on to the next Ingleby Mackenzie in the Alexander and Felix genetic line, it's interesting to explore the family that John had married into – the Rebenacks. Here there are some fascinating people who experienced famous periods of British history.

Rebenack and Sartorius

Captain Charles Coenrad Rebenack

Captain Rebenack was the father of Emily and therefore a great, great, great, great grandparent of Alexander and Felix. He was born in Bombay

on 5th April 1800; as a small child he was sent by his parents to England
to Stone Hall School in Bexley and returned to India as a young man to
join the East India Company in 1819. He was in the 25th Regiment of
the Native Infantry.

Charles was 19 when he applied to the Company for a cadetship and
was nominated by John Morris, one of the Directors. In his application he
explains that his parents are dead (both died in Bombay; his mother in
1807 and his father in 1817). His guardian is Major Goodfellow,
'residing in Bath', an officer in the Bombay Engineers. He reports that
he has studied mathematics at school. A glimpse of his personality (an
assured self-confidence?) is given by his succinct answer to the question in
his application:

Do you believe that any person has received, or is to receive, any pecuniary
consideration, or anything convertible, in any mode, into a pecuniary benefit,
on account of your nomination?
His reply: 'certainly not'.

He had to provide evidence of his baptism. This had taken place at
Cannanore (Bombay) on 19th May 1800 into the Church of England.
His younger brother, John Samuel Frederick Rebenack, applied for a
cadetship two years later. He had attended the same school but was
obviously a greater scholar as he reports that the 'nature of education' was
'classical *and* mathematical'. It's sad to think that both boys had left India
when they were very young and may not have seen either of their parents
again. Given that communication was by ship it must have been months
after their father died before they would have known.

Charles married Elizabeth Turville Bowzer (b. 1806 in Glamorgan) in
Bombay. The wedding was in April 1838 and their daughter Emily was
born in 1839. Charles's father was German (or to be more accurate from
the part of Europe we now call Germany) – Johannes Friedericus
Rebenack was born in 1775 in Zarbrucken (today spelt Saarbrucken).
His mother, Caroline, was probably also from the same city. Johannes
joined the East India Company, anglicised his name to John, and became
a captain in the Bombay Engineers. He was just 43 when he died in 1817.
He too had had to submit proof of baptism. The original document is in
German and can be found in the British Library, with an English
translation, attached. The documents explain that his parents were
Andreas Rebenack, Chamberlain of Zarbrucken, and Sophia Carolina
Rebenack (maiden name Sartorius). The city is in southwest Germany
and during the Napoleonic Wars it had been occupied by the French

from 1793 to 1815. Johannes was 18 when this happened. Was that the reason he left his native town and ended up in India – to escape Napoleon's soldiers?

Charles died within a few years of marrying. His military record is held in the British Library, and it reports that he was appointed an ensign on 2nd October 1819 and then a lieutenant a few weeks later on 15th October, but he then had to wait twelve years before he become a captain in December 1831. There is a brief history of his service and periods of leave in Bombay. He was appointed for a year to act as an agent for 'clothing the army' from October 1838, and then 'to act temporarily as Assistant Garrison Engineer'. He returned to regimental duties from August 1840.

He was then posted to Kotra in Bombay Province. An appraisal by his commanding office (Col. Marshall) read:

. . . that he highly appreciated the steady and soldierlike way in which he led the light company in the successful attack made on the 1st December '40 on the force of the Insurgent Brahooees near Kotra in the hills adjoining Culchee.

He survived this and four months later he was 'directed to proceed to Kotra to resume his appointment as Commissioning Agent at that station'. The final note on the report says: 'Died at Kotra 4th June 1841'. No cause of death is given. Did he sustain a wound during the attack a few months earlier? Or did he die from an illness? He was 41. His younger brother survived only five years in the Army and died in September 1826 – just 22.

Emily and her mother Elizabeth returned from India to live in England. There is only one census record that tells us anything about Elizabeth's life after her daughter's marriage. In 1861 she was visiting friends at Hendon. She died in Rugby in 1875, so it seems likely that she was living with or close to Emily and John at the time of her death. There are no other census or Births, Deaths and Marriage records in England during the Victorian period for any other Rebenack. It is a unique family name.

Admiral Sir George Rose Sartorius

When Charles Rebenack applied for a cadetship he was proposed by a director of the Company, but on 'the recommendation of George Sartorius'. This man was a naval officer who had been born in Bombay in 1790 (his father was Major John Conrad Sartorius of the Bombay Engineers). It looks likely that George was a relative of Charles. On John

Rebenack's original application to join the EIC the English translation of the German affidavit says that his mother's maiden name was Sartorius, so this suggests that George and Charles were related. There were a number of German families living in Bombay at that time; for example Charles's mother's maiden name Heineman. But whatever the precise relationship the Sartorius family and the Rebenacks were obviously close and appear to have a common German grandparent.

George Sartorius had a long and very distinguished life. He became an admiral of the fleet and three of his sons also became senior army officers, two of them winning the Victoria Cross. George entered the navy in June 1801 at the age of 11. He was a midshipman at 15 and fought at the Battle of Trafalgar on the *Tonnant 80*. Immediately after the battle he was placed with Lieutenant James Stuart on board the *Bahama,* a Spanish ship captured during the battle. He was promoted to lieutenant by the age of 18 and was in action protecting the Greenland fisheries and defending Sicily. He became a commander in 1812 and a captain in 1814 (and held this rank in 1819 when he supported Charles' application).

He saw lots of action but surely one of the things he must have recalled to his own grandchildren in later life happened in August 1815 when he was present at the surrender of Napoleon Bonaparte to Captain Maitland of the *Bellerophon.*

After the war his life took another adventurous turn when he commanded the Portuguese regency fleet for Dom Pedro against Dom Miguel from 1831 to June 1833 and was created Visconte de Piedade. His name 'was struck off' the English navy list but restored in 1836. He was knighted at Windsor Castle in 1841 and appointed as Captain of the *Malabar* in the Mediterranean from 1841 to 1844. He also received the honour of being a naval Aide-de-Camp to Queen Victoria. Many of his children, he had six, were born in Portugal during this period. He was made a rear admiral in 1849, admiral in 1861, and Admiral of the Fleet in 1869. He and his wife appear in the census returns for 1851, with a house in Hampstead, from where they moved to Lymington in Hampshire. He died in 1885 aged 94.

His three sons (all distant great uncles of Alexander and Felix) entered the army. Major-General Euston Henry Sartorius had joined the 59th Regiment in 1862 after training at the Royal Naval School in Woolwich. It was during the Afghan War that he was awarded the Victoria Cross:

Euston Henry Sartorius, Captain (now Brevet Major) . . . on 24 October 1879, in leading a party of five or six men of the 59th Regiment, against a body of the enemy, of unknown strength, occupying an almost inaccessible position on the top of a precipitous hill. The nature of the ground made any sort of regular formation impossible and Captain Sartorius had to bear the first brunt of the attack from the whole body of the enemy, who fell upon him and his men as they gained the top of the precipitous pathway; but the gallant and determined bearing of this officer, emulated as it was by his men, led to the most perfect success, and the surviving occupants of the hill top, seven in number, were all killed. In the encounter Capt. Sartorius was wounded by sword cuts in both hands, and one of his men was killed. From the wounds he received he partially lost the use of his left hand. (*London Gazette* 17th May 1881 as reported in '*The Victoria Cross 1856–1920*' Creash and Humphries 1920.)

His older brother Reginald also became a Major-General. He served during the Indian Mutiny and in the Kossi and Bhutan campaigns. During the Mutiny he was present at the Relief of Azimghur where he volunteered to carry dispatches through the encircling enemy lines. He succeeded but had his hat shot through and his head grazed!

He won his VC in Africa in the Ashanti War of 1873–74:

Reginald William Sartorius, Major of the 6th Bengal Cavalry . . . Act of Bravery 17 January 1874. For having during the attack on Abogoo . . . removed under a heavy fire Sergt-Major Braimah, Doctor, a Houssa non-commissioned officer, who was mortally wounded and placed him under cover. (*London Gazette* October 1874.)

He continued his career in India and was made a Major-General in 1895. He retired in 1897 and died at Cowes aged 66 in 1907.

The oldest brother must have been considered a bit of a failure as he neither rose to general nor got a VC. However, Colonel George Sartorius did serve in India and the Afghan Campaign and he had a passion for shooting:

Recreations – shooting in India and Africa, tiger in India, also biggest bison ever shot (horns across widest part 47 inches, height at shoulders 18 hands 1 inch) in Africa lion and buffalo.

He died in 1925.

The second doctor

John Ingleby Mackenzie's second son (and Alexander and Felix's great, great grandfather), **Kenneth Walter Ingleby Mackenzie** followed his father's profession. In one way he was the first *Ingleby-Mackenzie* because though John and Emily had given all their children the forename *Ingleby*, Kenneth used it as a surname. He may have done this so that patients would not be confused as to which Dr Mackenzie they were seeing. In all the medical registers John was Dr John I (or Ingleby) Mackenzie while Kenneth was Dr Ingleby-Mackenzie. This confusion could have been an issue when Kenneth first went into practice as he and his father worked together in London (33 Powis Square) for a short time from 1887.

Kenneth was born in Sidmouth in 1864. He studied medicine at St Barts, and was licensed as a doctor by the Royal College of Physicians in 1886 when he was 22. After working with his father he took up the post of house surgeon at the Royal Isle of Wight County Hospital, and then entered private practice (the National Health Service was still 57 years away) living in Ryde for the rest of his career. He was obviously well respected as a doctor and had a reputation for being 'very successful with children'. He held many posts during this time such as medical officer to the Island Volunteer Battalion and the Ryde Police Force. In the early years he did some work on the mainland, as he was an assistant at the Central London Ear and Throat Hospital.

Like his father he married very soon after qualifying. He was a committed Anglican and served on three occasions as churchwarden in the parish church, and this strong involvement may explain his choice of lifelong partner. Soon after arriving on the island he married Florence Sale; Florence was the niece of the Ryde vicar, Canon Poole.

Florence was a few years older than Kenneth; she was born in 1858 at Normanton in Derbyshire. Her father, Richard, was a land tax commissioner and the Sale family were well off farmers. Her mother Mary was a vicar's daughter, her father being the Reverend Alexander Poole, vicar of the not too distant town of Chesterfield. Mary's eldest brother was also called Alexander and he too became ordained. His first parish was at Clifton in Bristol, and then in the early 1890s in Ryde. Mary died very young, leaving Florence and her two younger sisters to look after their father (with the help of three servants). But when her father died it was to her uncle on the Isle of Wight that Florence turned; she stayed at the vicarage and when she got married it was Canon Alexander Poole who provided the Christian name for her first son.

Kenneth and Florence had two children, Alexander, born in 1892 and Keith, born in 1899. All their married life was spent at Ryde, much of the time in Lansdowne House which was a fair sized grey stone building close to the parish church. It had a big garden and stables where the car was garaged that he used to visit his patients. Besides work and his involvement in the church, Kenneth was very keen on all kinds of sport and eventually became president of the Ryde Sports Club. He rarely missed a football match at the local ground and often acted as the doctor patching up the injuries. This interest was obviously passed onto his older son and grandson, as both became noted sportsmen. The Victorians and Edwardians, for that is what this family of Ingleby-Mackenzies were, had a great love for membership of societies and clubs of all sorts. Kenneth was a freemason. He joined the Ryde Lodge in 1892 and rose to the office of 'provincial assistant grand director of ceremonies'. By 1932 he was honoured with the title of 'provincial junior grand warden'. Later in the century much scepticism, and even suspicion, of freemasonry became the accepted view, but for middle-class people who wanted to be active in their communities it was quite a normal and acceptable 'club' and we will see elsewhere in the ancestral line a number of other men who were freemasons.

The beginning of the twentieth century was a period of huge change but one event more than any other was to bring shock and sadness to the Mackenzie family and to millions of other homes – the Great War. Both sons went off to fight, but only one survived. Keith joined the Argyll and Sutherland Highlanders and was attached to the 16th Squadron of the Royal Flying Corps. He was one of the very earliest pilots. In May 1916 he was sent to the Military School at Catterick Bridge and learned to fly on a Maurice Farman Biplane. As a second lieutenant he went to France and just eleven months later, aged 18, he was killed. He is buried in the cemetery at Bois-Carre, near Thelus.

Keith's war records are held in the National Archives in Kew, and they give us something of an insight into his character. He attended Little Appleby School in Ryde till he was 11, and then went to Winchester College for a few years before moving to Repton. Like most young men he was in the Officer Training Corps at school and applied to join the Royal Military Academy when he was 16. When he applied to join the army he wasn't quite sure about his nationality. On his application he wrote that he was Scottish – perhaps an understandable exaggeration as he was applying to a Scottish regiment, but then he crossed it out and stated he was English. The Mackenzies had been south of the Border for more than a hundred years so it was pushing it a bit. His headmaster wrote a recommendation and said that though he had initially failed in maths and science his tutor reported he had 'improved greatly and would now qualify, I think'. He went on to say that he was as yet too young to be a

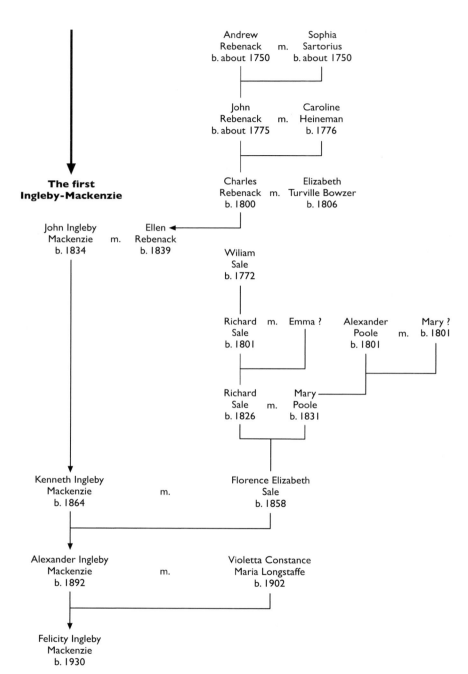

Figure 7: The Ingleby-Mackenzie family tree

leader but he had it in him. The application specifically asked about 'any special characteristic the candidate exhibits?'. The headmaster commented: 'a very pleasant person with very many friends; this type is best indicated by the fact that he is "dressy" and very careful of his appearance. But he is quite a sound person'. Because he was so young the application asked if it would be better that he stayed on at school a little longer before joining up, the headmaster answered: 'yes, except for the fact that like everyone he is very anxious to be doing his bit now'.

Immediately after his training in August 1916 he was sent to join the 5th Anzac Division in France, but by December he was appointed as a flying officer in the 16th Squadron. At Christmas he was given two weeks' leave and went home to Ryde. When they waved him goodbye on 6th January it was for the last time. Pilots did not live long – the average was a matter of days, not even weeks. The Squadron Record Book of his flights gives an insight to what he did as a pilot:

Counter Battery Patrol: flashes observed at . . .; three men seen on road; factory chimney smoking . . . six barges seen at . . .
Counter Battery Patrol Had to come down twice as aerial would not unwind; lorry on road . . .
Bomb Raid. Bombs dropped on railway sidings at Denain
Artillery Regn: 4.5 inch How on tramway
Bomb Raid; 112lb bombs dropped on Houbourdin railway yards.
Photography: Unsuccessful owing to camera trouble

And then on the afternoon of 8th April just a few words had been written on the record sheet:

Photography 3pm. Failed to return.

The shock of receiving the news of his death must have been made much worse as notification came in two parts. The first telegram stated:

Regret to inform you 2/Lt K I Mackenzie Arg & Sutherland Highlanders attach RFC 16 Sq missing April eighth. This does not necessarily mean either killed or wounded and any further news sent when received.

But another came shortly after:

Deeply regret to inform you that 2/Lt K I Mackenzie previously reported missing now reported killed April 8th. The Army Council expresses their sympathy.

Paperwork flowed back and forth between the army and his parents; official notification for insurance purposes, the description of the cemetery and perhaps the most bureaucratic of all, his final pay: 'Number of days' pay claimed 186; rate 12 shillings. Amount £111 12 0d.'

We can imagine the shock of receiving the news from the War Office. As a doctor Kenneth must have been called on many times to support grieving families after they had got a similar notification and like these families, he and Florence must also have been praying for the safety of their other child. Their eldest son, Alexander, did survive and, as his daughter relates in *Felicity's Story* they were to have many happy summers and parish church fetes together. Alexander's first son, Angus, remembers those summer holidays with Grannie Mackenzie (or Old Flo as she was known, probably behind her back). She was very High Church and the services went in for a lot of incense, which made Angus sneeze, and even years later he hated its very thought. Kenneth continued as the local doctor until his retirement; he died in June 1935. Florence lived for another three years.

The naval surgeon

Known as *Alec* **Alexander Ingleby-Mackenzie** followed his father and grandfather and became a doctor. After school at Repton he went to Trinity College, Oxford and read medicine. Also like his father he was very good at sport. He was a hockey blue, eventually becoming university captain. But he was a good all rounder – golf, tennis, and squash. There is an amusing story of his prowess on the running track. During a competition between the athletic teams of Oxford and their rivals Cambridge, the Cambridge captain confidentially approached the Oxford captain and suggested that as Alec was sure to win the 880 yard race there was little point in running it, so how about a practical joke. The Oxford Captain agreed and when the starting gun went off Alec sprinted out into the lead all the other runners turned round and raced round the track the opposite way. About halfway Alec met them coming towards him! The umpire was in on the joke so he pretended to disqualify Alec on the grounds that it was *he* who had gone the wrong way.

After Oxford he studied at St Bart's Hospital becoming a member of the Royal College of Surgeons in 1916, and he was licensed as a doctor in 1917. By now the Great War had been going for three years and as there was no obvious end in sight he joined the Royal Navy as a Surgeon Lieutenant at the age of 24. His younger brother had chosen the Army, but perhaps Alec joined the Navy because of the thrill of living as a child in Ryde and seeing the yachts and steamers passing around the island. During this time studying in London he had met Dorothea Twining (née Charington), whose husband, a member of the famous tea business, had recently been killed in France. They married in 1917 and for a short while had a flat in London but then Alec was posted to his first operational ship, HMS *Cardiff*. She was a light cruiser and was in a fierce action during November in the Heligoland Bight, off the coast of Denmark. Later she patrolled in the Baltic and had the honour of leading in the escort to the surrendered German High Sea Fleet at the end of the War.

The year 1918 must have been one of double joy for Alec; the war ended and his first son, Angus, was born. After the war he decided that he wanted to stay on in the navy, and in 1919 was posted to the battleship HMS *Iron Duke*, and then to another battleship, the *Queen Elizabeth*. But unhappiness was to follow when he and Dorothy divorced in 1923. This must have been a very difficult time, especially in view of the social attitudes to divorce during this period both within the Services and in wider society.

It was to be quite a long time before he was appointed to another sea posting, and so during the six years up to 1930 he held a number of short shore appointments. One consolation of being on dry land was that he could take part in sport. He represented the Royal Navy and Marines at cricket, tennis, hockey and squash; and not just playing but getting to national finals and playing internationally. In 1929 Alex married Violetta Longstaffe, the daughter of Judge Amyas Longstaffe, and the next year he was posted as Fleet Medical Officer East India Station in HMS *Effingham*. In September 1930 Felicity Jane was born in Colombo and baptised in the ship's bell (see Chapter Six – Felicity's Story). After the *Effingham* he had a shore appointment in 1932 as Medical Officer in Charge at Dartmouth College in Devon. In 1933 Violetta gave birth to a son, Alexander Colin David Ingleby-Mackenzie. Though Alec was good at sport his son (who was known by his second name, Colin) proved to be brilliant, Captaining Hampshire Cricket Club when they won the county championship in the 1960s and becoming President of the MCC.

After Dartmouth he was in the Mediterranean for a short period and then the RN Hospital in Plymouth. Rather inexplicably he decided to retire from the Navy in 1937 and became the secretary of the Union Club in Chelsea. But it was obvious that another war was looming and the following year he rejoined and was posted to HMS *Resolution*. At the outbreak of the Second World War he was Squadron Medical Officer on

Plate 2.2 Surgeon Commander Alexander Ingleby-Mackenzie and Violetta
at the time of their Presentation at Court.

HMS *Hood* and saw considerable action in the Atlantic and North Sea, and later in the Mediterranean in the famous Force H. He had a long period as Medical Officer in Charge of the Hospital Ship *Vita*, which took part in the capture of Sicily and the landings on Italy.

When the War ended he stayed on in the Navy and steadily rose in rank. In 1952 he was appointed Medical Director General Royal Navy as Surgeon Vice-Admiral, and later that year he was knighted and created KBE. There is a wonderful photograph of Alec and Violetta (Surgeon Vice-Admiral Sir Alexander Ingleby-Mackenzie and Lady Violetta Ingleby-Mackenzie as they had then become) in their coronation dress. It must have been a proud moment for them both to be present at Westminster Abbey to be part of the crowning of Queen Elizabeth. Two interesting notes can be found on his official Navy record: the granting of £30 10s. 0d. for alterations to his uniform at the time of the coronation; and that 'Name is now to be Ingleby-Mackenzie'. The hyphen was official.

On his retirement in May 1958 a banquet was given in his honour in the Painted Hall at Greenwich. His first son Angus was present and wrote a description:

This was an occasion to be treasured. The painted ceiling beautifully lit – the silver table ornaments with candles warmly reflecting in the huge U-shaped table, seating a host of uniformed officers from the three services, civilian and foreign representatives, flanked down the walls by a legion of pristine mess waiters in their white jackets.

Alec left the world of uniforms and mess dinners but it was not the end of his active life. Sir Hugh Beaver, the chief executive of Guinness, the brewers, invited him to become a director. He worked on the personnel and health side as well as taking an interest in the company's sporting activities in both Dublin and Park Royal in London. He became a committee member of the All England Lawn Tennis and Croquet Club and so had no difficulties getting seats for Wimbledon!

He died in January 1961 aged 69. He had led a full life and was a very talented man both physically and intellectually. He had been born at the end of the Victorian era, when very clear norms existed as to how fathers related to their children, and how much time they spent with them, and as a sailor he had long periods away. His children, Angus, Felicity and Colin, did not have the same opportunity to have fun with their father as Alexander and Felix have with their parents. It must have been especially difficult for Angus because after his parents' divorce he saw very little of his father. Much of this section on Alec's naval career has been provided by a short history that Angus wrote in 1988 (in order that his children and their children would know 'who was who in the zoo'). Angus's account of his father finishes with a moving reflection:

I must have confused the relationship even more when, with his full and ready agreement in 1939 on my 21st birthday . . . I added by deed poll the name of Charrington to Mackenzie . . . The outcome was that Admiral Sir Alexander Ingleby-Mackenzie worked for Guinness and Angus Mackenzie-Charrington worked for Charrington & Co, two brewery directors of different firms whose relationship was not realised by the world at large.

Few family lines have given so much to others or seen so many great historical events as this one. It is unlikely that Vice Admiral Alexander Ingleby-Mackenzie would have known that the famous Admiral Sartorius, who died a few miles across the Solent from Ryde, and just seven years before his own birth, was in fact a great, great, great, great cousin. Their two lives as sea-going naval officers encompass the period from the battle of Trafalgar to the dropping of the atomic bombs on Japan and the end of the Second World War; from a time when a ship's surgeon cut off limbs with nothing more sophisticated than rum, a saw and hot tar, to a modern hospital ship like the *Vita*.

It is Felicity who carries on the Ingleby-Mackenzie line, but before she tells her story the family tree needs to look at Felicity's mother Violetta and her fascinating lineage.

Unna, Lewis, Taylor and Longstaffe

Four family lines and two centuries of history have given Alexander and Felix a very interesting paternal grandmother – Felicity. Here are some of the stories of these great, great, great uncles and aunts, grandfathers and grandmothers.

The Unna family

Jacob Arnold Unna was one of the great, great, great, great grandfathers of Alexander and Felix. He was originally German, being born in Hamburg just a few weeks into a new century, on 5th February 1800. One of the early memories that he recalled to his own children and grandchildren was in 1813 when the city was besieged by Napoleon's army and eventually captured and occupied. His first job was in Hamburg as a 'confidential clerk' in a large commercial business (or *house* as they called them in the

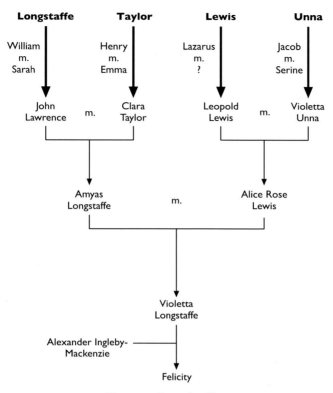

Figure 8: Four families

early nineteenth century). It was this job that brought him to England when he had to visit the cotton and wool markets in Manchester and Bradford. He was obviously good at his job and in 1836 S. L. Behrens, a company dealing in worsted cloth, asked him to set up and manage a branch of their company in Leeds. The business prospered and in 1844, two years before the railways came to the area, he moved the office and his home to Bradford, and in the following year became a naturalised British citizen.

This part of Yorkshire had traditionally made woollen clothes but by the end of the eighteenth century worsted goods had become the main commodity with mills being set up to produce worsted tops and yarns. It was this that Jacob was buying and then selling in countries across Europe.

Jacob was Jewish. Many Jews had started to settle in Bradford during the 1820s, coming from Germany and Denmark. It was quite usual for

Hamburg merchants to send their sons overseas for a few years to gain experience and build trading networks. For Jewish people there was the added advantage of experiencing a more liberal attitude in England towards their faith than existed in many parts of Germany after the French wars. The Jewish merchants found in Bradford an economic and political freedom that many had not encountered on the mainland of Europe. Because of this they were able to take an active part in the civic life of the town. By the time that Jacob died in the 1880s Bradford had a population of 200,000 but the middle and upper classes of mill owners, industrialists and businessmen was small and so the Jewish merchants, who comprised about 100 families were able to make a great mark on the city. Jacob became a leading figure both in the business of the town and in Jewish life. He was a founder member of the Chamber of Commerce and a promoter of the Bradford District Bank.

The most famous immigrant to Bradford in the nineteenth century was Jacob Behrens, a close friend of Jacob Unna. These early German merchants knew little about the manufacturing side of the industry, but they had the knowledge and expertise to know what the European markets would buy. They set up businesses in Bradford because they couldn't get the English manufacturers to package the cloth in the way needed by the European merchants. So they packaged it themselves. To do this they built large warehouses where tens of thousands of textile pieces – a *piece* was a length of worsted cloth about 60 yards long and 60 inches wide – were delivered from the mills and stored. The district where Jacob Unna established his business soon became known as 'Little Germany'.

The woollen industry thrived over the next 50 years or so and the manufactures and the merchants prospered. Jacob Behrens was knighted by Queen Victoria and in 1863 Bradford had its first Jewish mayor in Charles Semon. Jewish families became very much part of English life. For much of this period there was no synagogue in the town because the Jewish community did not want one. The Chief Rabbi visited and urged them to form a Jewish Association and hold services, but he had little success. As one observer commented: 'England was their home . . . Without knowing they developed an intense patriotism'. (*The Jewish Connection*, Katie Binns, Bradford and Yorkshire Local History.)

Jacob married Serine Solomon about 1836. She had been born in 1813 in Copenhagen but her family had moved to Germany and her younger sister, Henrietta, was born in Hamburg in 1826. There is a mystery surrounding Serine's background; family tradition has it that she was the illegitimate daughter of a Danish courtier – perhaps even a member of the Royal Family. Whatever the truth of her parenthood, she obviously came from a well off family because the famous European Court painter, Franz Winterhalter, painted a full-length portrait of her in a blue dress. Jacob and Serine's first child Charles, was born in 1838, then Violetta in 1840, Caroline in 1843 and Emily in 1853. After the move from Leeds to Bradford the family remained in the town as a well-off Victorian family with their cook and house servants. In the census returns Jacob is described as an 'Export Merchant of yarns and stuff goods'. A sad time struck the family in 1851 when Caroline died at the very young age of eight. When another daughter was born a short time after they gave her the name of Emily Caroline.

Jacob was obviously respected in the town. He was an active Free-mason, and a founder and first Worshipful Master of the Lodge of Harmony. The Chief Rabbi may have despaired at his efforts to get the community to build a synagogue but Jacob supported the Anglo-Jewish Association in Bradford and became its President. Most of the Jewish families were not Orthodox Jews but belonged to the Jewish Reform Movement; Bradford had one of the earliest Reform communities in England. In 1871 they recruited from Germany a young Reform minister and a synagogue was eventually built. A plaque on the wall tells us: '. . . *opened on 6th April 1880 by Jacob Arnold Unna*'. Not all the Jewish community stayed with their faith; many joined the Unitarian Church because of its liberal theology and progressive philanthropy, making it attractive to those seeking cultural assimilation.

Serine died in 1877. Three years later Jacob celebrated his 80th birthday. A grand party was held and though his son, Charles, could not attend, his 12 year-old grandson did, and wrote a letter to his father describing the event:

14 Feb 1880. My Dear Papa – I am sure we were all very sorry that you were not here on Grandfather's birthday. I had breakfast at 8am then went down to Eldon Place. Lewis was already there. Waited quarter of an hour & Grandpa came down. We sang a song while we waited. Presents from Auntie Else: Alice: Auntie Emily: Auntie Fanny; Auntie Annie; Uncle Leopold; Auntie Yetta; Fraulein Jeinsen; Nellie & I; . . . Mama . . . Doctor Juffs' choir and the new school master Mr Steele. There were 45 visitors & 35 letters. The day consisted of family, visitors; dinner and a party in the evening . . . (Letter from Jacob Unna's grandson, Bradford Town Hall records ref:71D83.)

Jacob died the following year. His will, which was very long and complicated, gives more insight into the life of this interesting ancestor. He remained true to his faith but also held a Victorian fear of being buried alive:

... I die in the persuasion of my forebears in the belief in one God Most High and in the hope of a life after this temporal one. I desire that my body shall be examined after my decease by two medical men and to be kept above ground for five days and to find my resting place near that of my beloved wife in Schalemore Ground and having been a Freemason for many years I expect that my brethren will pay me the last honour ...

He gave instructions as to how his most personal effects were to be distributed:

... to my son Charles Frederick ... my library and books of account papers and writings ... and the silver salver ... the walking stick used for many years by my father and grandfather ... and to my daughter Violetta ... my silver bowl and the full sized painting of my dear lamented wife Serine and bequeath my other jewellery worn by my late wife together with the photograph pictures and paintings to my daughters Violetta and Emily ... to my housemaid Mary Briggs the sum of two hundred pounds and an annuity of ten pounds per annum ... and bequeath to my cook Mrs Margaret Winterbottom an annuity of five pounds per annum ... (the maid was obviously better at cleaning then the cook was at cooking!)

Jacob was buried in the Jewish section of the Scholemoor Cemetry. There was a short religious service in the house and then his body was taken to the cemetery. The funeral was a grand affair, with the procession being led by a detachment of borough police and followed by a hundred gentlemen. At the cemetery chapel the prayers were in English and Hebrew, and the preacher, the Reverend Doctor Strauus, likened Jacob's loss to 'an evening of a long summer day when the sun goes down at the borders of our horizon, and a longing desire overcomes us to feast our eyes yet a little longer upon the beauteous site, and a regret creeps into our bosom ... Similarly we are grieved when a dearly beloved face passes away ...'. Perhaps it is the obituary in the *Bradford Observer* that captures very simply the essence of his life:

It was largely due to the energy, the keen insight into foreign requirements, and the general business capacity of German gentlemen like Mr Unna that Bradford owed the development of the textile trade which resulted in its assuming such a position of importance in the commercial history of the world . . . In private life he was the embodiment of undemonstrative goodness . . .

His son Charles continued in the family business and for a time they obviously prospered, as his daughter Helena Unna was presented to the Queen at Buckingham Palace. The grandchildren did not remain in the Jewish faith and became Christians. Charles died just eight years after his father and his will suggests that he was in dire financial straits. Whereas Jacob had left an estate of £16,000, Charles's amounted to only £587, with the administration of the estate . . . granted to 'Barthold Blenheim of Bradford, Gentleman, a Creditor'. Some of Jacob's family in Hamburg eventually went to live in the new state of Israel, and the first Israeli Ambassador to South Africa was a member of the family – Yitzhak Unna.

The Lewis family

The family line leading to Alexander and Felix continued through Jacob Unna's eldest daughter, **Violetta Ann Unna.** At the age of 18 in 1858 she married another Bradford merchant, **Leopold Lewis**. Leopold was born in 1832 in Mecklenburg, a region of Northern Germany, and like Jacob had become a naturalised British citizen. It seems likely that he was also Jewish as his father's name was Lazarus Levy Lewis, and also because Leopold and Violetta were married not in a church but a registry office. Leopold was also a stuff merchant, and the census returns tell us he employed 18 men and 11 boys. This was a period when many children died when still very young, and like her mother, Violetta suffered the loss of a daughter, Amy Caroline was born in 1859, soon after the marriage, but died within a few weeks. Alice Rose was born in 1861 and survived, and then another daughter, Agnes was born the following year. Their first son, Albert, was born in 1864 and then Frederick Gustave in 1874.

Violetta's children like her brothers, became Christian and the family remained in Bradford until Leopold retired. Their daughter Alice Rose Lewis was married in All Saints Parish Church in 1883. Her husband was an up and coming young barrister Amyas Longstaffe. By the early 1890s Leopold and Violetta were living on their own as all the children had left, and possibly because Alice and Amyas had set up home in Paddington they moved to London (69 Evelyn Gardens, South Kensington). Violetta died in September 1897 and Leopold a few years later in 1905. Violetta's will instructs what is to happen to personal jewellery and effects:

To my daughter Alice Rose Longstaffe wife of Amyas Longstaffe my diamond spray, my gold bracelet with blue enamelled centre, my painted opera glasses, white feather fan, my dark Hungarian feather fan with monogram, my diamond half hoop ring and my blue enamelled watch with fastener and earrings to match.

At the time of Violetta's death Alice Rose had one daughter and a son, and Violetta left jewellery to her granddaughter and an emerald and diamond ring to her grandson (John Lewis Longstaffe).

The Lewis family were rich, probably the wealthiest of all the Alexander and Felix's ancestors. When Leopold died eight years later he left an estate of nearly £45,000 – a sizeable amount at the turn of the twentieth century and equal to many millions of pounds in today's money. He obviously liked America and railways because the bulk of his wealth he left to his son Frederick 'to be invested in or upon Sterling gold bonds of any Railway Company constituted or carrying on business in the United States of America'. It was his smaller bequests that give a picture of his life:

To my son Frederick . . . my gold watch and chain which I am in the habit of wearing, my Errd Grand Piano, all my ivory, the two gilt cups which belonged to my parents, the two pastels of my maternal grandparents . . . the two old portraits of relatives of my late wife . . . To my son Albert Unna Lewis my platted coffee and tea service . . . To my daughter Alice Rose Longstaffe my old fashioned silver gilt basket, my silver grape dish and scissors, one pair of old silver hammered candlesticks which belonged to my parents, my open sugar basin and sifter and my two silver bread baskets with handles and my old small spoon basket . . . To my son-in-law Amyas Longstaffe my large oil painting by Gozzam . . .

He left all his other effects including carriages and horses to be divided equally between his children, and to Alice an additional sum of nine thousand pounds. The grandchildren also received bequests (though not the three year old Violetta Constance Maria, as she had been born after the will had been drawn up). And he remembered his maid, Harriet Smith, who got 50 pounds.

Unfortunately it is not clear whether the Winterhalter portrait of Serine that Violetta inherited from her father is the one of the 'two old portraits of relatives of my late wife' that went to Frederick. The portrait remained in the Lewis family until the 1940s and eventually was inherited by the famous actress Dame Peggy Ashcroft. It's not been possible to identify the portrait – there are more than 500 known pictures by the artist but none of the titles and dates obviously describe the young Serine (another possibility is that the portrait was by his brother, so it was a Winterhalter but not *the* Winterhalter). Peggy Ashcroft did have a legitimate claim to the picture, as her mother was Violetta Maud Bernheim, the daughter of Emily Unna, Jacob and Serine's youngest daughter. Peggy Ashcroft's mother had married William Ashcroft. Peggy was born in 1907 but when she was ten her father was killed in the First World War, and then her mother died when she was just 18, leaving her elder brother Edward as her only close relative. The Lewis family took her under their wing. Her brother was in Switzerland studying and so the young Peggy lived with her 'devoted guardian' first in Hindhead in Surrey and then in Addison Crescent in Kensington She went on to become a renowned classical and movie actor, being made a Dame in 1956 (with a theatre being named after her in Croydon). So the portrait is of Alexander and Felix's great, great, great, great grandmother but also of Peggy Ashcroft's great grandmother.

It is Alice Rose Lewis who continues the family line. With her marriage to Amyas Longstaffe in 1883 she became **Alice Rose Longstaffe**, and it was her youngest daughter, another Violetta, who eventually marries the naval surgeon Alexander Ingleby-Mackenzie. As a young barrister Amyas was a frequent visitor to the Yorkshire courts and he specialised in business and trade issues, so it may well have been in his professional capacity that he met Mr Lewis and his daughter. Amyas was obviously an energetic and intelligent man, and though he died quite young (in his fifties) he rose through his profession to become a judge. The Longstaffes were an interesting family – black sheep and all.

The Longstaffe and Taylor Families

Amyas Philip Longstaffe was the maternal grandfather of Felicity, and one of the great, great, grandparents of Alexander and Felix.

He was born in London in 1858, and though he was only 56 when he died in 1914, he had a distinguished career as a barrister, and during the last few years as a court judge. The Longstaffes came from Lincolnshire. Amyas's father was John Lawrence Longstaffe, who was born at Gedney Marsh in 1834. John's parents, William and Sarah (his mother's maiden name was Sarah Paine Lawrence), were farmers and very wealthy. The family owned 1700 acres and employed 140 workers. John's father was born in Leicestershire at Bushby in 1804 (where a generation later Manoah Peberdy lived – another ancestor) but his wife Sarah came from Dunsby in Lincolnshire, and it was just outside Lincoln where the Longstaffe family owned this very large farm. All the first sons in the family were named William; John's father was William, his father born in the 1770s was William, and John had an elder brother, William, born three years before.

John's mother became critically ill shortly after his birth. She went to stay with family in Hastings but died when John was only eight months old. John was brought up by his mother's sister who was married to a solicitor, and this may explain John's choice of a career, because as a young man he went to London to become an articled clerk. John's father remarried quite quickly after his wife's death. He and his new family appear in the census returns over the next 40 years. At one time they were living in The Close at Winchester, at later in Micheldever in Hampshire, and another son was born (named William!). They were a rich family but as John was not the first son it seems likely that he knew he had to make his own career, as he would not be inheriting the family's land. His older brother entered the army. Of all the great uncles and great aunts in our story, it is this William (John's older brother) who appears to have been the richest; his wife Selina was born in Farnham Castle in Ireland, and by the end of the century they lived in a grand style at Little Ponton Hall in Lincolnshire with dozens of servants, gardeners and even footmen!

Amyas's father John qualified as a solicitor in the same year that Amyas was born – 1858. John specialised in trade issues and went into partnership with a Mr Dad, the firm being based just off Oxford Street and known as Dad and Longstaffe. But here a mystery begins, and it is only possible to speculate about what may have happened.

Throughout his professional career John was known by his family name of Longstaffe, but in his domestic life he used another name. Amyas's mother, Clara Maria Taylor, was born in Highworth, Wiltshire in 1836. When Amyas was born his father's name was given on the birth certificate as 'Henry Taylor – a merchant' and the mother's name as 'Clara Maria Taylor – formally Longstaffe'. A second son, Amyas's brother, was born 15 months later and on his birth certificate it states that the father is 'John Taylor – solicitor's clerk' and the mother is 'Clara Maria Taylor, formerly Medhurst' – so two births and two family names. John, Clara and the children were certainly living together in 1861 and in 1871 (as they appear on the household census returns) and were recorded as Mr and Mrs Taylor.

At the age of twelve Amyas was sent to Westminster School, and the school records tell us that he was '. . . the eldest son of John Lawrence Longstaffe (formerly Taylor) of London, a solicitor, admitted to the school in January 1871 and left in 1877, he assumed the name of Longstaffe in lieu of Taylor in September 1873.' He went on to qualify as a barrister and moved to Birchington in Kent. His younger brother later qualified as a solicitor and joined his father in the partnership.

What might explain the dual names? The most likely explanation is that a certain young 23-year-old solicitor's clerk met the very pretty 22-year-old Clara Taylor, a dressmaker living in Billericay, and Amyas was the result. The father's name on the birth certificate was her father – Henry Taylor – not the child's father. There is no clue as to where the name Medhurst came from (though John's father, William Longstaffe, had friends staying with them called Medhurst at the time of the census in 1851). Whatever the explanation, in 1873 John decided to return to the name of Longstaffe. It is pure speculation as to the reasons for these name changes. Victorian society had very clear views on marriage and the social standing of husbands and wives in the professions. It's possible that the family went back to the Longstaffe name because John wanted one of his sons to join the family business, or perhaps an inheritance from the Lincolnshire Longstaffes encouraged the return. Whatever the reason, John and Clara eventually had four children and lived comfortable lives into the next century.

Amyas Philip Longstaffe married Alice Lewis in 1883. They had three children, all born in London – Mary Alice in 1885, John Lewis in 1887 and, 15 years later, Violetta Constance Maria, born in 1902. The naming of children is often significant. Amyas is of Latin origin and means 'loved'. His father would certainly have had a good knowledge of the language and given the possible circumstances of the boy's birth it is a very appropriate name. Amyas and Alice gave their children names that had come from their own parents and grandparents. Violetta had been named after her grandmother, Violetta Unna, but immediately given a nickname by the family – *Toodie* – the children's pronunciation of *intruder*. Well, she had arrived when her sister was 17 and her brother 15!

Amyas had a very successful career. Accounts of his life are found in legal biographies and Who's Who, but the best overview is given in *The Times* obituary of 15th June 1914:

The death took place on Saturday at 17 Cumberland Road, Leeds, of his Honour Judge Amyas Phillip Longstaffe in his 56th year.

Born in 1858 . . . he was called to the Bar at the Inner Temple in 1880. He read in the chambers of Sir Robert Finlay. In 1890 he became a Revising Barrister and was junior counsel to the Board of Trade in wreck inquiries in 1905. He was also Legal Commissioner for Formal Investigations under the Boiler Explosive Act. He was in 1911 appointed Judge at County Courts

Plate 2.3 Alice Rose Longstaffe (née Lewis) widowed in 1914.
She married again to another judge and became Lady Tindall-Atkinson.

(Circuit No. 12 – Halifax, Huddersfield and Dewsbury). Shortly before his death he had received intimation that the Lord Chancellor had transferred him to the Bristol County Court.

References to Amyas appear frequently in the newspapers because of public interest in accidents at sea that he helped to investigate. For example, in October 1909 *The Times* gave a lengthy account of the proceedings of an accident in the harbour at Ryde on the Isle of Wight, involving the passenger ship the *Duchess of Kent,* carrying 400 people, and a transporter vessel. The two ships collided but fortunately both vessels were safely beached and all the passengers got to shore. Amyas's detailed court questioning of the crew on both ships was fully reported.

What this newspaper account did not say but we can imagine, is how

Plate 2.4 Judge Amyas Longstaffe and his youngest daughter
Violetta Constance Maria (Toodie) – circa 1905.

shaken many of the passengers would have been. Some may have needed
the attention of a doctor and who better than the local Ryde GP – Dr
Kenneth Ingleby-Mackenzie. By coincidence it was his eldest son
Alexander who 20 years later was to marry Violetta Longstaffe.

Amyas was young when he died. Of course his work involved great
responsibility and much stress so perhaps it is not too surprising that
Amyas was only 56 but there may have been another factor. Just two years
before his death his only son, John (who was known as 'Jack') had been
killed in an accident. As *The Times* obituary reported:

His son John Longstaffe was killed while flying at Long Island, U.S.A., on
September 28. 1912.

It must have been a terrible shock. John only 35. Family tradition has it
that he was the 'black sheep' of the family. Perhaps he had inherited
Grandfather John Longstaffe's adventurous spirit. He was obviously a
daring person, as 1912 was in the very earliest days of flying. The Wright
brothers had achieved the first flight in 1903, just nine years before, and it
was only in July 1909 that the Frenchman – Bleriot, had made the first
flight across the Channel from France, landing in Dover. In these early
days flying was seen as an eccentric pastime pursued mainly by French
sportsman. This channel crossing marked the start of modern aviation as
politicians and military leaders saw the implications for potential
invasions if planes could now go over the heads of battleships. Within

a few years Britain's first squadron of biplanes came into service, and by another small coincidence Dr Ingleby-Mackenzie's younger son Keith was killed just five years later in France, also in one of these early planes. Later members of the family knew virtually nothing about either John's life or the manner of his death, and this may have been because he had been seen as a 'black sheep'. The newspaper accounts of his death give a clue to at least one aspect of his life – he had been a gun-runner during the early days of the Mexican Revolution.

Mortally injured in Aeroplane mishap. Wire became jammed and the Farman Biplane overturned. John L. Longstaff, a former English army officer . . . was mortally injured this evening . . . (*The Daily Journal and Tribune*, Knoxsville, Tennessee, September 29th 1912.)

A fuller account was given in the *New York Times*:

John L. Longstaffe, the English aviator, was carrying his mechanician to the finish of a flight at Hempstead Plains Aviation Field late this afternoon, when his biplane buckled and plunged to the ground. Longstaffe picked from the wreckage with a broken skull died four hours later in Nassau Hospital. His passenger Pierre Chevellier of . . . Manhattan lies in hospital unconscious and seriously injured but he will recover.

Longstaffe with Chevellier as his passenger had just made a graceful circle of the field and was heading for the door of the hangar. He had started to volplane and was not much more than fifty feet above the ground when suddenly with a report that sounded across the field like a thunderclap his machine buckled in the middle and shot to the earth, where it landed with such a force it was completely wrecked . . .

Chevellier was thrown clear of the wreckage and lay unconscious. The attendants and spectators ran forward and found Longstaffe pinned beneath the twisted and broken remnants of his aeroplane . . . One of the spectators offered his automobile for ambulance duty, and in this the two were hurried to the Nassau Hospital. There it was found that Longstaffe had no chance of recovery.

In the opinion of those who observed the accident the trouble began first with a slackening and then a tangling of the control wire. Those who had been watching knew that something was wrong with his biplane and that he was afraid of it. Although he took passengers into the air with him and made graceful circles every afternoon, he made them cautiously, and he was satisfied that it would not be safe to fly at any greater height than 150 feet . . .

Longstaffe was born in Leeds, England, some thirty-five years ago. He was formerly an officer in the English Army, and his name is well known on the

Plate 2.5 Farman biplane. John Longstaffe carried guns at night time across the Texas-Mexico border in a plane similar to this in 1911.

Continent. He got his pilot's licence from the Royal Aero Club of England. He had been flying as a scout with the insurgent army in Mexico until recently and he came to Hempstead Plains field as one of the Gressier exhibition flyers. Mrs Longstaffe and his step-daughter, Miss Jackson-Taylor, who recently came from England to Newport, arrived in New York a few days ago and had intended flying with him this evening'.

The shock for his family must have been great. Another newspaper account a few days later reports that 'Mrs Longstaffe gets body. Aviator's widow goes to Hempstead to claim the body of her husband . . .'

He was obviously working on Long Island as a pilot taking up paying passengers, but earlier in the year he had earned money in an even more dangerous way:

During the rebellion of General Pascual Orozco two Moisant Bleriot 2 airplanes of the Federal Army participated, flown by the North American Hector Worden and the Mexican Francisco Alvarez. During this year the first instance of the contraband of arms by air by the English pilot John L. Longstaffe. Flying a Farman biplane, he established a sort of mail service and he also transported arms to the rebels from Laredo [Texas] during the night (*Fuerza Aerea Mexicana*, Historia, Inicios, website, translated from Spanish).

But was he a good gun-runner or a bad one – well, in terms of the revolution he was supporting? Fortunately for his descendants it looks as if the cause was a just one. The man that John was giving support to was

General Orazca, a Mexican revolutionary leader. The Mexican Revolution was an armed struggle that started in 1910 with an uprising to overthrow the dictator Porfirio Diaz. Though Diaz had brought some modernisation and industry to Mexico he had made the lives of ordinary rural people much worse. Human rights were ignored and the Catholic Church's power undermined. The revolution was fought as a populist uprising promising liberal reforms and better conditions for farmers and

Plate 2.6 Toodie dressed for her Presentation at Court in June 1925.

workers. In fact it was the first major revolution of the twentieth century. General Orazca led the revolutionary forces in the north. The United States gave some quiet support to the Revolutionaries, which is why it was possible for John to be flying guns from Texas, and for the fact to be so openly spoken about. The man he worked for didn't live much longer than John. The General fell out with his fellow revolutionaries and fled to America. In 1915 he and his supporters were mistaken for bandits and were pursued by a posse of marshals, Texas Rangers, and troops from the Thirteenth Cavalry, before being gunned down in the best Western Movie tradition, in a shootout in the Van Horn Mountains.

Back in England Judge Longstaffe was to live for only a few more years. Alice remarried after her husband's death, to another lawyer, and became Lady Tindal-Atkinson. **Violetta Constance Maria Longstaffe** (Toodie) was only ten when her brother was killed and 12 when her father died. In 1930 she married the young naval surgeon Alexander Ingleby-Mackenzie, and in Ceylon later that year Felicity was born. Alice must have been a very proud grandmother as she immediately took ship from Italy to be in Columbo with mother and daughter. More of that in *Felicity's Story*.

CHAPTER 3

Peberdy: a Leicestershire Family

It wasn't until 1795 and the birth of William Peberdy that the spelling of the surname became fixed in its present form. William's father John was 'Pepperdy', and in the hundred years previously variations included Pebody, Paybody, Pebodey, Peabidy and Pepperday. Many of these forebears were illiterate, and so it was the vicar or his curate at the time of baptism, marriage or burial who interpreted the pronunciation and determined how the name should be spelt. Paybody remained in use (or that was how it was pronounced) until the mid eighteenth century.

The majority of Peberdys up to the mid 1800s lived in Leicestershire, with some in Northamptonshire, Warwickshire, Nottinghamshire, and even in New England. Alexander and Felix's line of the family, from the end of the seventeenth century to the 1830s, were farmers in the village of Saddington. This is a village in the south of the county, about nine miles from Leicester; a place today of small grass fields, hawthorn hedges, low hills, a church and a reservoir. It's not on any major road so it's the sort of place you get to because you intended to be there. There were 50 families living in the village when the first Peberdy arrived. By 1801 the population was 241. It rose to 279 in 1841 but then fell to 182 by the 1890s after many villagers, like our forebears, moved into the towns. In the churchyard are at least ten Peberdy graves; the earliest headstone is for John, who died in 1772, and the latest, for Thomas who died in 1895.

The history of the Peberdys during this period is bound up with the flourishing, and subsequent decline, of yeoman farmers. The effect of the Enclosure Acts in the eighteenth and nineteenth centuries, followed by the impact of new farming methods, resulted in the larger farmers getting bigger holdings and the smaller ones losing their land and becoming farm labourers. As new agricultural machinery replaced the need for labourers, and as the city of Leicester grew as a centre for hosiery manufacturing, the pull of industry resulted in the drift of families from the countryside to the town. This process for the Peberdy family took place over eight generations and involved three moves within a location no bigger than

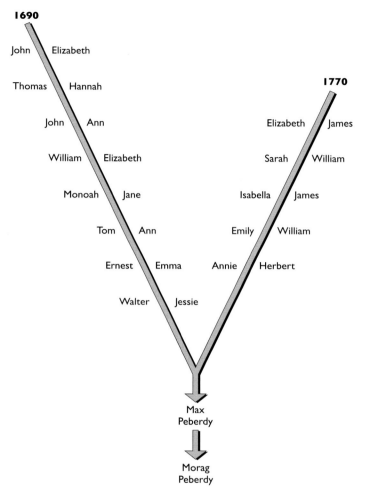

1690

John   Elizabeth

Thomas   Hannah

John   Ann

William   Elizabeth

Monoah   Jane

Tom   Ann

Ernest   Emma

Walter   Jessie

1770

Elizabeth   James

Sarah   William

Isabella   James

Emily   William

Annie   Herbert

Max
Peberdy

Morag
Peberdy

Figure 9: Fathers and mothers

twelve miles by six: Saddington to Shearsby (two miles), Shearsby to Thurnby (eight miles), and Thurnby to Leicester (two miles).

Saddington 1690s

John Peberdy was born about 1678 and probably in the village of North Kilworth, but he moved a few miles eastwards and became the first of the Saddington Peberdys. The church records make reference to him as the father of Robert, who was baptised in September 1699. Our line descended through Thomas Peberdy, who was born in 1719 and was John's fifth child.

   John was described in the church records as a *yeoman*. He was obviously of some standing in the village, as he was churchwarden in 1730, thus we know that the Peberdys were Church of England, which is not surprising as there were less than ten people in the village who were non-conformists. Little else can be gleaned from what remains of the written records except his will. John died in 1747 and the will he made shortly before his death gives an insight, not only into his possessions but also the way he provided for his wife Elizabeth and their three sons:

In the name of God amen I John Paybody of Saddington in the County of Leicester yeoman being weak in body of good m [em]ory of sound disposing mind and memory and considering the certainty of death and the Uncertainty of the time therof do make and ordain this my last will and testament manner and form following [viz] first I give to my son Robert Paybody one five shillings and his son Thomas Paybody one Guine and the sum of two hundred pounds of good British money I give and bequeath unto my said son Thomas Paybody the money to be paid to him one month after my Decease by Ex[ecutor]s herein after named I give to my son Thomas Paybody the three year old colt of the rideing sort and the cheast [chest] that was my fathers and my son Thomas Paybody to pay his mother duering her life one pound ten shillings a year and to be paid every halfe year fifteen shillings to his mother . . . [original text crossed out] . . .

   . . . also all the rest of goods cattel [cattle] chatte [ls] implements of husbandry and personal estate what so ever and where so ever I give and bequeath unto my two sons John and William Paybody they paying my debts and dischargeing my funeral Expenses and the legacy aforesaid whom I make sole ex[e]c[ut]ors of this my last will and Testament Revoaking all former by me maid and my son John Paybody to pay his mother one pound ten shillings every year to be paid every half year of fifteen shillings and my son William Paybody to paye his mother one pound tenn shillings every year and to be paid ever[y] halfe year fifteen shillings of this my last will and testament revoaking all former by me maid. In witness wherof I the said John Paybody the testor have here put into my hand and seale this five and twenty day of July of the year of our Lord 1746.

He wasn't literate and therefore didn't know how to write his name. Instead he made an x. The will had been drawn up by William Wagstaffe and William Horton, who were local attorneys, or the equivalent in the eighteenth century and there was a final instruction:

Ye household good to be parted bettwex my wife & John & Wm and Thos Peybody & everyone to have an eaquell part as they agree upon as are living. To my brother Edward Paybody I give Two Guines to be paid by Ex[ecutors].

The style of the will is interesting. As he died shortly after, it was probably made when John was lying seriously ill in bed and dictated by him to an attorney or his clerk. That may help to explain the repetition and the lack of a clear structure to the bequests. The style also reflects the state of English grammar at this time; there is little punctuation, and no consistency of spelling (even the surname had variations!).

The will also gives an insight into custom and family relationships. Elizabeth does not inherit any property or money directly but only a share of the household items which as the inventory below shows is worth less than a twentieth of John's estate. It is quite confusing as to who gets what, and there is no mention of land. Was John a tenant farmer or had he already handed on the farm to his oldest son Robert? Or was it that as this was before Saddington had been enclosed there was no need to refer to land or land rights, as this would follow local custom? He is described as a 'yeoman' which generally referred to a man who cultivated his own land or rented at least 50 acres; a tenant (who rented a smaller amount of land from a landowner) was usually called a husbandman. On balance it seems most probable that John was a tenant.

Within months John had died, and he was buried on 7th August. Elizabeth lived another nine years. They were both about seventy, and so had reached their three score years and ten. A month after John's burial the inventory was made. The estate was worth £684. A farm labourer earned about 12 pence per day at this time. That is less than £18 a year, so John's estate was equivalent to 38 years of a farm worker's pay. His gift of £200 to Thomas (Alexander and Felix's great, great, great, great, great, great, great grandfather) was equivalent to more than 11 years' pay.

The inventory was made in the autumn immediately after harvest, and so it is not surprising that the crops, probably peas, beans, barley, wheat and oats, were the most valuable item. Leicestershire is a county of grass and this was a mixed farm with cows, sheep and pigs. Today a typical farmer would have a lot of very expensive machinery, for John the implements were relatively small in value but his horses and mares (the tractor, landrover and car of their day) made up an eighth of the value of the estate. There is no mention of hens, ducks or geese and perhaps this is because traditionally poultry belonged to the farmer's wife, money from the sale of eggs and meat was hers to dispose of as she wished. So they don't appear in the inventory because they were already Elizabeth's. The mother's allowance from the sons is very little; far less than a farm labourer's wages, so it's likely that she was to live with her eldest son and be supported within his family.

The inventory shows the value of the things that John owned:

	£	s.	d.
Purse and Apparell	60	0	0
The household goods	30	0	0
Wool and Cheese	25	0	0
The implements of husbandry	30	0	0
The Crop of all Soils of Grain	130	0	0
The horses and mares	84	0	0
Cows	46	0	0
Sheep and lamb	50	0	0
Swine	9	0	0
Money upon Bond	220	0	0
	£684	0	0

Thomas Peberdy was 28 when his father died. He married Hannah Tauveley in 1764 when he was 35 – quite a late marriage by the standard of the times. They had four children: Elizabeth, Hannah, Thomas and our direct ancestor John (who had been given his grandfather's Christian name). The leading landowner – the lord of the manor – at this time was William Wollaston, and it was he who petitioned Parliament in 1770 to have the village land enclosed. Some of the land had been fenced earlier but now the three open fields (Peasehill Field, Mill Field and Limborough Field) were divided between 27 landowners. Of these only the vicar and Wollaston himself got more than 200 acres. There were five allotments of between 50 and 100 acres, and ten of 10 acres or under, one of which went to the churchwardens. Unfortunately we don't know how well the Peberdy family did out of this carving up of the village.

Thomas was only 53 when he died and so his children were very young – the girls seven and five, the boys three and one. So John Peberdy, the youngest, would never have known his father. Thomas made his will on 3rd March 1772 and he was buried just four days later. In his will he says:

As to my Worldly Estate I Give and Dispose that as follows I give and Bequeth unto my two sons Thomas and John Pebody the sum of One hundred and fifty pounds A Piece Also I give unto my two Daughters Elizabeth and Hannah Pebody the sum of Forty Pounds a Piece All which said Legacy I will and Direct be paid to my Executrix herin after Named unto my said children at their respective ages of Twenty One Years or Days of Marriage which shall first happen . . . Also my stock of cattle crops or corn grain and Hay Implements of Husbandry Household Goods and furniture and Personal Estate whatsoever Not herein before Disposed of I Give and Bequeth unto my Dear and Loving Wife Hannah Pebody.

His words about Hannah are very moving. They had been married for less than eight years and when these words were written he obviously knew that he had only days (or hours) to live.

Unfortunately there is no inventory remaining with the will so we can't compare his estate to his father's. But the amounts of money are much less than with John's will, so we can deduce that as a second son he had been less wealthy than his father (though the amounts are still substantial). Also by now Saddington was enclosed, with the loss of traditional common grazing and other benefits. This would have had a serious effect on the livelihoods of the smaller farm families and cottagers.

Thomas's son **John Peberdy** was described in the church records as a *grazier*. This may mean that unlike his father and grandfather who had both arable and pasture, he had only grass fields and therefore no crops. John married Ann Norman around 1791 (there were many families named Norman living in the area in the nineteenth century) and they had at least five children. He died in 1833 aged 62. Unfortunately his will, though very long and very detailed, is extremely difficult to read and so only parts can be understood:

. . . unto my daughter Hannah Mason, wife of Samuel Mason of . . . in the county of Nottinghamshire my best worsted coat and drawings and Bed covers belonging in my best bedroom and unto my son John Peberdy the bedstead with hangings and other furniture belonging . . . I usually sleep and unto my son William Peberdy the bedstead with Drawings and other furniture belonging to the rooms where my sons have usually slept and unto my daughter Elizabeth . . . the sum of one hundred pounds and to my daughter Hannah the sum of two hundred and twenty pounds and unto my sons John Peberdy and William Peberdy the sum of thirty pounds . . . and to my maid servant Elizabeth Warner £40. My late daughter Sophia . . .

It appears that not only had one daughter died but so had his wife Ann. It's likely that later in the Will the cattle and other farm items were bequeathed to John and William but as William, is the younger he may have got far less than his brother. By 1833 the land around Saddington had been fully enclosed and the fortunes of our branch of the Peberdy family decline.

Just a few years earlier in Saddington a John Peberdy was transported for stealing a lamb. In the records of the Leicester Summer Assizes the verdict of his trial is recorded starkly across two pages, with on one side of the entry – *John Peberdy – sheep stealing* and on the other page just one word – *Death*. The sentence was obviously commuted to transportation however, and a few weeks later there is an account in the diary of William Gilbert, a painter and odd job man who lived in a neighbouring village. His diary entry for 15th September 1828 read:

This morning went through Harborough from Leicester Goal on a Coach with other convicts John Peberdy the son of John Peberdy of Saddington in this county on the way to New South Wales to where he is Transported for Life he was convicted of stealing a Lamb belonging to Perkins, Baker of Fleckney value 3s 6d I have been intimately acquainted with his family for some years.

In the 1990s when as a family the Peberdys were travelling by car through New South Wales in Australia they drove over a small river; its name – 'Peberdy's Creek'. In the local town of Tamworth there were many families named Peberdy listed in the telephone directory. Were they descendants of John? It's also not clear which family in Saddington the transported man belonged to; it was obviously not 'our' John Peberdy as he was still living in the village when his father died in 1833, but there was at least one other of that name during this period. A cousin, descended from the first Saddington Peberdys (John and Elizabeth) was born in the village in 1803. If it were him he would have been 25 at the time of the theft. However, another Peberdy – Thomas Peberdy of Leicester – was also transported at the next court sitting. His crime was larceny and obviously considered less serious, as Thomas only got four years' transportation. By coincidence both John and Thomas were on the same convict ship, the *Layton,* which left England on 23rd March 1829, arriving in New South Wales on 17th June (almost three months in the hold of a sailing ship!). John disappears from the records but Thomas is given his Certificate of Freedom in April 1845, so it is more likely that it was his line that led to the Peberdys of Tamworth and the naming of the river. More research is needed to identify which Peberdy settled in this part of Australia but the fact that a man like John,

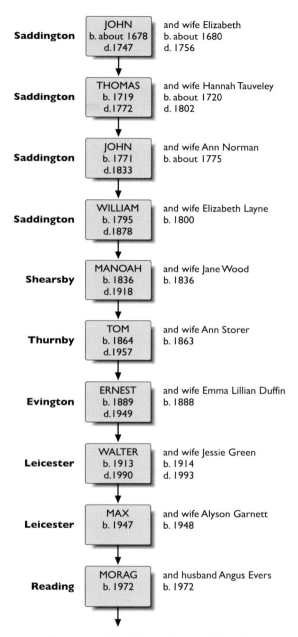

Saddington	JOHN b. about 1678 d.1747	and wife Elizabeth b. about 1680 d. 1756
Saddington	THOMAS b. 1719 d.1772	and wife Hannah Tauveley b. about 1720 d. 1802
Saddington	JOHN b. 1771 d.1833	and wife Ann Norman b. about 1775
Saddington	WILLIAM b. 1795 d.1878	and wife Elizabeth Layne b. 1800
Shearsby	MANOAH b. 1836 d.1918	and wife Jane Wood b. 1836
Thurnby	TOM b. 1864 d.1957	and wife Ann Storer b. 1863
Evington	ERNEST b. 1889 d.1949	and wife Emma Lillian Duffin b. 1888
Leicester	WALTER b. 1913 d.1990	and wife Jessie Green b. 1914 d. 1993
Leicester	MAX b. 1947	and wife Alyson Garnett b. 1948
Reading	MORAG b. 1972	and husband Angus Evers b. 1972

Figure 10: Ten Generations – Peberdy

from a farming family, took the extreme risk of stealing a lamb, knowing the consequences, may well indicate just how severe poverty had become.

Another relative and another John, 'John Pebody' was in court a year later in 1830. This was the year when almost two million sheep died from disease. It was the worst year for foot rot in either the eighteenth or nineteenth centuries, and led to even lower farm wages at a time when food prices were rising. Farm labourers blamed the new machinery such as threshing machines for their poverty. Riots took place with attacks on farms, breaking of machines and the maiming of animals. In July John Pebody was acquitted of burning a straw stack at Little Bowden (about nine miles south of Saddington). The acquittal was in spite of considerable circumstantial evidence of his guilt and it shows that jurors were in sympathy with what men like John were doing.

Out of Saddington 1833

William Peberdy, John's second son, was born in 1795, and it is he that takes forward the family line. A notable change took place at this time in the village, with the building of a reservoir between 1773 and 1797. This acted as a catchment basin for the supply of water to the Grand Union

Plate 3.1 St Helen's Church, Saddington where in the 17th and 18th centuries the Peberdys were baptised, married and buried.

Canal. A natural hollow was banked to hold water from two brooks and feeder streams were made to carry the water to the canal. The reservoir took about 60 acres of land. It would be interesting to know if any of this land had been used by the Peberdys. Saddington was still a mainly agricultural village but with a few people employed as framework knitters and in the traditional rural trades. There was, for example, a blacksmith, a tailor, a shoemaker, a joiner, a miller, a baker and a publican at the Queen's Head.

William married Elizabeth Layne in about 1829. She had been born in Birdingbury, Warwickshire. Though in a different county it is only 20 miles away from Saddington, and if her father had been an agricultural labourer, as seems likely, he may have moved to Leicestershire for work. Their first child was Sophia (also the name of William's older sister who had died) and though she was born in Saddington their second child, Manoah (a great, great, great, great grandfather of Alexander and Felix) was born in 1836 a few miles away to the west in Shearsby. After 140 years as farmers this branch of the Peberdys had become farm workers.

William and Elizabeth were very imaginative with their children's names: after Sophia and Manoah there was Elijah, Phoeby and Amos, plus a grandchild living with them called Thirza. Manoah is a biblical character (Judges 13:8–21) whose wife could not have children. An angel told her she would have a child but she 'must not drink fruit of the vine, nor eat unclean food and obey God's laws'. She gave birth to Sampson. The next account in Judges after Sampson's birth is Sampson killing a lion and finding a swarm of bees in its stomach. This leads him to set a riddle for the Philistines: what out of the strong comes forth sweet? A riddle that as children we all knew because it was on the label of tins of Golden Syrup.

None of the previous Peberdys had Old Testament names and so it is probable that Elizabeth chose them. Possibly her father had been Manoah Layne, and to surmise further, had his parents or grandparents waited a long time for a child and so when a baby was eventually born they chose a name from the Bible of a person who similarly had waited a long time? Or perhaps there is something in the genes of the Layne family that compels them to give extraordinary names to their children. Laynes live in Warwickshire today and recent offspring have been called Horizon Aurora Layne, Jamell Troy Layne, Jayden Di-Kai Layne and Jeremiah Daniel Layne.

Shearsby is still a small, rural community. If you visit the village today quite early on a spring morning, when nobody is around, then some of the atmosphere of the 1840s can be felt. At this time of the year a temporary fence is placed around the graves in the churchyard and a flock of sheep have breakfast among the stone crosses. William and Manoah would have been familiar with the scene.

In 1851 **Manoah Peberdy** was 15 and an agricultural labourer and no doubt a farmer's boy before that. He was living with his parents but they had now moved to Knaptoft, a village a few miles to the east of Shearsby. William was also an agricultural labourer and Manoah's younger brother Elijah worked on a farm. The oldest child Sophia was a 'duff maker'.

Manoah married Jane Wood when he was 24. Jane had been born in Bushby, a village close by, and her mother was recorded on the household surveys as a 'labourer's widow'. In the 1840s and 1850s there was no state provided education and both Jane and her mother Catherine were illiterate. A day school and a Sunday school had been opened in Saddington in 1828 by subscription and were attended by 70 children, so it is likely that the young male Peberdys got some education. But it is moving to see on official documents such as birth registrations that many adults could not write their names and had to make a simple *x*. Jane's father must have died when she and her brother John were very young, because at the age of 14 John Wood was living as a farm servant in Bushby. For us today it is difficult to understand what all these occupational classifications meant, but a farm servant was an unmarried farm worker who lived with the farmer's family and received food and accommodation as well as wages; married farm labourers lived in a tied cottage provided by the farmer.

In the years when William and Manoah were employed as farm workers rural poverty in England was still severe. After the Enclosures many of the traditional rights had been lost: gleaning (picking up the ears of corn that had fallen on the ground at harvest), collecting wood for the fire and tethering stock in the lanes. They seem very small things to us but often made the difference between having enough to eat or going hungry for much of the time. Living conditions were harsh and there was no safety net for the very poor other than going on 'parish relief', which usually meant entering a Union House – the workhouse. Charles Dickens describes (for example in *Oliver Twist*, 1837) the terrible conditions in these places – conditions that were deliberately made harsh to deter people from entering unless they were facing destitution. There was no workhouse in Saddington but the records show that around this time 50 adults and children in the village were receiving out-relief; that is getting money from the parish to feed them but being able to stay in the village and not forced to go the workhouse in Market Harborough (a town a few miles away). Poor people lived with this fear and everyone knew families on poor relief. In 1850 about 17% of the population in England was receiving support, and even 20 years later it was still as high as 14%.

Wages were low and a worker like Manoah would receive about six or seven shillings a week (in other words it took three weeks' wages to earn a pound). This level of wage was just enough to buy basic foods: bread which was always the main item, potatoes, tea, sugar, soap, candles, coal, wood, butter and cheese. Only a few pence would be left from this for replacing worn clothing. Some of the richer people in villages like Saddington had left money when they died that was used to help the poorest. For example one vicar left £2 12s for bread for the poor which could be distributed fortnightly at the church. A farmer left money for the purchase of an ox each Christmas to be cooked and eaten on the day.

A farm worker's family did get a cottage with the job but it was likely to be small, cold and very damp. William Cobbett, the early-nineteenth-century campaigner for better rural conditions visited Leicester in the 1830s and wrote:

Leicester is a very fine town; spacious streets, fine inns, fine shops, and containing they say thirty or forty thousand people. It is well stocked with gaols, of which a new one, in addition to the rest, has just been built covering three acres of ground! Nothing speaks the want of reflection in the people so much as the self-gratulation which they appear to feel about these edifices . . . Instead of expressing shame at these indubitable proofs of the horrible increases of misery and crime, they really boast of these 'improvements' as they call them . . . You have nothing to do but to walk through these villages [outside Leicester] to see the cause of the increase of the gaols . . . look at the miserable sheds in which the labourers reside! Look at these hovels made of mud and straw; bits of grass, of old off-cast windows without frames or hinges frequently, but merely stuck in to the mud wall. Enter them, and look at the bits of chairs or stools, the wretched boards tacked together to serve for a table; the floor of pebble, broken brick, or the bare ground; look at the thing they call a bed, and survey the rags on the backs of the wretched inhabitants; and then wonder if you can that the goals and dungeons and treadmills increase . . .' (William Cobbett, *Rural Rides*, vol.2' Midland Tour' pp. 265–266.)

If you lived in rural poverty it is not difficult to understand that the town could well have held out the hope of something better. Leicester had reached a population of 31,000 by 1831. St Margaret's parish saw the biggest increase and it was to here that many of our forbears arrived (both on Alyson's side and Max's). Viewed by modern standards conditions in the city were appalling. There was a total lack of sanitation; both rich and poor only had outside privies that emptied into cesspits usually yards away from the houses. It was not until the 1850s that the first piped water came to the city and so everyone drank from wells or the River Soar, all of which were frequently polluted by sewage. The streets were lit by burning oil lamps until the 1820s when gas mantles were introduced. To us it sounds like a place to avoid, and yet compared to the conditions in the villages it did offer a chance of improvement. But unlike today you couldn't just move from a village to the town. There were restrictions. Parishes in the city did not want more poor people, especially those who needed support out of local taxes, and did everything they could to limit those eligible to poor relief. There was an economic depression in the hosiery trade, a main business of Leicester, after the Napoleonic Wars, so jobs as framework knitters were scarce. Different also from today was the fact that a person could not just 'do a job'. In many trades you needed to have served an apprenticeship. The records of the Leicester court illustrate the types of offences you could commit if you did try to work or reside in the town:

Thomas Carte, Syston, yeoman, for trading as a butcher unapprenticed.
Nicholas Richmond, framework-knitter, for illegally lodging John Keen in his house.
Joseph Thornton, framework-knitter, for illegally lodging Eleanor Stephens, a common stroller, in his house.

There were many other restrictions, even to what you could say:

John Sherrard, framework-knitter, for swearing 6 profane oaths: to wit 'God damn you', 'God damn you'. 'God damn you', God damn you', 'God damn you', 'God damn you'.

The town parishes did what they could to prevent the destitute being their responsibility, but many did come and plead for help:

William Lauder, labourer: is of the age of Threescore and Ten yeares and upwards and is a broken man by a Rupture of his Belly so that your poor and humble petitioner . . . is not able to work . . . and . . . desires from the parish of St Margarett only a habitation for himselfe and his wife having layen Seavon Nights in a Hay Rick . . . so that your petitioner may lye noe more out of doors. And your Petitioner as is duty bound Shall ever pray for your worshipps etc.

But Leicester did continue to expand. In the 20 years after 1851 its population rose by 50% to 95,000. This is an almost unimaginable level of growth. By 1871 the city wanted the able bodied for the hosiery factories. At the same time there was much less need for workers on the farms as new technology had replaced many of the labour-intensive activities. Unemployed farm families were a burden on local rates and were encouraged to move out. One strategy that landowners and farmers adopted was to deliberately reduce available housing. Cottages would be pulled down or allowed to fall into disrepair. Thus by the 1870s the forces acting on poor families were like a vacuum cleaner sucking towards Leicester, and a huge fan blowing through the villages.

Into the Town

By 1871 Manoah and Jane had four children and had moved to Thurnby. Today Thurnby is a suburb of Leicester city (it became a city in 1919) but it would still have been rural when Manoah moved there. He is now a shepherd. Another ten years on and they are still in Thurnby, and the family has grown to eight children. Their oldest son John is 18 and an agricultural labourer, but living at home. Tom Peberdy (great, great, great, great grandfather) is 17 but he has made the break from farm to city. He has moved into lodgings in Leicester and is working as a butcher's apprentice.

Another ten years on and in 1881 Manoah was a cow keeper. The family had now moved a little closer to the city and into the village of Evington. This is on the easterly edge of Leicester and soon to be absorbed within the city. Manoah produced milk, which his son William (20) was selling on a round. John was 28 and an agricultural labourer and Hephzibah (16) was a shoe machinist. By the turn of the century they had made their final move: into Humberstone. Humberstone had been rural, but it was now urban; the city had crept out and taken them: the Peberdys were no longer to be villagers. Manoah had retired and the family business was in the hands of John. Many of the Peberdys in the extended family did continue to live and work in the countryside, and 40 years later the wonderfully named John Conquest Peberdy converted his coal delivery truck into a bus and started a regular passenger service from Fleckney to Leicester. But from this point onwards most of the family were townspeople.

Manoah lived to be 83, a year older than his father William, and died at
the end of the First World War. There was a household census in 1911
and Manaoh completed the form in his own hand; he may not have had
much schooling but his handwriting is clear and almost artistic in the
swirls that form the *M* of Manoah. In the return he reports that he and
Jane have been married for 51 years, had 11 children of whom eight are
still living. Only Ruth is still at home and she does the dairy work in their
cowkeeping and milk business. Manoah died in the autumn of 1918; the
cause of death was given as bronchitis, which, the doctor reported, he'd
had for 20 years. His will shows that in later life he had become
reasonably well off. The original will was written in November 1905
and his son Tom and daughter Ruth were the executors.

I bequeath all the consumerable stores and provisions which shall be in or
about my Dwellinghouse at the time of my decease unto my wife Jane Peberdy
absolutely. I also bequeath to my said wife . . . the use and enjoyment of my
house furniture, plate, linen, china, glass, books, prints, pictures and other
household effects and after her decease I bequeath the same to my daughter
Ruth Peberdy absolutely. I bequeath to . . . Jane Peberdy a Pecuniary Legacy of
one hundred pounds . . . I bequeath to my son William Peberdy my business
of Milk Purveyor and my milk float and harness and other things of a like
nature . . . and one horse . . . I devise all that my Messuages numbered 102
Baggrave Street, Leicester . . . and also my two Messuages numbered 5 and 7
Meynell Road, Leicester in the respective occupations of John Shenton and
Frederick Turner with the outbuildings and appliances . . . to my wife Jane
Peberdy during her life . . . I bequeath the residue of the personal Estate to
Tom Peberdy and Ruth Peberdy . . . to invest the monies . . . in government
real or other sufficient security and to pay the annual income . . . to my wife . . .
to divide equally between all my children . . . and the issue of any child . . . in
equal shares.

Six years later Tom was replaced as an executor by Harry. It is an
interesting will because it gives us a picture of the family at the turn of
the century. William was running the dairy business, Ruth was at home
unmarried, and the family were comfortably off. Besides the business and
their house Manoah owned two other properties (messuage means a
dwelling and outbuildings with adjacent lands) that he rented out. We
even know that he read books! He was concerned to ensure Jane had a
good income and that his children all inherited fair shares. There is even
an echo of the will of Manoah's great, great grandfather John who had
been concerned that part of the inheritance he passed on would be in

'good British money'; Manoah wanted to ensure that his money would be invested in safe British government stock.

Of all the ten generations it is Manoah who appears like a patriarch; with his biblical name, his eight children, and all the changes he had experienced – from being a yeoman farmer's grandson to seeing his own children become factory workers in a Midland town. He is the link between pre-industrial England and the very different world that emerged after the shock of the Great War. Life had materially improved. No longer did the family live on the edge of destitution and the workhouse; by the end of the War they had property and for the elderly Jane the security of a hundred pounds a year. Max's father Walter was five when Manoah died. His parents also lived in Humberstone and so surely he must have had some memory of his great grandfather, but to Max's great regret, he never said.

Tom Peberdy was born in 1864 and was Manoah's second son. He married Annie Storer in 1884. She and her parents (Thomas Storer and Elizabeth Noon) were all born in Leicester or at Enderby just outside the city. As a family they had moved out of farming before the Peberdys. By 17 Annie was a servant in Aylestone; her sister Rachel was in service and her brother Thomas was also a servant. Tom Peberdy obviously did not remain as a butcher's apprentice because in the 1901 census he was described as a 'labourer', living in Leicester, and with five children. Of all the Peberdys there is least to say about Tom. He lived to a good age, dying in 1957 at the age of 93. It was his second son Ernest who took forward the genetic line.

Ernest Peberdy was born in 1889 and married Lillian Duffin in February 1911. The Duffins are the first family which we have a photograph. It must have been taken in the mid 1890s as it shows Lillian about eight with her parents George and Elizabeth, and older brother Alfred (b. 1887), younger brothers William (b. 1889) and Herbert (b. 1895) and sister Edith (b. 1893). Both parents had similar family histories to the Peberdys. George was born in Walton on the Wolds, a grassland farming area, which was also situated in the north of the county. Elizabeth, whose maiden name was Adkin, was born in the village of Shepshed. They had moved into Leicester about the time of their marriage. George's father Charles Duffin had been an agricultural labourer, and his wife Ann Copeland was born in the same area as Walton. Like the Peberdys the Duffins did not look far afield for brides.

Plate 3.2 The Duffins circa 1895. From left to right: Alfred, Lilian, Edith (sitting), George and Elizabeth, Herbert on his mother's knee and William.

A sad aspect of the Duffin family history is that George's youngest sister Edith, born in 1881, became blind and in the 1901 census she is a 'residential pupil' at the General Institution for the Blind in Birmingham. Her occupation is described as 'basket maker'. George died when he was only forty and his last job was as a waggoner.

The twentieth century

The marriage of Ernest and Lillian in 1911 was probably a quickly arranged one, as their first child, Lillian Ruth, was born three months later. She died at age four months. Walter was born in 1913 and his sister Margaret two years later. They had no more children and it was from this time that the Peberdys started to have small families (Walter had only one child and Margaret two sons). Ernest joined the Fire Service and by the time of Walter's marriage in 1938 had become a district fire officer. The photographs of him show a smallish man with a smiling face. He played cricket and was a member of the fire service band.

Plate 3.3 Ernest Peberdy on the steps of a cricket pavilion.

It seems likely that Ernest became a fireman just after his marriage. This was a historic period for the Leicester service, as it had just made the change from horse- drawn fire appliances to motor drawn engines. He started in the Rutland Street Station, but in 1927 he was among the first officers to be based in the newly opened Central Fire Station on Lancaster Road. It must have been an exciting time as the station was considered as being at the forefront of new technology. In fact the *Leicester Mercury* hailed it as 'one of the best equipped fire stations in the world'. There was a grand opening ceremony attended by the city's important folk and Chief Fire Officers from around the country. The reporter sent by the local newspaper rose to the occasion in his description:

A kindly sun reposing on a cushion of warm blue sky shed a thousand glorious beams on the gleaming brass and the crimson pomp of Leicester's Fire Brigade Pageant to-day . . . The 'get-at-it-lads' clanging of alarm bells, the wild dash through the streets of burnished engines, the rhythmical chug

chug of the pumps – all the frantic evolutions associated with the stern and romantic business of combating the flames made a picture that will linger in the minds of all who saw it.

Ernest and his young family lived at the fire station and paid five shillings a week rent. His son Walter was 14 at the time of the move. It was a big station covering more than three acres with specially constructed buildings for the machinery and accommodation for all the officers. The technology was innovative. The electrical appliances and alarms could be monitored from just one control room, and it was the Chief Fire Officer Henry Neal who had designed the new system. From this room 45 street alarm-call points could be responded to and individual call-bells activated in each fireman's house. In an emergency individual officers or specific teams could be immediately summoned. The doors to the engine houses were all automated and a master clock recorded how long it took to respond to an incident. The fireman was on call at most times, in fact it was not till the end of the Second World War that their 124 hour weeks were reduced to just 60! In other words there were only a few hours each day, or perhaps a long afternoon, when the men were not on duty or

Plate 3.4 The Leicester Fire Service Band, circa 1935.
Ernest Peberdy is playing the guitar.

standby. Ernest played a part at the opening – he demonstrated the new turntable ladder and a photograph appeared in the *Mercury* of him at a great height spraying a hose as spectators looked on.

In 1932 Ernest gave evidence at a coroner's inquest into the death of a woman in a house fire. The death was suspicious and the proceedings were reported in *The Times*. It seemed that Ernest had gone to the fire and brought the woman's body down from an upstairs bedroom. He laid it out on the ground and the husband came up, but rather than ask about his wife he wanted to know whether his cash box had been found. Ernest swore at the man for his lack of concern (the coroner said he wouldn't write down what Ernest had shouted!). The inquest tried to ascertain if there was other suspicious evidence. The man was in debt and the house and life insurance would have cleared what he owed; he admitted that he should have done more to save her but said 'he'd lost his head'. At the end the coroner concluded: 'I must say on the evidence before you that you have no direct evidence against Mills'. The jury returned a verdict that Mrs Mills had died through the fire but had no evidence as to how it had started.

Ernest was promoted to station officer in 1933 and became the district officer in charge of the Ashfordby Street Substation in 1937. With the coming of the War he was based back at HQ. In 1939 there were 53 regular firemen, which was obviously far too small a number to cope with the expected air raids, so the Brigade recruited almost 2000 auxiliary fire fighters who were based at 16 small stations set up around the city.

The lives of Ernest and Walter (great, great grandfather and great grandfather) encompass an entire century. This was a century of huge changes, not only in technology and the well-being of ordinary people, but in cultural identity and behaviour. The first cars were on the streets of Leicester when Ernest was a child, and in the City Museum there is a photograph of a car built in 1907 by Earp and Peberdy. By the time that Walter died in 1990 most reasonably well off families owned a car and a range of appliances like washing machines, giving them more leisure time and a freedom to do things that their grandparents could not even have imagined.

The two world wars and their after-effects dominated the first half of the century. Neither Peberdy was in the armed forces as Ernest was a fireman during both the wars and Walter a policeman in the Second World War, but like everybody else their histories were shaped by the consequences of the wars. The economic depression and the poverty of working people during the 1920s and early 30s affected the way they thought. Ernest had a secure job and so his family did not face hardship, but the experience of that time made them careful people who did not do anything that would put the family at risk, and certainly didn't do anything that might get them into debt.

Ernest was the first generation of the family to benefit from the educational reforms of the late nineteenth century. The 1870 Education Act, perhaps more than any other legislation, was an important one for the Peberdy family as it gave them *schooling*. The Act made the State accept responsibility for ensuring every child had access to an elementary school of reasonable quality. Ernest had gone to school till aged 14 and was literate and numerate. Similarly Walter had a good level of education, and though he, like most children from his background, didn't go to college, he was very supportive (and proud) of his son when he went to university.

It was also these two generations who benefited from the social and welfare legislation introduced during the middle of the twentieth century. Both lived in good housing with inside sanitation. When Ernest died the National Health Service had been established, and in the last years when he was dying from lung cancer he experienced a level of free support unknown to Manoah and Tom. Both Ernest and Walter had secure old ages with pensions, and certainly by the time of Walter's death he had no worries about destitution in the way that the Peberdys from Tom back to John almost certainly would have feared. The Peberdys had gently and unremarkably, gone from surviving to thriving.

But they had also made another transition. Tom was a labourer. His great grandfather may have been a yeoman farmer, but he was most definitely urban working-class. It was Ernest who had taken the first 'step up'. As a district fire officer he had become, in occupation and attitude, 'respectable working-class'. Walter went further. By the second half of his life he saw himself, and was seen by others, as middle-class: he had an almost professional job, was a homeowner, an *Express* reader and a lifelong Conservative voter.

Walter Peberdy was Alexander and Felix's maternal great grandfather. He was born in 1913, just a year before the outbreak of the First World War. As a child he lived with his parents and sister in a fireman's house. His first job was in a hosiery factory, Rudkin and Lauden, and there he met Jessie Green. He became a policeman in 1936, and in 1938 they married. In holiday photographs they look happy (well, people generally

Plate 3.5 Jessie Green aged about 20 in 1934.

do!), and those taken camping at the seaside, swimming in the canal or posed in a garden, show a healthy, smiling mid-20s couple; Walter with his pipe and Jessie in a pretty dress that she had almost certainly made. He owned a small sports car, and one of the memories that Walter related was being on holiday in Cornwall in August 1939. The war was imminent, and as a policeman he was ordered to return immediately to Leicester. This was the time before motorways and the trip back, on roads full of other fearful returning holidaymakers, went through 20 or more towns and took them 12 hours. Walter never spoke of the war and hardly ever of his time in the police. The only exception was his macabre story of patrolling a railway line in the middle of the night to pick up the body parts of a man who had committed suicide.

But from Leicester police archives it is possible to gain something of a glimpse of his time as a copper. Walter was 23 when he joined the Leicester City Force in September 1936 and became PC 134. He wasn't the first Peberdy in the Force; that honour goes to John Peberdy, who was appointed as a constable in 1839 to patrol the Leicester Union Canal. The Force had come into being in 1836, so Walter joined in its Centenary Year. Why did he become a policeman? He had been brought up as a

Plate 3.6 Jessie at the wheel of Walter's MG sports car.

fireman's son and spent his childhood years living in a house alongside the fire-station, so following his father into another of the services was not too big a step. An important factor may have been that the job provided a house and so enabled him to marry Jessie. After training he was based at the new Police HQ in Charles Street. This had just been built and was an impressive three-storey fortress of a building faced with Portland stone.

Police officers in this middle part of the century were respected authority figures. Constables had *beats* that they patrolled on foot. So got to know, and be known by, the community. In the 1930s they had few of the modern pieces of equipment that we take for granted, not even radios, though the Leicester force did introduce VHF radios into its small fleet of cars the year Walter joined. There were about 300 constables, and walking their beat and traffic duties were the two main routine jobs. In the mid 1930s a new system of working was introduced. It involved *police boxes*. These were small wooden cabins placed at points around the city, painted a distinctive shade of dark blue, they measured seven feet high and five and a half feet square, with a single door at the front. Inside was a table bolted to the wall, a stool and a single bar electric fire. One light bulb dangled from the ceiling. A telephone that directly linked the box to police HQ was on a shelf, and the public could access this in an

Plate 3.7 Jessie and Walter on honeymoon, 1938.

emergency (very few private homes had a phone) by lifting a flap on the outside. These constructions became famous two generations later when the science fiction television series *Dr Who* had a time ship within one of these traditional police boxes. At the start of each eight-hour shift Walter would phone from the box to the Charles Street HQ to get his orders for the day. He'd then walk his beat or direct traffic, and halfway through return to the box for a snack. The time spent in the box was regulated to the minute, and sergeants would visit each constable twice a day to check they were not slacking.

The uniform was the traditional children's story book representation of PC Plod – the stiff dark jacket and trousers, shiny buttons and the distinctive domed helmet with cap badge. In the 30s and 40s constables wore white gloves – cotton in the summer and wool in winter (hence Auden's lines in his 1936 poem *Funeral Blues*, 'Put crepe bows round the white necks of the public doves, Let the traffic policemen wear black cotton gloves') and with the addition when directing traffic, of long white sleeves to ensure that drivers could see when they were being allowed to cross the junction. Walter's salary was about £200 a year, which doesn't sound much, but you could buy a house on one of the new estates for £500. He was keen on sport and played cricket and football for the police teams. A surviving photograph of him in the force was taken in April 1938; he is dressed as a goalkeeper in the back row of the team photo as they proudly show off their cups. Alongside him is PC Charles Smith, his best friend, who a few months later was his best man.

The year that Walter became a policeman, officers started receiving training in war duties and the things that would need to be done if the expected air raids happened. By mid 1939 it was clear that war was coming. In mid-August all off-duty officers could be seen outside the Charles Street HQ, in their vests and braces, filling bags to protect the window from bomb blasts. Almost every constable helped out, earning an additional 1s 6d an hour to shovel 800 tons of sand into the bags. Walter and Jessie left in mid August for their annual holiday to Cornwall. He had to provide a telephone contact number, and on 25th August his sergeant called to say that all leave had been cancelled and he was to return immediately. Nine days later, on 3rd September, war was declared.

Plate 3.8 Walter (bottom right) with members of the police football team, circa 1938. He was the goalkeeper.

Leicester at War

Unlike in the First World War when the conflict and destruction was *over there,* it was understood by everyone that the entire population would be potential targets, not just soldiers but civilians too. The advances in technology meant that German planes could reach every Midland industrial town.

When Walter was on duty in the city he must have encountered his father, also on duty as a district fire officer. Like the fire service, the regular police force recruited a range of civil defence volunteers – air raid wardens, police auxiliaries and the Women's Voluntary Service – and trained them in what to do when the expected bomb and gas attacks began. Every household with a garden was given an air raid shelter that they could build below ground while larger communal shelters were made for people in the city centre. On 5th September the Town Clerk set up a food control committee in anticipation of food and petrol rationing. Leicester had a population of 240,000 and in spite of the depressed years of the 1930s was reasonably prosperous, and so in the early months of the war, though everyone was nervous of what was to come, things were not too bad. The rural parts of the county were considered to be safer than the city, and streams of evacuees from northern cities soon started to arrive at the railway stations to be allocated to families in the rural towns and villages.

At Charles Street Police HQ preparations were made for the expected gas attacks. Walter and the other officers were shown how to use the protective suits, and showers were installed so that they would be able to wash thoroughly after an attack. One problem to be solved was the street lighting. All houses and factories were blacked out at night – this involved covering the windows with dark material to ensure no light could be seen from the air. But if all the streetlights were put out it would be both difficult and dangerous for essential people to get about. The city engineers developed a low intensity system called *starlights,* which enabled vehicles and pedestrians to move around but were invisible to enemy planes. Yet even with this system many road fatalities happened as people stepped in front of trams and buses. Because of the fear of invasion all place names and road signs were taken down, and even the word Leicester was painted out on the tramcars. If the Germans did arrive they would be lost!

In 1940 the bombing started. Two daylight Luftwaffe raids took place in August, causing a lot of damage, and then, in November another raid followed on the 19th by the biggest raid on Leicester of the War. At about

7.30pm enemy planes dropped flares over the city, the precursor to a
targeted attack. At eight a first wave of high explosive bombs hit houses
and the town hall. Just after nine o'clock the Highfields District was hit,
killing 60 people, and then shortly after midnight a group of police
officers from Walter's station were sent out to help. They had only just
arrived at a severely damaged street when a huge explosion buried them in
rubble. Two were killed outright and another died of his injuries a few
hours later. When daylight broke the full extent of the attack could be
seen – 550 houses destroyed, 4200 damaged, 11 factories reduced to
rubble and 72 no longer able to function. One hundred and eight people
were dead and 203 injured. The month of November was horrific for the
whole country. The neighbouring city of Coventry suffered terribly, with
400 tons of high explosive being dropped and 1350 causalities. Over the
whole country 2000 civilians died during the month and 8000 were
wounded. For Ernest and the fire service their worst night was also 19th
November, but in total they faced 55 major fires during the war, with
each one seeing them out on the streets trying to make things safe as the
bombs rained down.

The raids and the threat of raids kept the police busy and yet normal
police work also had to be done. With so many weapons in circulation
gun crimes became common. There was a spate of armed robberies on
cinemas in 1944, and perhaps surprisingly low level crime also increased,
especially caused by young people. The Chief Constable, Oswald Cole,
believed this was due to the absence of fathers, and mothers having to be
out at work. The more disciplinarian attitudes of the time can be seen in
his solution: 'adventurous trumps or the driving away of a car as an outlet
of boyish energy might be overlooked, but in my opinion, children who
despoil others' property should be whipped!'

The war ends

Finally, on 8th May 1945 the war in Europe came to an end. At 12.01
flags were flown over the offices, factories, schools and the Town Hall;
shops closed and children were sent home so that they could join the
celebrations. Large crowds gathered in the Town Hall Square and sang
Rule Britannia accompanied by the Salvation Army band. As the day went
on street parties and dancing took over every public place. The Specials
Police Band provided the music in the city centre and coloured lights were
switched on for the first time in five years. On Victoria Park an
enterprising man sold American hot dogs (an exotic foreign food) that

he cooked in the headlights of an army motorcycle. In the streets effigies of Hitler were burned on bonfires.

After the dropping of the atomic bombs on Japan in August and their surrender, the global war finally came to an end in September. Walter left the police force and Ernest retired as a fireman. But it was a very different world from 1939. Rationing continued into the early 1950s, and in fact many food shortages became worse in the years immediately after the war. The boot and shoe industry and the hosiery factories prospered, and it was into the hosiery business that Walter entered when he left the police. Along with the rest of the country the city experienced a *baby boom,* with the city growing from 239,000 at the outbreak of the war to 285,000 by 1951. Ernest retired from the Fire Service but he did not have a long retirement as he died from lung cancer in January 1949. Did Ernest get a chance to hold his baby grandson Max in that last period of his illness? Let's hope he did.

Walter left the police in January 1946, the year before Max was born. On holiday he and Jessie had met a businessman, Harry Pereira, who owned a hosiery company in Leicester. They became good friends and when Max was baptised Harry was one of the godparents. Walter went to work for him and financially this was a good time. They bought a house and in 1951, when their son was four, they moved to Buckingham so that Walter could develop the company's sales in the south of the country. They returned to Leicester however, in 1953, as Jessie was not happy living away from her friends. Eventually Walter was made a director, and it was with great pride that they bought copies of the *Leicester Mercury* to see the announcement of his appointment.

He had been a keen cricketer in his younger days, but by his forties when he wasn't working Walter spent his time making things. Mostly he did carpentry (but with the skills of a cabinet maker!). A Welsh dresser that he made when he first married is still in the family, and will officially be an antique in 2037. He was always making something. His biggest project was a house. In the early 1960s he designed it, got an architect to draw up the detailed plans, then scoured south Leicestershire for some land, and eventually contracted different builders and tradesmen to build it in the village of Great Glen. After that he built garden walls, paths and more walls as well as maintaining the house.

The move to the country was Walter's idea, not Jessie's. In the mid 1960s things did not go well for them. They separated. She went back to Leicester while Walter and Max stayed in the house. Harry Pereira retired and it was agreed that the business should be sold. Max went away to agricultural college and Walter was on his own. It was a lonely time for him. He sold the house and used some of the money to buy a menswear shop in Tamworth. After a few years he married again, to Barbara Hands, and they moved to the village of Ratby just north of the Leicester city boundary. By now he had retired, and the last ten years of his life were very happy. They were quiet people, but both *doers*. They had a small group of friends and while Walter kept the house in a superb state of repair, Barbara maintained the inside to an even higher standard.

Walter died in 1990, and there is a headstone with his name in Ratby churchyard. With his death the link between this Peberdy family and Leicestershire came to an end. It was **Max Peberdy** who continued the family but first there is an important genetic line that comes through Jessie Peberdy and the generations of mothers that led to Miss Green and her marriage to Walter Peberdy.

It is possible to go back a little over two hundred years from Max's birth in 1947 to his maternal great, great, great, great, great grandmother Elizabeth Shirley who was born in 1760. From Elizabeth to Max's mother Jessie there are six generations of mothers (and thus six generations of ancestral grandmothers of Alexander and Felix), and all but Jessie were born in rural Warwickshire.

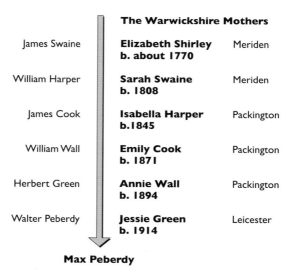

The Warwickshire Mothers

James Swaine	**Elizabeth Shirley** **b. about 1770**	Meriden
William Harper	**Sarah Swaine** **b. 1808**	Meriden
James Cook	**Isabella Harper** **b.1845**	Packington
William Wall	**Emily Cook** **b. 1871**	Packington
Herbert Green	**Annie Wall** **b. 1894**	Packington
Walter Peberdy	**Jessie Green** **b. 1914**	Leicester

Max Peberdy

Figure 11: Six Generations of Mothers

This family line can be said to be truly middle England, because Meriden has claimed for many centuries to be the exact centre of the country. A 500 year-old sandstone monument stands on the village green proudly telling the passing world this fact, though more recent analysis by the Ordinance Survey suggests that the true geographical centre is a farm some 11 miles to the northeast. The village obviously goes in for memorials as another was erected in 1921 to all the cyclists who died in the First World War. It would be interesting to know if Thomas George Evers (Alexander and Felix's paternal great grandfather) visited the site, as the first regiment he joined in 1916 was the 2/1 Essex Yeomanry – a regiment that became cycle mounted in the latter half of the war.

Little is known about **Elizabeth Shirley** other than she may have been born in Meriden in the late 1760s and married James Swaine in Birmingham in 1787. They married by licence, which indicates they went to the city to get married instead of waiting to have banns read. They had a daughter, **Sarah Swaine,** who was baptised in Meriden on 18th September 1808. At this time Meriden had a population of about 800 with 150 or so houses. They were a poor family, James being an agricultural labourer. He had died by the time that Sarah was a teenager because the Meriden Church Vestry Book records in 1823 that Widow Swain and some other villagers had asked for financial help to pay their rent but it was refused 'on account of their daughters being capable of going to service being kept at home'. The following year she applied and got a weekly payment of one shilling. The next year (1826) the minute book records 'That Widow Swaine having given up her house to Widow Knight that the house be repaired'. Over the next ten years the entries show she got annual relief from the parish of about 26 shillings. She lived to a good age and died in 1840.

In 1842 her daughter Sarah Swain married William Harper, a man 20 years her senior. William was Meriden born and a brewer. It may seem strange to us today that so many people were occupied in making beer. We are used to big commercial breweries, but for several centuries up to the middle of the twentieth century there were numerous small, family-run beer makers, many of whom would have sold their own beer from their house. It was quite common for even small villages to have two or three public houses. Beer consumption was high and farm workers and labourers had some of their wages paid in beer or cider, so most communities would have had a number of families involved in brewing. Because so much beer was drunk – often gallons (many, many litres) per day – and as it was a bulky commodity to transport, most beer was consumed within four or five miles of where it was made. A few brewers had started making beer by the 1790s on an industrial scale, Samuel Whitbread being the most famous, but it wasn't until the establishment of the railways that non-local beer was drunk in rural areas.

It is more accurate to say that the Harpers were primarily maltsters not brewers. A maltster was a man who either made malt for beer or was a dealer selling malt to brewers. Malt was made by coarsely grinding barley grains and then mixing them with hot water. This process converted the starch into maltose sugar, and the resulting liquid was called *wort*. This was then boiled with hops to give flavour. Most brewers bought the malt rather than do this process themselves, hence why there were two types of occupation. Many of those who brewed at this time would have been large farmers. Malt was taxed and in fact in the early part of the century up to a seventh of the government's revenue came from this source. Excise officers could inspect the maltster's premises to ensure the correct amount was being paid but in rural areas their visits were infrequent so it's likely that most produced far more than they declared. It was a skilled job as the maltster had to make judgements about the quality of the barley and how best to combine different types. The busiest time was October to May when the cooler weather meant it was easier to control the temperature of the malting process, which usually took 12 to 15 days for each batch.

Many poor labouring families spent more on beer than any other commodity and given the poor quality of the water it was often a safer thing to drink: 'strong beer and ale for adult men . . . table beer and small beer for family and servants'. The temperance movement had not yet taken off, and in fact people like John Wesley and William Cobbett actively supported beer drinking, as they believed it far preferable to consuming spirits, especially gin. It was even considered far better than tea. As Cobbett wrote: 'I view the tea drinking as a destroyer of health, an enfeebler of the frame, an engenderer of effeminacy and laziness. A debaucher of youth and a maker of misery in old age.' (William Cobbett, *Cottage Economy,* pp. 14–22, 1926 ed.) Not only were our ancestors contributing to the health of the nation they were also considered to be patriotic, as true Englishmen drank home produced ale, not foreign imported wines!

Sarah and William moved shortly after their marriage to Great Packington, just a few miles north of Meriden, and the next three generations lived and worked on the Packington Estate. Packington Hall was the home of the Earls of Aylesford. The hall was built in 1693 and was extended and improved in the Palladian style in 1732 by the Italian architect Joseph Bonomi. The park was landscaped with a lake and woodlands and by the time Sarah and William arrived in the 1840s it was a very grand mansion employing many dozens of servants and gardeners. There was no village of Great Packington, the parish consisted of about 60 estate houses and cottages and the church of St James that had been built in the park 50 years earlier. The population when Sarah and William arrived was about 340 people and the way of life on such an estate had not changed greatly for a 100 years. But in 1839 a change did happen when the London and Scottish Railway opened a line that crossed the neighbouring parish of Little Packington; before the turn of the century this area was to become a centre of British industry, with Birmingham and Coventry reaching out and eventually surrounding this narrow belt of 'old England'.

William and Sarah's first child was born in Packington in 1843 – a boy – and following family tradition he was named William. **Isabella Harper** was born the next year. It seems likely that they were running a pub, as their address at the time of the 1841 census is the *Malt Shovel.* Isabella's father died at some point between 1851 and 1861 and her mother married again – to Joseph Tustin, so at the age of 15 she was living in Packington but with her mother and new stepfather.

In a neighbouring house was the Cook family; the father Charles and the mother Prudence (née Shuttleworth) had both been born in Packington at the turn of the century. Charles was a bricklayer cum mason. They had a big family – nine children – and it was their youngest son, James, born in 1841, that Isabella married. Packington was a very close-knit community or perhaps a more accurate word is *enclosed* because families stayed together and intermarried in a way that is not common today. For example the Shuttleworths had been on the estate for many centuries. Charles Cook and Prudence Shuttleworth married in Packington Church in 1821 and that same year both Prudence's mother Deborah (b. 1781) and her grandmother Catherine (b. 1743) died and were buried in the churchyard. The church and the Christian rites of passage were to some small degree levellers of the great class differences between those living in the 'big house' and those employed as labourers on the estate, as for example Prudence's first child Caroline was baptised in January 1822 and the next entry in the church register was the baptism of Augusta, daughter of the Earl and Countess.

The marriage of James Cook to Isabella took place in Packington in February 1867; Charles had followed his father's occupation and was a bricklayer. They had six children but Isabella died when she was just 41. The cause of death was *phchicus,* this is not a word that we recognise today but it was the old medical term for tuberculosis, a disease of poverty and poor living conditions. It is easy to have a cosy and rather romantic view of rural life in the nineteenth century without the stresses of our modern day living, but the reality was great hardship and very poor housing. And of course this was well before the time when modern medicine even understood the causes of many diseases, let alone had drugs to cure them. It is her sister in law whose signature appears on the death certificate, except that it isn't a signature but an x; rural families like these, especially the women, had little if any formal education and certainly could not read or write.

It was their third child **Emily Cook** who continued the family line of mothers – she was born in 1871. A momentous event overtook the Hall when Emily was a little girl of six; the Earl and his wife became involved in scandal! The Aylesford family were frontpage news both in England and overseas with the *New York Times* running many articles on the antics of the English nobility. The 7th Earl and his wife fought a bitter divorce in the High Court. Lady Aylesford had eloped with a certain Lord Blandford, but the Earl was also having an affair with the wife of a neighbouring landowner. The Dilkes family lived in Maxstoke Castle, not far away, and when Mr Dilkes discovered that his wife was being unfaithful he committed suicide. All these details became the stuff of numerous newspaper articles throughout the world, and when the case ended the Earl fled the publicity and settled in the States. He was not to live long after the scandal, and in the Packington Church is a memorial brass plate that reads:

Heneage 7th Earl of Aylesford, the Cowboy Earl died Big Springs Texas emigrating after Royal scandal on 13th January 1885.

The Earl's brother inherited the title but life for the ordinary folk on the estate carried on much the same. Emily and her siblings and cousins all attended the local Packington School. The record books give a picture of what school life was like. Often it was closed; in February 1876 when Emily was five and just starting school an entry states: 'Floods again on Tuesday. Premises entirely under water during Wednesday and Thursday'. In the following Spring 'A heavy gale with driving snow kept all away but 3'. In February 1878 'four fifths of children affected by colds. Were given cough mixture'. Other events also encouraged the children not to attend: 'Attendance very irregular, children acorn gathering; Boys absent due to bird-keeping; lingering harvest, small irregular attendance'. With poor families the children were an important source of income, and in fact some farmers would insist that the children of their workers helped out at busy times, so it's not surprising that the teachers recorded such happening as normal events. There were three holidays per year. two weeks at Christmas, Whitsuntide week in May and Harvest Holiday from mid-August to mid-September. Even with these holidays, if there were pennies to be made the children could be away for long periods. One of Emily's young cousins, Charles Cook, is recorded as 'returned to school after an absence of ten weeks'. However there were occasional treats, and one is recorded in August 1875 – 'Half holiday on Monday. Public tea at the Old Hall on the occasion of Lady Anne Murray's wedding'.

Emily married in 1890, and not surprisingly to another young Packington-born estate worker, William Wall. She was 20 and he was 27 and employed as an undergardener. A tithe house came with the job and they lived at Brook Cottage. A cottage in the nineteenth century was a cold and damp place where the family lived in very close proximity. The only heating was usually a wood fire in the kitchen; all the other rooms would be very cold in winter. As Thomas Hardy wrote: 'in cottages the breath of the sleepers freezes to the sheets'. There were usually only two bedrooms, so the children would all sleep together when they were young, and as they got older a daughter would often live at a grandparent's house. Cooking was confined to what could be done on the open fire, so mostly things that could be boiled, stewed or pot-roasted. Tinned food was just becoming available and a treat on Sundays was a tin of salmon, corned beef and possibly condensed milk with a cup of tea. Virtually no cottages had piped water so rainwater falling on the thatched roof was collected in water butts or water was taken from a well. There were no indoor toilets, and the *privy* would be at the back of the house, usually a brick outbuilding with a seat and a hole. Taking a bath consisted of placing the washing tub in front of the kitchen fire, and as this was the common room of the house the opportunity for the parents and older children to wash thoroughly was infrequent. A bowl of cold water in the bedroom was the more normal custom. Of course there was no electricity so at night oil lamps would be lit. These only gave a weak arc of light and so the edges of the rooms would be dark, allowing the mice to run around just

Plate 3.9 Park Gate at Great Packington – the home of the Wall family and where
Annie Isabella was born in 1894.

feet away from the sitting family. It's not surprising that country people
went to bed early as other than conversation and mending clothes there
was not much to keep you up after a hard physical day.

William's father Richard Wall had been born in the adjoining county
of Northamptonshire in 1825. In 1848 he married a second cousin, Eliza
Fulford, and a few years later moved to Packington to live with an uncle.
Richard emerges from the records as a strong character. He and Eliza had
five children, though Richard was a manual worker at the age of 76 he was
described on the census as a 'labourer on the road'. He was obviously a
reasonably educated man as he held the post of *parish clerk* in 1891. Emily
and William had four children, Eliza 1892, Charles 1893, Annie Isabella
1894, and William in 1898, four children but they may have had others,
for as the Packington Church records show, many, many children on the
estate died before their fifth birthday.

Annie Isabella Wall is Alexander and Felix's great, great grandmother.
She went to school until her teenage years and then left the family home
like many country girls, to go into *service*. By now the railways had been
established for 60 years and many Wall relatives had started to move away
from Packington. One aunt had become a housekeeper to a family in
Leicester, and at the age of 14 Annie was put on the train to become a

maid in the 'mistress's house'. It is difficult for us today to imagine just how big a change this was for Annie; she may have been lucky and seen a little of the world outside Packington – perhaps on a charabanc day-trip to the seaside – but it's doubtful if she had stayed away from home for even one night before going off to this big city. Yet she took with her a lot of good sense, and the belief that there was little point in complaining about the cards life had dealt you. She also had acquired much Midlands country folklore, like the imperative to turn over one's money on hearing the first cuckoo of Spring – a good luck belief she passed onto her daughter and then to her grandson, who in turn passed it on to Alexander and Felix.

   Knighton was the smart part of Leicester and it was to a large house in Knighton that Annie went to work as a housemaid. A housemaid was responsible for cleaning the windows weekly, mopping the floors, washing the household clothes and generally doing what the housekeeper and cook told her to do. She would eat in the kitchen with the other servants; breakfast was usually bread and butter, hot meat and vegetables for dinner, and bread and cheese for supper. This sounds a very restricted diet to us, but compared to what Annie had back in Packington she was eating well. Looking out of the window she would have seen a young man tending the garden, Herbert Green. Herbert was five years older than Annie. He had been born in 1889 in Rothley, a village to the north of the city, and was the youngest son of ten children. His parents, Edwin Henry Green and Eliza Holmes, were both first generation city dwellers. Edwin had been born at Admaston in Shropshire and his father George was a farmer, first with 40 acres in Wellington and then moving to a larger farm of 103 acres at Little Wenlock, an area made famous by A. E. Housman and his *A Shropshire Lad* poem:

> On Wenlock Edge the wood's in trouble;
> His forest fleece the Wrekin heaves:
> The gale, it plies the sapling double,
> And thick on Severn snow the leaves.

It seems probable that there was some family rift that led Edwin to leave home and find labouring work in Leicestershire. As a result it was his younger brother Thomas who took over the farm at Little Wenlock at about the turn of the new century. On Herbert's mother's side the family had lived in villages in the northern part of Leicestershire and worked as agricultural labourers or builders for at least two or three generations back.

Plate 3.10 The Wall family: Annie centre with her mother and father
(sitting left front) circa 1914.

Annie Wall and Herbert Green were married back in Annie's home
church at Packington on 19th November 1913. A short time later Jessie
was born and the following year another daughter Elsie. They had very
little time together as in September 1914 the war with Germany began
and Herbert joined the Royal Welch Fusiliers. There is a family
photograph taken at this time – the two small girls with the young
Annie and Herbert in his uniform. That was to be the only memory his
daughters were to have of him, as in 1917 he was killed. Unlike the tens of
thousands of British troops killed by German bullets and bombs, Herbert
died from a British made hand grenade. He and another soldier were
moving boxes of grenades when they accidentally exploded. Annie
received the stark notification from the War Office of his death and
then a few weeks later his last letter to her was delivered – surely this must
have made her grief even more intense. He had written it on the night
before he died:

July 2nd

My Dearest Wife

    I now write these lines thanking you for parcel which I have just received
quite safe. A lot of the small cakes are smash up dear, but the large one is
alright dear. I have enjoyed my tea dear, once again. It came just right, for I

had just finished my last bit of writing paper. Did you send a parcel before this one dear. Those Fruit Flavours are alright dear. Remember me to Mother and Dad when you write dear, and tell them I shall not be over for haymaking now, worse luck. Have you wrote to the Duffs lately dear for I have not. Remember me to Mrs Clarke hoping she is keeping well I don't expect I shall know our little home, when I do get back dear, by what you say the children will be altered so, but there is one thing I shall know it with, and that is you dear, so now my dear don't you go and altered or I shall be lost. Well my darling I shall have to close now, so good night and God bless you and the dear children.

I remain your Ever Loving
Husband xxxxxxx
for the children
xxxxxxxxx

The war ended the following year. Annie received a small widow's pension from the Army but it was a time of great hardship. She remained in Leicester and Jessie and Elsie went to school in Knighton. On Tuesday 10th June 1919 Annie and thousands of other Leicester people gathered in the centre of town and in Victoria Park to welcome King George V and Queen Mary. The king had come to grant the town city status. This was probably the largest public event ever seen in Leicester – before or since. There was a huge procession and excited children waved their union flags.

Plate 3.11 1916 Herbert Green and Annie with Jessie and baby Elsie – probably the last time they were together before he left for the trenches. He died in July 1917.

But it must have been a day of some sadness for Annie as she watched the march past of regiments and soldiers who, unlike her Herbert, had survived the war.

Life for most working class people was about to get even more difficult. The early 1920s saw the start of the terrible economic depression. Even as early as 1921 work in Leicester was difficult to find and the numbers of unemployed rose rapidly; with the Wall Street Crash in 1929 things got worse. Annie eventually remarried. Frank Amey was a First World War Veteran (and proudly showed off his hand with its missing fingers shot off by a German sniper). He worked as a conductor on the trams, and they bought a small house in Knighton Church Road. Within a few years the Second World War started, and like her neighbours Annie and Frank witnessed the destruction and horror of a modern war. Though there had been air raid warnings during 1914–18 the city did not experience any bombing, but things were very different in this war. On the terrible night of 19th November 1940 about 30 German planes dropped bombs close to where Annie lived. A parachute mine landed on houses close to the junction of Knighton Road and Newstead Road. It destroyed two houses and killed eight people. Then minutes later another bomb landed in Knighton Road itself, demolishing a house and killing two more people. Annie and Frank lived just a short distance away and it must have been a frightening night for them and their neighbours as they waited below ground in their shelters for daybreak.

Annie had always been thrifty and knew how to *make do* so rationing was a challenge she could understand. Meat was the first food to be restricted (to 1s. 5d.'s worth per person per week), and then butter (4 oz a week), sugar (12 oz) and bacon (4 to 8 oz). Eggs were soon replaced by egg powder and though bread was never rationed till after the war, Annie throughout the rest of her life did not waste bread or any other leftover. The war ended and she kept herself busy earning money as a babysitter or cleaner right up till the last few years of her life. She remained in her little house at 57 Knighton Church Road till her death at the age of 94 in 1988.

She was a strong character, a survivor and as such not always an easy person to get on with. Jessie and Elsie left home in their teens. Both finished schooling at 14 and went to work in local hosiery factories as machine operators. Elsie was always the more daring and ambitious of the two. With the coming of the Second World War she met an English Army officer and for the next twenty years or so until his death lived with him on Jersey as Mrs Penny Scott-Kiddie. She had a daughter, Jill, who Grandma Amey brought up.

Jessie Green fell in love with one of the young supervisors at the factory, Walter Peberdy, and when he became a police officer they were married in Evington Church. In the early years they were happy except for one thing, they wanted children but none came, then after nine years of marriage Jessie had a son. In 1947 Maxwell Adrian Peberdy was born, and the tale continues in *Max's Story*.

CHAPTER 4

Garnett and Seven Mothers

Mothers are important. Like fathers they contribute half the child's genetic roadmap, but because they usually spend much more time with their children than others, it is from them that their son or daughter acquires much of their social and cultural inheritance. Going back seven generations embraces mother to great, great, great, great, great grandmother, and to the beginning of the 1800s. In genetic studies the family

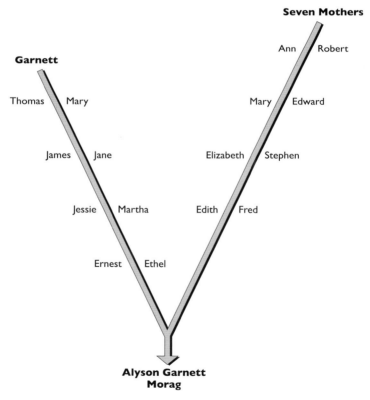

Figure 12: Arriving at Alyson and Morag

tree that looks at mother to mother is called the mitochondrial line. For Alexander and Felix it is inherited from Morag, and from her mother Alyson, and then through Ethel, Edith, Elizabeth, Mary and Ann and of course beyond them through hundreds of earlier generations. Each of the mothers has passed on to her children (almost) identical pieces of material crammed inside every cell of her son or daughter's body. These mitochondria act as a kind of battery in the cell. Although there are occasional mutations these changes are rare, and therefore these little organelles that Alexander and Felix carry around with them are essentially the same as the ones that Ann Holmes carried around as she skipped over the Derbyshire Peaks on the day of the Battle of Waterloo.

Because the maternal line is so important this chapter is structured in a different way from the previous three as its focus is on the maternal line till it reaches and joins the Garnett family in the mid 1930s – Garnett being the family name of the fourth Alexander and Felix grandparent, Alyson Garnett. The story starts back in the early nineteenth century with the seventh generation mother.

Baslow, Derbyshire

Ann Holmes was born in 1814. Baslow village is on the northern edge of the hilly Derbyshire Peaks and sits beside the river Derwent. The village is divided into three distinct areas with names that sound as if lifted from the pages of Tolkien – Over End, Nether End and Bridge End. In the nineteenth century there were two big landowners; the Duke of Rutland, and the Duke of Devonshire whose home, Chatsworth, lies just to the south.

It was in Baslow that Ann was born. Her parents were John Holmes (b. 1780) and Mary (b. 1790). John was an agricultural labourer and the couple had at least two other younger children, Alice and Charles. The earlier generations of the Holmes family had lived in the village during the eighteenth century and the old records give a few clues to their lives. Ann's father paid 25 pence to the Duke of Rutland for the rent of a 'homestead', while his father Robert had paid eight pence in tax to the local curate in 1772. This indicates that they were not well off as the richest families in the village were paying £1. 9s. 4d. to the church, but they were not the poorest as these were only paying 4d. It seems likely that the Holmeses had moved into the area in the early part of the 1700s, as there is no reference to them in the records of the previous century. Interestingly, we know that Robert and his wife Ann went to church and even the pew in which they sat! Baslow church listed all the pews and seats – there were 380 in 1789 – and who was eligible to sit on them. Anne's grandfather Robert Holmes sat on pew 23 and her grandmother on pew 35. Not surprisingly, given that he was the largest landowner, the Duke of Rutland owns most of the pews, and each of his tenants were eligible for one of his seats. The social divisions were important even at times of prayer!

We know little about Ann. As a young girl she may have worked in the village cotton mill that had been opened in 1785. But opportunities in the countryside were very limited and though the towns were grim there were attractions there for a young women, some independence from parents, and a greater chance of finding a husband who wasn't a farm labourer. Eventually she left home at Cherry Tree Farm in Upper End where her parents farmed a few acres and moved the 40 miles to Manchester. It's probable that she got a job as a servant or worked in a cotton factory. She was still very young when she met and married Robert Waterhouse, and only 17 when she had her first child. Of all the seven generations of grandparents of Alexander and Felix she was, by far, the youngest when she married.

Manchester

By the 1830s when Ann arrived in the city, Manchester was already a very big place. During the 1770s and 1780s demands for workers in the cotton factories had led the population to increase sixfold to 142,000. It wasn't just growing, it was exploding! By the time Ann's daughter had reached 20 the city had 338,000 people, and had become one of Europe's most important commercial centres. The growth was seen not only in the newness of the buildings, but also in the awful squalor. Even in the years before Ann arrived it was a city of clear divisions between the mill owners and workers, between the factory hands and the handloom weavers. In 1819 the Peterloo Massacre had taken place; this had been a protest by thousands of workers about their living conditions. The authorities responded with force and many deaths resulted when troops tried to restore order.

Manchester had both cotton and wool industries. The cotton spinners were the aristocracy of the new workforce, and though there was an economic boom in the 1820s, shortly after Ann arrived there was a slump, leading to more riots and unrest. It was a city of whose like had never been seen before. It had many very dynamic, and visionary entrepreneurs who became a new English class. They guarded their independence from the government in London, and so many of the reforms in urban living conditions were much slower in coming to Manchester than in some other British cities.

But in contrast to this elite was the great mass of ordinary people like Ann and Robert who poured in from the surrounding rural areas and from Ireland. It was to a life so very different from what they had experienced or could even imagine. Ann would have known poverty in the village but not this mixture of disciplined, time bound work in a factory with a return home at the end of a 12 or 14-hour day to the horrendous conditions in the basement accommodation or back-to-back terraces. Conditions in many areas of the city went far beyond anything we can imagine today. Life expectancy could be as low as half that found in rural England. Sanitation barely existed. Waste of all sorts was thrown into the courtyards and none of the terraced houses had toilets, bathrooms or running water. Cholera and typhus epidemics were frequent.

Ann married Robert Waterhouse in about 1829. They had nine children, well nine who survived. The first was Mary (b. 1830), then John (given her father's name), Eliza, Jane, Robert, Sarah, William, Charles and Emily, the last child being born in 1855. All births were in Manchester except the first son John who came into the world in Derbyshire. Ann has obviously made a visit to her family during the second pregnancy. Her husband was a butcher in the city. He was nine years older than Ann and had been born in Lancashire and probably came from a family who owned a butcher's shop. It is surprising for us today to see how many butchers there were in nineteenth century towns: in Manchester alone there were more than 500, but as there was no refrigeration each shop was only able to stock small quantities of freshly killed animals. Ann and Robert obviously had a very stable life as they appear on every census from 1841 to 1861, and with their children living at home until they left to get married. So it seems probable that they had quite a prosperous life compared to many.

Mary Waterhouse was their eldest child and Alexander and Felix's great, great, great, great grandmother. She married into a large and extended Manchester family – the Cockshoots. By the early 1800s there were a number of Cockshoot brothers working in their father's coach business. This was of course before either the car or railway, and they owned and ran horse drawn coaches, today's equivalent of buses and cabs, the taxis of nineteenth century England. Two of the brothers, Joseph and Edward, were employed in the business and some of their sons worked as drivers. Edward had a son, also called Edward, and Mary married Edward junior in 1848. At the time of their marriage Edward was a butcher and we can imagine them meeting at the Guild of Butchers Christmas Ball, which Mary attended on the arm of her father, or perhaps more mundanely, Edward may have been a boy apprentice in her parents' shop!

Edward didn't stay as a butcher but became a coach owner in the family business. The Cockshoots were a close family. Three brothers and their spouses lived as neighbours and their children would often sleep in the home of the relative next door. By now Manchester was a very big city, both in population and physical size, and there was a need for hundreds of horse drawn cabs. The Cockshoots were one of 49 Hackney *Coach and Cabriolet Owners* businesses registered with the council.

An account in *The Times* of December 1853 gives some idea of what it could be like in the smog and confusion of such a vast place:

A dense fog prevailed in Manchester during the whole of Tuesday . . . and approaches from the suburbs were so dark that many people lost their way and sought their homes in the directions directly opposite to their destination . . . the drivers of cabs had to get down and lead the horse, lantern in hand. Some ludicrous scenes presented themselves in the outskirts, where the slight indications of the course of the roads given by the gas lamps did not exist, and in several instances the drivers of omnibuses being met on foot, at the horses heads with lamp in one hand and a horn in the other producing the most unnatural sounds while the passengers walked behind . . . Yesterday frost set in and there were hopes of improvement though the fog is still very dense.

It was coal that was a main source of heating and energy in the factories, so Manchester, like all the big towns, had frequent smog that made seeing even 20 steps ahead difficult. General Napier, who was sent by the Government to put down unrest a few years before, had described the city as 'the chimney of the world. Rich rascals, poor rogues, drunken ragamuffins, and prostitutes form the morals, its soot made into paste by rain . . . what a place. The entrance to hell realised!'

Generally cab drivers had a reputation for adjusting their charges according to what they believed the customer would pay. Earlier that year, in April 1853, the Government had introduced the licensing of cabs. This laid down that for a distance of under a mile or a journey of less than 15 minutes, the charge was to be no more than sixpence. If a dispute arose and a magistrate was sitting, the driver was to go to the nearest police court for the disagreement to be settled.

An important event had taken place in Manchester just a few years before, in 1851. It was the year of the Great Exhibition in London, but as

Plate 4.1 Hansom Cab

part of the celebrations Queen Victoria travelled to the big cities. Tens of thousands of Manchester people lined the streets to see her. Hopefully Mary with her small son Joseph, and baby Sarah, were in the crowd, or perhaps they travelled in the family cab, as the newspaper accounts report that hundreds of cabs followed the Queen's procession. Victoria wrote in her diary about the enthusiastic crowds, and how well behaved they were, more so, she said than in Glasgow or Dublin or Edinburgh. But they were '. . . a painfully un-healthy looking population, men as well as women, but the white rosettes were as evident as their white faces.'

Edward and Mary had five children: Joseph, Sarah, Edward, Elizabeth and Robert, all born between 1845 and 1863. It is Elizabeth, born in 1858, who takes the maternal line forward, when she made the move from Manchester to Liverpool. She appears to be quite an independent young person, for she lived, not with her parents but next door in her Great Uncle Joseph's house. His wife must have died, because in the 1871 census, when Elizabeth was 12, there was also a cousin, Maggie Selina Cockshoot, in the house, and an older cousin, Mary Ann, acting as housekeeper.

Liverpool

Elizabeth Cockshoot married Stephen Betteley in 1879 when she was 21. While Elizabeth came from a family in the business of people conveyance, and owned coaches, Stephen's family were in alcohol and owned a pub. Just as Elizabeth's father Edward had been named after his father, so Stephen was the son of a Stephen. His father, Stephen Ravenscroft Betteley, was born just before the turn of the century in

1799 at Audley in Cheshire. He'd married Ann Cooke from Bromyard in
Herefordshire and set up a business in Liverpool in the area called West
Derby. They started as 'wine and spirit dealers' but by 1860 they ran a
pub.

They had nine children; eight sons and one daughter. Stephen junior
was son number three. It is interesting to see what jobs the boys went into:
a cotton broker's clerk, an ironmonger's apprentice, a watch finisher and a
tailor's apprentice. It was the young Stephen who worked in the pub as a
barman. Their mother must have died quite young and when the father
retired he went to live with his unmarried daughter Ellen.

After their marriage Elizabeth and Stephen took over the running of the
pub. Stephen had been previously married a few years before and had a
son (also called Stephen) but both the child and his first wife had died.
This second marriage to Elizabeth was also to be a short one. They had
two daughters, Alice Betteley, born in 1880, and Edith Betteley born the
following year. But then Elizabeth died and Stephen was soon to follow
(1893), leaving the two girls at the ages of 12 and 11 without parents. It's
not clear what happened to them immediately after their father died, but
it seems probable that it was a Cockshoot uncle who became their
guardian.

Alice and Edith were obviously high spirited and independent girls,
and with no parents to keep a close eye on them trouble followed. Alice
fell in love with her music teacher at school and got expelled. She and Mr
Beaumont ran off to London, eventually got married, and opened a music
shop in Hammersmith. They had a son and daughter but both had tragic
deaths, the son falling off rocks on Puffin Island and the daughter dying in
the London Blitz. The maternal line continued with **Edith Betteley.** Like
her sister she had inherited some money after her father's death, and living
on that income she went to stay with her older cousin Elizabeth Ann, who
she referred to as 'aunt', in Caernarfon.

Caernarfon

Family tradition has it that 'Aunt Elizabeth Ann had married badly'. Her
husband, a Mr Hughes, had been a 'consumptive Welsh barman' (it's best
not to try and analyse which element of this was considered worst). They
ran a pub in Caernarfon called the Pontrhythalt Inn. By the time that
Edith arrived, in the late 1890s, Elizabeth's husband had died, leaving her
with the pub and four children. One of these children was Emily, a second
cousin to Edith and a few years older. It was Emily Hughes who married a

man called Henry, and to add complication to the family tree, he also had the surname Hughes. It was this union that gave the maternal line its one famous person, well, famous in North Wales and among historians of the Labour Party. Henry was a quarry worker, but he became ordained as a Baptist Minister.

The Reverend Henry David Hughes and Emily had a son, Cledwyn. Cledwyn was born in Holyhead in 1916. He was a bright young man and went to Aberystwyth University, and after serving in the Second World War he set up a firm of solicitors in Holyhead. He was interested in politics and became the Labour MP for Anglesey. Eventually he was promoted to the post of Minister for Commonwealth Relations, and this took him to Rhodesia at the time of Ian Smith's declaration of UDI. He became Secretary of State for Wales and in 1961 Minister of Agriculture. In 1979 he was made a peer, Lord Cledwyn of Penrhos, and was the Leader of the Opposition in the Lords for ten years until his death in March 2000.

At one level the biological connection between Cledwyn and Edith Betteley seems a little distant, as they were only third cousins. But there are some closer links. Firstly, because when Edith married, her children stayed quite regularly with Cledwyn and his parents, and secondly, because of a birthmark.

In all the public photographs of Lord Cledwyn he is shown in profile, from the right side. This is because he had a 'ruby wine' mark on his left cheek. Alyson Garnett, Edith's granddaughter, has the birthmark on her hand, and Stephen Billing junior, another grandchild, on his cheek. Assuming that the mark is genetically inherited, then it must be via the Cockshoot line. Of course, many other Cockshoots may have had the mark but as a person's appearance is not recorded on the census data we have no way of knowing. The ancestor common to Cledwyn, Stephen and Alyson, is the father or mother of Joseph and Edward born at the end of the eighteenth century. The gene can obviously be inherited from both males and females, and so the carrier was either 'Father Cockshoot' or 'Mother Cockshoot' back in the 1770s.

Edith Betteley lived with her aunt for a few years. No doubt she felt quite accustomed to her new home being a pub as her own parents had run one in Liverpool, but attitudes in the local community were very different from those in West Derby. This was a strong non-conformist part of Wales that didn't approve of drinking and would not readily have

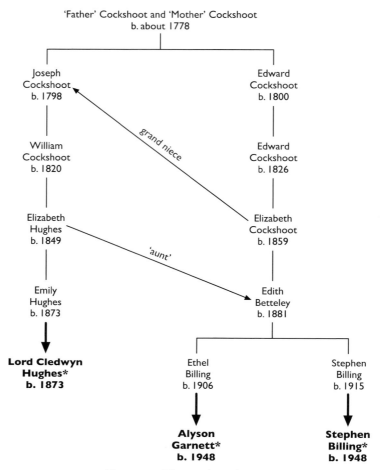

Figure 13: The Birthmark Gene
(* those known to have the ruby wine birthmark)

welcomed an independent-minded young Englishwomen. Because of the money she had inherited after her father's death she did not need to get a job; the 1901 census records that she was 'living on her own means'. But she didn't have a very long stay with her aunt, because in 1903 she married a young man in the town, Fred Billing.

The Billings were also an English family in Caernarfon. They had originally come from Northamptonshire. By the time Edith met Fred they were well established and ran a pub called the Alexandra Hotel. But Edith had at last escaped living in pubs because Fred, being a bright young man, had qualified as a dentist. Edith Betteley became **Edith Billing** and the matriarch of a respectable middle-class family.

Billing as a family name originated in Northamptonshire, there being two villages called Great and Little Billing. The first recorded person in the county with the name was a certain Osbert Billing in 1195. Many modern day Billings have researched their families and a number of books and articles tell of the Billings who were grazier farmers just to the north in Leicestershire. Some of these researchers claim that the name goes back even further than the villages and to a family group of Angles called the *Billingas,* who came from the island of Funen, in present-day Denmark, and settled in eastern England. The most famous Northampton Billing was Sir Thomas Billing (1410–82), who was the Chief Justice at the time of the War of the Roses.

Our ancestors were not so grand and their lives in the nineteenth century had been bound up with the growth of the railways. Fred Billing's grandfather was the Moses who took the family out of rural poverty and into a much more prosperous life in Wales. Joseph Billing was born in 1818 at Weedon, a village about ten miles to the west of Northampton. His wife Eleanor, who liked to be called Ellen, came from a family of shoemakers. Joseph and Ellen married about 1842 and had four children, the first two, Ann and Sarah, in Weedon, and then a son, John Eldred Billing (b. 1848) in Oakham, Rutland. A final son, Frederick, was born in 1851.

At some point in the 1850s Joseph became part of a 'revolution' that was to change the way the countryside looked and how people lived. He helped to make the railways. This was the period of the 'railway mania' when hundreds of new lines and dozens of railway companies were coming into existence. Joseph was not a navvy – navvies were the men who physically dug the tunnels and embankments – but an organiser of these workforces. On the census returns he is described as a 'railway contractor' or 'railway excavator'. The family now started a period of moving around the country. In 1861 they were living at East Dean in Gloucestershire and both Joseph and his eldest son were working as excavators.

A huge number of men were employed in the construction of the tracks at this time; it's estimated that by 1850 there were 250,000 navvies throughout the country. Building the line between Shrewsbury and Ludlow involved 2000 men and 400 horses, so these were immense construction projects. The bulk of the work was done by hand, the typical

tools being the pick, shovel and wheelbarrow. The word 'navvies' is a
shortened form of 'navigators'. They were organised in gangs and lived by
the newly constructed line in so called shantytowns. Huts would
accommodate twenty men and they would pay a little over a penny for
a night's bed. The fact that the Billing family were living in a house
suggests that they were reasonably well off compared to the men they were
employing. By the standard of the times the navvies were well paid, they
could earn 25 pence a day, which was about twice that of a farm labourer.
But their drinking was notorious, 'going on a randy' was navvy slang for a
drinking spree that could last for days. Only the tavern owners were
happy about the high spending on alcohol, while people living in towns
close to the construction sites closed their shops and recruited temporary
constables to defend their inhabitants.

East Dean, where the Billing family had their home in the 1850s and
60s, was part of the Forest of Dean, where most of the local people were
employed in coal and iron ore mining. In the 1840s Swindon to the east
had become an important locomotive works, and the Great Western
Railway extended its broad gauge lines to Bristol and then up to Gloucester.
Here it encountered a problem because the line from Birmingham that had
reached the city from the north was narrow gauge. But after much
negotiation a deal was struck, allowing the Great Western to build more
lines westwards using mixed gauges that enabled both broad and narrow
gauge trains to run along the same tracks. The Billings were living close to
the new Hereford, Ross and Gloucester line. This had been opened in

Plate 4.2 A gang of railway navvies in the mid-nineteenth century.

1855, and they may have moved to the area to help construct the track. They were also just a mile or so from another new construction, the Monmouth to Ross line that was eventually opened in 1873.

Perhaps this connection of railway construction and pubs explains how Joseph and Ellen came to Caernarfon. In 1850 the Britannia Tubular Bridge across the Menai Straits from Caernarfon to Anglesey was opened. This enabled the railway line to run, without a break, from London to Holyhead where it connected with the ferry to Dublin. The town of Caernarfon benefited from the increase in traffic and the need for accommodation and refreshment. The Billings moved to the town and became the licensee of the Alexandra Hotel sometime in the early 1870s. In 1872 the older son, John Eldred married Anne Goode. Joseph died, and so it was his widow Ellen, with son John and his new wife Anne, who ran the pub.

Anne seems to have been a very strong, hard-working woman. It might have been expected that son John would have found a wife in Gloucestershire or Wales, but he didn't. John had left East Dean and took a job as an ironstone miner in Wellingborough (he was on the 1871 census as lodging with a family in the town). It was here in the Billing's ancestral county of Northamptonshire, specifically to Weedon, that he found his wife to be. Anne's father, Samuel Goode, was a shoemaker in Weedon. In fact John had sought an even safer bet because not only was she a Northampton girl; she was also his cousin. Anne's mother had been a Billing before marrying and becoming a Goode. Thus Anne's maternal grandparents and John's paternal ones, were the same: John and Elizabeth Billing, born in the 1790s and also shoemakers. The families were neighbours, and as a child Anne had lived, at times, not with her parents but with grandma and grandpa. Though in theory tracing seven generations should identify 252 grandparents, Anne and John deprived Alexander and Felix of two, so they have only 250!

Caernarfon has always been known for its magnificent castle. It has a small harbour which was important for shipping out the locally quarried slate, and two railway lines that had opened around this period, so the town was a busy place with hundreds of very thirsty men eager to spend money in the local taverns. No photographs exist of John and Ann, but we get some idea of them as a couple and of their lives in the Alexandra Hotel from a short description written by one of their granddaughters, Freda Billing lived to be almost 101 and in her nineties recalled some memories of them from her childhood in Caernarfon:

. . . kindly gentle people; I associate them with many small pleasures. Grandpa once brought us a posy of meadow cranesbill. He had a nice round bristly face, was an excellent gardener and nature lover; he walked out early every morning, and ate only two meals a day. Granny was a dear old lady with a pair of rimmed spectacles pushed up into her fluffy grey hair.

Pubs didn't open on Sundays, and so the grandchildren would visit and be allowed into the 'snug' bar for a taste of port wine, and a Marie biscuit. This introduction to booze was obviously in expectation that as future publicans they needed early exposure to the product of their trade. The children were fascinated by the sawdust scattered on the floor of the bar, the polished spittoons (many of the customers would have had tuberculosis), the horsehair sofas, and the brass sugar crushers that men used when drinking a glass of hot toddy to sweeten it to their taste. If they stayed overnight it was in a four-poster bed with curtains, the bed having been warmed with hot coals from the fire in a copper bed warmer – 'what bliss' recalled Freda.

Christmas was a special time at the Alexandra, and there was always a party for the children. The hotel had 14 rooms, and the one where the party was held was up two storeys and immense, covering the whole

Plate 4.3 1912: A guard of honour in front of the Alexandra Hotel, Caernarfon. Is it great, great, great grandmother Annie Billing at the window?

upstairs floor of the pub. There were games, 'Sally go round the moon' being Freda's favourite. Grandma's toilet was remembered with pleasure. It had to be mounted by a series of steps, and was so large that as children they had to be careful not to fall in. It had a Wedgwood bowl decorated with flowers, and Freda was fascinated by its beauty; after being given a disappointing Christmas present, such as a pair of gloves or a prayer book, it was some consolation to be able to admire the loo. The Alexandra is still a pub today and is known locally as the 'Alex', rather appropriate given the name of the Billing great, great, great, great grandson.

John and Anne had eight children but only four survived, Fred (b. 1873), Joseph (b. 1878), John Eldred junior (b. 1879) and Florence (b. 1880). When Grandma Ellen died in 1893 John and Ann became the official licensees. Their oldest boy had obviously done well at school, and after graduating as a dentist in 1897 set up a practice in the town. Perhaps Edith Betteley was one of his patients; if so she would have had plenty of opportunity to stare into his eyes as she sat in the chair having her teeth drilled. In 1903 Fred and Edith got married. He was thirty and she twenty-two.

The new husband and wife were very different in attitude and aspirations. Edith, like her sister who had run off with her teacher, was a strong character and socially ambitious. Because of the money she had inherited she hadn't worked before their marriage, and like most women with reasonably well-off husbands, never had a job after she married. The exception to this was during the First World War when she was a volunteer nurse, and we have a photograph of her in uniform, marching through the streets of Caernarfon in about 1914. Once married to a professional man she expected to live in the style appropriate and to some extent that happened, they lived in a comfortable ten-room house with servants to help cook and clean. But two things made life difficult. First was Fred's personality; he was 'a very benevolent figure occupying the background' (Freda's recollection). But while Fred was quiet, Edith was stormy. She would rail about him to her daughters if he left her in the evenings to go to his club, and as a last resort turn on all the house lights to annoy him with her extravagance. Ultimately she made the pretence of leaving him, and took the children to stay with a friend in Newport. Fred came and brought her home but it was clear after that who was in charge. In 1911 a momentous event happened in the town. The Royal Family, eager to demonstrate their Britishness during the growing tensions with Germany, proposed that their eldest son Edward should be made the

Plate 4.4 The Billing family circa 1908 – Fred standing on left behind Edith
with daughter Freda on her knee and Ethel at her feet.

Prince of Wales at an investiture ceremony at Caernarfon Castle. In July
the future King Edward VIII was invested, and the Billings would
certainly have been on the streets with the cheering crowds, waving
their Union flags.

The desire to be part of respectable Caernarfon society led Edith to
wear very showy clothes. Some of the styles she copied from her sister who
came for breaks from her life in London. The children were obviously
embarrassed by their mother's flamboyance and Freda remembered with
some pain the particularly large hat decorated with a stuffed seagull! The

Plate 4.5 Edith Billing in nurse's uniform marching through Caernarfon 1914
(second from left in rear row).

second difficulty the family experienced in trying to achieve Edith's
aspirations was that the Billings were foreign, and though the daughters
learned to swear in the vernacular, as a family they did not speak Welsh.
But almost as bad as being English, Fred was a Conservative in a
predominantly Liberal town, in fact David Lloyd George was the local
Liberal MP and went on to be Prime Minister. Also they were Anglicans,
not Methodists or Baptists, and to cap it all, Fred's father ran a public
house.

The dental practice provided a living but it did not do well, and Fred
suffered frequent ill health. But he remained a dentist for more than forty
years, retiring in 1941. The couple had four children: Winifred or 'Freda'
(b. 1905), Ethel (b. 1906), Stephen (b. 1915) and Norman (b. 1918).

The second sister, **Ethel Billing,** continued this line of mothers. She was
intelligent and self-confident, and though the younger of the daughters
she was the adventurous one. Whereas Freda was originally educated at
home, Ethel's nature led her parents to send her to a small private school
close by. Neither daughter was allowed to play with local children, but
they had their own world in a nursery upstairs.

As a treat the girls were allowed to go and stay with Aunt Emily and the
Reverend Hughes at their house in Holyhead. The thing they liked best

Plate 4.6 Ethel and Freda Billing circa 1935.

was the freedom to read any book in their uncle's library. Towards the end of the war in 1918 when food supplies were short, they stayed and were amazed that their aunt had eggs and butter, and even sugar, the perks of being a country minister's wife, enough even to make them cakes. Their only duty was to take the two-year old Cledwyn for his morning outing. They could take his pram anywhere within reasonable distance, except onto the beach with its dangerous quicksand. But like the grandson in *Peter and the Wolf* who was forbidden by Grandfather to go into the meadow, it was just the place they did want to explore. It was Ethel who led them down to play. They had a wonderful time and got back to the safety of the sea wall, but they were seen. A parishioner reported back to the Manse. Their punishment was not too severe, and when they returned home to Caernarfon their mother was too preoccupied to tell them off, as she had just given birth to Norman. Cledwyn survived and so the history of North Wales and the Labour Party were shaped, just a bit, by two little English girls.

Wigston, Leicester

Ethel did well at school and went to Bangor University to study botany. This was an achievement for a girl in the 1930s and also says something about the encouragement and support that her father, and hopefully her mother, must have given. She became a teacher and took a post at a school in Leicester. It was there in Wigston, a village suburb to the south of the city, that she met and married Ernest Garnett.

To those with an interest in local history, the name of Wigston is very familiar. In 1957 one of the first academic historians to research the lives of 'ordinary people' was Professor W. G. Hoskins, and his book *The Midland Peasant* was a study of Wigston Magna from its beginnings as an Anglian settlement in the sixth century, until the turn of the 1900s. The nineteenth century, when many of our immediate ancestors lived in the village, was a period of rapid population increase and industrialisation as families moved from working on farms to making 'things'. The *thing* that was made in Wigston was hosiery, mainly woollen long socks and gloves. It was the invention of the knitting frame that was to change the lives of the Hacketts, Garnetts, Masons, Arthurs and Leonards.

Wigston people had been framework knitters for many centuries. The original machine was invented in 1589 by the Rev William Lee of Calverton, in the neighbouring county of Nottinghamshire. At the time it was revolutionary, as nothing like it had been devised before. But using an ingenious design of needles laid out horizontally on a wooden frame, it was possible to knit thread made of wool, cotton or lace into lengths that could then be sewn together to make a variety of garments. The new invention was adopted by the hand-knitters of the East Midlands, but each area specialised in just one type of yarn; in Derbyshire it was silk, in Nottinghamshire cotton, and in Leicestershire, because sheep were so important on the farms, it was wool. In the eighteenth and early nineteenth centuries Wigston made woollen hose, a type of long legging sock that gentlemen wore with knee length breeches.

As the changes in farming became widespread, fewer people were needed on the land and they took up knitting, either in their own homes or in small village workshops. A family could rent a knitting frame for about two shillings a week from a master hosier; the husband and wife would work on the frame, the older daughters would sew the seams and the youngest children would wind the thread onto bobbins to feed the machine. The finished goods were bought by the master hosier who took them into Leicester where they would be sold to merchants at the Globe Pub.

The population of Wigston grew. In 1700 it was about a thousand, by 1800 it had increased to 1500 and in 1831 to 2200. By the middle of the nineteenth century there were more than 500 knitting frames in the village. But the wearing of hose went out of fashion, and the countrywide depression of the 1820s and 30s resulted in great hardship. Of the 480 families in Wigston more than 200 were in regular receipt of poor rate relief, surviving on a small amount of money given to them from local taxes on the richer people. When there was work the knitters would be at the frames for 10 to 12 hours a day, but often the master hosier would pay them in tokens that could only be used in certain village stores. The largest employer at the time was George Loveday who was also a shopkeeper, and he paid much of the wages in bread from his shop. This practice was made illegal in 1831 by the Truck Act, but was still happening in Wigston in the 1840s.

Those in charge of parish relief had the power to force the destitute into some form of work. For example, orphans would be put into apprentice-ships to prevent them being the responsibility of the parish, but conditions for these young people could be very bad. An article in the *Leicester Journal* of 1802 reports from a local magistrate's court:

William Goode and John Collin two apprentices to Thomas Smith of Hinkley framework knitter, were discharged from their apprenticeships. It appears on examination, amongst other complaints that Smith frequently obliged his two apprentices to work from the early part of the day till two o'clock the next morning.

The Magistrates were also pleased to direct that Smith should deliver up all their apparel and pay the Overseers of the Poor four guineas for re-apprenticing the boys to more humane masters.

By 1870 things in the village were changing. Steam powered knitting frames had been invented in the 1820s, but their use was resisted in Leicestershire as knitters wanted to continuing working in their own homes. But two Acts of Parliament hastened the end of this cottage industry. The 1870 Education Act meant that children had to go to school rather than working at home, and in 1874 an Act ended the practice of renting frames out to householders. By 1880 a few of the master hosiers had set up small workshops employing a dozen or so workers, but by now there was other employment available, on the railway and in the boot and shoe factories. The ancestors of ours that moved from the land into Wigston towards the latter half of the century did not work as framework knitters, but they did marry into families who were knitters.

The Garnetts were an established Wigston family by the time that Ethel Billing moved to Leicestershire. They ran a newspaper shop and were agents for the retailers W. H. Smith's, providing Sunday papers to all the other newsagents. Ernest's father, Jesse Garnett, and his father, James, had opened the first shop at the end of the 1890s. Jesse had married Martha Hackett. A look at the family tree shows that once the Garnetts were established in Wigston they married into families who had been in the village for many generations. These families had mostly been employed as framework knitters.

It was James Garnett who was the patriarch. James had been born in the Northampton village of Cold Ashby in 1845. The village is about two miles from Naseby, the site of the famous Civil War battle, and Cromwell had stayed in the village the night before the battle. Northamptonshire is mainly a county of rolling lowland grass pastures, but Cold Ashby is on a 200-metre ridge – hence its name. It was probably quite a miserable place in winter and during snow could be cut off for weeks. James Garnett's father Thomas (b. 1804) and his father William (b. 1778), had both been agricultural labourers. They had big families; James was one of six, and he had nine children, Jesse being the youngest. James, like Manoah Peberdy, had made the move from rural worker to town worker. He married Jane Arthur in about 1870. She was also from Northamptonshire, and her father, James Arthur, had been an agricultural labourer. But her parents both died when she was very young, and by four she lived with a family called the Bosworths. They appear to have been a childless couple, and at 14, Jane was still with them and working as a servant in the house.

When James and Jane married they moved away from Cold Ashby and went to Kent. In the history of both the Peberdys and the Garnetts this is remarkable in itself, as generally agricultural workers moved only a handful of miles for a new job. James had travelled almost 100. But the migration was similar to the other Northampton ancestors in our history, the Billing family. It was due to the railway. James became a railway porter at Bexley Station. He may not have got this job immediately but would have had support to make the move because his mother, Mary Colesworthy, had been born in Dover in 1845. The Colesworthy family were shipwrights and lived around Chatham, Medway and the Kent coast. So it seems likely that when James and Jane got married they went to live with his grandparents. James may even

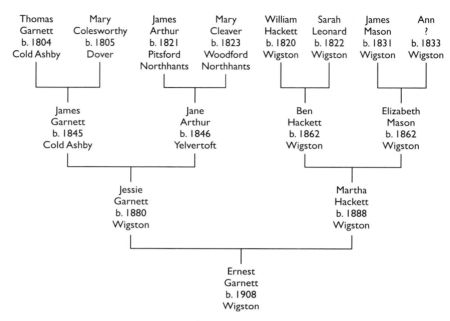

Figure 14: The Wigston Family Tree

have worked with them, because later in Wigston he used his carpentry skills to repair wagons.

Their first three children were born in Kent: Florence at Lower Ham (b. 1871), Maud in Bexley (b. 1872), and Amy at Willesborough (b. 1874). But soon James left the railway and returned to Northamptonshire, and there the wonderfully named William Henry Boswell Garnett was born (1876). Ann's gratitude to the couple who had looked after her as a child was repaid, at least in a small way, by giving her first son the Christian name of Boswell.

They stayed in the county for almost another ten years but in the early 1880s moved to Kilby Bridge, a small hamlet a few miles south of Wigston. James was a labourer and at the time of the move had six children. By 1891 they had set up home in Wigston; they had their full complement of nine children, and this was when James became a wagon repairer. It's likely that he worked for the Clark family, who were wheelwrights. They had a workshop in Kilby and another in Wigston. Even years later Wigston people remembered the Clark-made wagons with their brightly coloured decorations, the paint being made by the Clarks themselves from a lead base and their own local pigments. But by the turn of the new century James had left this job and was a newsagent. Their youngest son Jesse was a 'newsboy hawker', which meant he sold papers on the street corner, while his older brother was a shoe machinist and the girls machine hands.

Even from the very little that is known about James he stands out as a determined character in the family history. He had the courage to try new things and to take risks. He obviously wanted his family to do well, and it was he who started the business that was to last almost 100 years and to provide for three generations of Garnetts.

Jesse Garnett took over the business. He married a Wigston girl, Martha Hackett (always pronounced 'Matha'). The Hacketts were Wigston folk through and through and all Martha's grandparents back into the eighteenth century had lived in the village and married within the

Plate 4.7 Jesse Garnett and Martha Hackett on their wedding day, 1907.

Plate 4.8 A holiday in Oxford circa 1934.
Ernest with a bruised eye from cricket. Ethel in middle front row.

village. Another pub now comes into the story: the Old Crown Inn, of which Martha's father Ben was the licensee. It's still an active pub today, only a few hundred yards from the Framework Knitters Museum, a building that has been converted from its original use as a small knitting factory and where for sure some of the Hacketts, Leonards and Masons would have worked. Before Ben ran the pub he had been a hosiery worker. The Hackett family lived in Moat Street and all the children had quite ordinary English names – Mary, Ann, Henry, John, Emma, William, Arthur and Ben – but with one exception, a little Alonzo, born in 1860. He only survived for two years but when his older brother John married he named his first child after the little boy who had died 20 years before. Jesse and Martha had just three children, Ernest in 1908, and then twin girls, Nora and Bessie. Bessie died at birth. When Ernest Garnett was old enough to leave school, he worked in the shop with his parents. In the mid 1930s he met Ethel Betterley Billing who taught in a nearby school, and they married in 1936. Ethel became Ethel Garnett and is one of the four great grandmothers of Alexander and Felix, the others being Jessie Green, Violetta Longstaffe and Dorothy Lamond Walker.

Ethel stopped teaching when her children, Carol, Elizabeth and Alyson, were born. During the Second World War Ernest served in the Military Police, and spent much of his time, according to his own account, playing cricket in Hampshire. In middle life, and even when

Plate 4.9 Ethel sitting in the sun in her eighties.

she was in her eighties, Ethel had a great deal of energy and was always active. Once the children were at school she returned to teaching, but Ernest and she were very different in temperament. They developed a way of living together. Ernest worked long hours and had few interests outside the business. But he, like Ethel, was also a keen gardener, and so it was agreed that to reduce conflict, there would be a clear demarcation of territory, Ethel did the flowers with the exception of the rose bushes, and Ernest the greenhouse and the vegetables. They kept to this arrangement for more than thirty years!

Ethel was slim. She had a passion, well, more than a passion, an addiction, to the sun. At every opportunity she would be outside with her face tilted up to the sky. In the winter her daughters would laugh from inside the warm living room at 'mother' sitting in a chair on the lawn, wrapped in a scarf and blanket catching the precious rays. As a result by the time she was old she resembled a well-travelled gypsy woman.

She died aged 93 in the last year of the twentieth century. At her funeral something happened that made those who knew her laugh. The coffin was placed on its carriage by the altar. It was an overcast day, but for a few minutes the sun broke out of the clouds. A ray of light came through the chancel window and onto the floor a few feet from the coffin. The carriage brake had not been set, and it gently rolled forward into the patch of sunshine. The undertakers were embarrassed, but the congregation laughed. Ethel had got her final wish.

But perhaps not quite her final wish; after the cremation her daughters discussed with Aunt Freda where the ashes should be scattered, in the garden at Wigston or in a meadow of wild flowers? Freda revealed that when Ethel was a young woman, she had fallen in love with a quarry worker's son. The young man's family lived in a village a few miles from Caernarfon. One weekend when she was visiting he was taken ill and died. Like so many of his generation he had consumption.

Carol, as the oldest daughter, was tasked with seeking Ernest's views on where the ashes should go. He agreed that it should be Wales, though it is doubtful if he fully understood the real significance of the location, and one Saturday afternoon Ethel's daughters gently scattered them under a pine tree in the churchyard of Betws-Garmon. The final grandmother in this genetic line is **Alyson Garnett**, Ethel's youngest daughter.

All four of the family lines have now been described and it has brought us to Alexander and Felix's four grandparents, Kenneth, Felicity, Max and Alyson. In Part Two the grandparents tell their life stories.

PART TWO

The Grandparents' Stories

CHAPTER 5

Kenneth's Story

Kenneth Austin Evers died in March 1991. He lived to see his eldest son Bruce marry Marie-Ann but not the marriage of Angus to Morag. Thus there is one grandparent that Alexander and Felix do not have an opportunity to know and who is not able to write his *own story*. This account of his life has had to be compiled by his family and from the records that have survived from his school and university days, his time in the army and his career as a tea broker. Though the dates and facts are hopefully accurate, a story written by others can rarely capture the things that were really important to the person, and we can only guess at what Kenneth might have said to his two grandsons if he had been alive to write this himself. But he lived through interesting times, born at the end of the First World War, going to school and university in the 1920s and 30s, being an army officer in the Second World War and then marriage and a career that took him back and forth from India. In fact his life is the stuff of books, and much of the literature of the first half of the twentieth century is about people just like Kenneth, from the children's boarding school stories of *Bunter* and *Jennings and Darbyshire* to *Biggles* and Evelyn Waugh's *Brideshead Revisited,* set in the Oxford college where Kenneth was an undergraduate.

Kenneth was born in London in September 1918. His parents had returned temporarily from India two years earlier so that his father, Thomas George, could enlist in the Army. His older sister Elizabeth Jean (known as *Jean*) was his senior by three years, and his mother lived during the war years in Wimbledon with her parents or grandparents, the Walkers. With the ending of the war and his father's demobilisation they took ship back to Calcutta. Thomas George resumed his work as a tea trader and had huge success racing horses at the Calcutta racecourse. Another Evers was born, Thomas Hugh in 1922, but India was not considered a good place to raise European children and most were sent home once they reached school age and so it was to be for young Kenneth. At the age of five he took passage with his parents, nanny and sister on the

Plate 5.1 1922 Nursery tea party. Kenneth Evers with his sister Jean and
Nanny holding the new baby Hugh.

Khyber (Cabin 11 in First Class, with Nurse Smith in Second) back to
Southampton. Kenneth stayed in Streatley with his Aunt Rose and his
parents returned to Calcutta. His first school was in Wallingford, which
even in the 1920s still maintained the description of a *dame school*. A
contemporary at the school was Tony McCaw, who was to remain a
lifelong friend. But he was not to be away from his parents for too long, as
in 1926 his father retired from the business in India and bought a house
in Wiltshire.

Hill House in Little Somerford was to become the family home until
his father's death in 1942. Even after their return the strong connections
with India were still important. His mother, Dorothy had many of her
family in Madras and would visit occasionally. Probably the last time all
three children went to India as a family was in 1932; Jean was 16,
Kenneth 13 and Hugh 9, so we can imagine that they were probably quite
a handful for their mother on the long trip back aboard the *Viceroy of
India*. Photographs of young Kenneth show him on horseback; he shared

Plate 5.2 Young Kenneth in Calcutta with a stern nanny.

Plate 5.3 Learning to ride. Kenneth with his father Thomas George
in India circa 1923.

his father's great love of riding and in his teenage and army days had a
passion for polo and racing, both of which he was very good.

School days

An important part of most peoples' lives is their time at school. For better
or worse this experience profoundly helps to mould the person we

become. Kenneth went to prep school in Worcestershire, Abberley Hall, and then to Winchester. We can get some idea of what this time was like from the memories of Kenneth's half brother Timothy Evers. Though Tim was more than 20 years younger, school life at Abberley and Winchester had probably not changed that much since Kenneth's time and many of the teachers were the same. Tim recounts:

Gilbert Ashton, who happened to be a friend of my father's founded Abberley, but I am not sure how their paths had crossed. Driving to it you could see from afar the clock tower, which for a small boy like myself, moved as the road twisted. Normally however, I joined the school train at Reading which took us up to Worcester where we were collected by buses, which drove us past the usually flooded cricket ground – not unlike Hogwarts. Kenneth and Hugh would have been there well before the war but were still remembered by a lot of the staff when I was there in 1947. It was a good regime: up at 7.00 to 7.30 (earlier if you had Early Work, i.e. special coaching for Entrance Exams to public school), cold baths, breakfast, lavatory and then chapel before lessons until lunch – with a short break – followed by sport on various fields scattered around the grounds. For rugger (Easter term) we walked or ran about a mile or so down from the school to a field outside the grounds; after the game you had to run or walk back up the hill, quick sort of footbath to get mud off, and then lessons until 6 or so. Younger boys were read Biggles by the formidable Matron, Barbara Fawcett, before going to bed about 7.30. There were about 70 boys and about 10 dormitories of various sizes on two floors.

The school was a country house with lovely grounds – fine rhododendrons, water gardens, lawns and so on as well as all sorts of exciting bits like the Valley of Rocks which you could explore on Saturday afternoons at leisure unless some of us had behaved badly and had to go on a walk with Miss James. Occasionally Leonard Greenwood (a classics master and deputy head) or Mr Neale would take the school on a good walk over the Witley Hills. Mr Neale taught maths and had a delightful wife: during one's last year it was a great treat to be invited to tea at their house on Sunday. We also had a wonderful music teacher, David Gill, who enthused some of us for classical music and one year took me and another boy to the Edinburgh Festival where we saw *Meistersinger,* which I really enjoyed.

So we slept and ate. We saw our parents at half term only, although possibly they could come up on one other weekend, but we were very self-contained. Once a term we would walk down to the village for Sunday morning service. On Saturday and Wednesdays (half-days) various sporting teams from other prep schools would visit or we would visit them, travelling in a hired Bedford bus that smelt of boiled sweets. I could go on a lot more but I guess this is sufficient to give some sort of impression of a very rich and varied life. I haven't mentioned carpentry, productions of *Pinafore* and *Mikado,* athletics in the summer, the Fathers' Cricket Match at half term, annual open day when the villagers were shown round the school, films on Sunday, cubs and scouts and so on.

A school friend of Kenneth's at this time was Derrick Bailey and in later life they joked about Gilbert Ashton. If a boy misbehaved the master would tap the offending pupil on the head, and Derrick maintained the reason Kenneth became bald so early in life was a result of him receiving this treatment so frequently. After prep school Kenneth went to Winchester. The year was 1932 and he was thirteen. The school motto is *Manner Makyth Man;* established in 1362, the College is one of the country's most prestigious public schools, with a strong academic reputation. A public school is a world within itself; all have a strong internal ethos and codes of behaviour that instil, and are intended to instil, a set of values and attitudes that will be a foundation for the rest of the young person's life. The boys are boarders and live within *houses* that

Plate 5.4 'Drilling' in the garden – young Kenneth could be the model for the *Just William* illustrations. May 1928.

provide both support and a sense of identity and belonging. There are ten houses at Winchester and Kenneth, and later his younger brothers Hugh and Tim, was in Chernocke House and this was where Kenneth slept and ate. Each house was presided over by a housemaster. Chernocke House had a nickname, *Furleys*, derived from the surname of the first house-master. Houses competed at competitions, especially in sports, and everyone was expected to do their very best to ensure that their house was at or towards the top.

Schools had their own language and new boys had to learn very quickly what many strange words and customs meant. In fact soon after arrival they were set the 'Notions Test' to show they understood these traditions. For example *strats* was the name given to their straw hats (these were abolished in 1984), while *toytime* was homework, but as they didn't go home more correctly called *prep*. Because Winchester was proud of its academic reputation classes were carefully structured. Each form was divided into three ladders; 'A' ladder for classics, 'B' ladder for history and modern languages, and 'C' ladder for mathematics and science. There was a hierarchy in terms of progression through the school, from Junior Part to Middle Part, to Senior Part and Sixth Book. The *fagging* system was very much part of boarding school life at this time and at Winchester was not abolished until the 1970s. Younger boys acted as valets, essentially servants, to the prefects and would have to wake the older boy up with tea, clean his shoes and in fact do pretty much anything he was told to do or face often harsh punishment from the prefect. Caning was part of normal school life throughout Britain at this time and was considered very necessary to install the right behaviour in the young.

Tim Evers followed Kenneth to Winchester:

Winchester I find more difficult to talk about than Abberley Hall. One thing that interested me as a new man, you lost friends that you had at 'tother' [your prep school]. If they went to a different house, particularly if you were in an Old Tutors House and they were in a Commoners House. Nonetheless links were maintained and every autumn term Gilbert Ashton, the prep school headmaster, would come to Winchester to take all the Abberley boys out to tea on Sunday, and probably to lobby the College for future entrants.

When you arrived in your house you were allocated for the first two weeks to a TJ [a play on the word protégé]. This older boy was meant to show you the ropes, where everything was in the house and around the school and town; where to sit for chapel, where the various playing fields were and the classrooms and so on. It was a sort of mentoring and I often think it would be useful as a training method in other walks of life. At the end of two weeks you were subjected to a notions exam to test your knowledge of houses, the masters and house colours, and the surrounding geography, the river, the steeplechase course, and the whereabouts of playing fields.

My housemaster was Eric Emmet, a mathematician, who succeeded Harry Altham who had been Kenneth's housemaster. Mr Altham was still a house tutor at Furleys and took an interest in how I was getting on academically and socially; he was a link with my older brother's time. He was an exceptional man, president of the MCC and owner of a formidable collection of porcelain that was on display in the museum. One day I had to write him a letter of apology for having broken a piece! The school was divided into houses and was full of bright eggs. Academically the lowest class was JP (Junior Part 2 and Junior Part 1), then Middle Part 3,2 and 1 and Lower VI and Upper VI, which I never made. I spent a lot of time in MP 2 and MP 1 but was top in the French and German sets.

You were a fag in your first year and learnt many useful skills like cleaning seven pairs of football boots in 30 minutes or pressing cadet uniforms and polishing brass and study floors or making sandwiches and fetching and carrying. In fact a prefect could put his head out of the study window and shout 'boy' and you went running to do whatever he demanded. I think that by the time I got to Winchester the prefects were less awesome than before the war, so Kenneth probably had an even tougher period as a fag. As you progressed through the school you were granted more privileges, like being able to take a certain path up to school or having your jacket undone. All of which served to support a system that probably made sense more before the war than after. I found it all agreeable without questioning it much but it totally confused my mother.

Oxford

Kenneth left Winchester in 1936 and went up to Oxford, where he read history at Christ Church. The world of Oxford in the 1930s was one that Kenneth would have fitted into very easily. The vast majority of under-graduates were from public schools and the customs and traditions an extension of the kind of thing he was familiar with at Winchester. Christ Church was one of the largest colleges and traditionally seen as the most aristocratic. It has produced 13 British Prime Ministers, poets such as W. H. Auden, and famous philosophers, theologians, Viceroys and Governors General. Eighty years before it was where Charles Dodgson, a maths don, writing under the name of Lewis Carroll, composed *Alice's Adventures in Wonderland* to amuse the Dean's daughters on afternoon picnics.

The Dean when Kenneth was an undergraduate was Alwyn Terrell Petre Williams, and though Kenneth was not one of the academic high flyers who would have had regular contact with the Dean, they would have met at the formal Dinners in the Great Hall. These occasions were very grand indeed following customs that went back centuries and with dons and undergraduates in tails and academic dress. Meals began with the Christ Church grace in Latin ('We unhappy and unworthy men do give thee most reverent thanks Almighty God our Heavenly Father for the victuals which thou has bestowed . . .').

The purpose of the public schools and the Oxbridge universities at this time was to produce men who would be able to run the country and the Empire, so the development of character and the right attitudes towards duty, social responsibility and fairness were seen as far more important than academic success and getting a good degree. Of course there were always *bright eggs* (to borrow Tim Evers' expression) who would go on to be the writers, professors and scientists, but at this period the top administrators, civil servants, lawyers and military men had walked the path that Kenneth was taking. Sport developed team spirit and healthy bodies, and Christ Church encouraged participation in cricket, rugby, athletics and of course rowing. Christ Church Meadows border the Thames and the Cherwell rivers, and Kenneth must have spent many a hot summer afternoon punting up the river for a beer at a riverside pub.

Kenneth loved sport and was good at shooting and golf. He had inherited his father's passion for horses and something of his skill. Early photographs show him being taught to ride, and when the family had returned to England and set up home in Wiltshire he had hunted with the Beaufort. At Oxford he kept up this interest and rode in point-to-point races as an amateur jockey. His great ambition was to ride a winner at Cheltenham Races, and he toyed with the idea of becoming a racehorse trainer. But events were to take his life in another direction; the war was approaching and he became a soldier.

A sad event happened in his first year at Oxford when his mother Dorothy died. Dorothy had been out to India during his last year at Winchester arriving back in March. She was taken ill and diagnosed with bowel cancer. In the autumn of 1937 she went into a nursing home in London where she died on 13th November. She was only 51 and Kenneth 19. The loss must have been very great for the three children and Thomas George. A memorial service was held in the church at Little Somerford. A sad coincidence was that when Kenneth died in 1991 his youngest son Angus was also 19 and in his first year at university.

The War

During Kenneth's last year at Christ Church it was becoming obvious that war with Germany was very likely. Kenneth had been in the junior Officer Training Corps at Winchester and the senior OTC at Oxford. Photographs show him at camp with friends on Salisbury Plain and by the time decisions had to be made as to what he would do after graduating, it must have been an obvious choice. He matriculated with a Third Class Degree in History and when war was declared in early September he enlisted in the Army, this was on 6th September, just three days before his 21st birthday. A frustrating time followed as this was the period of the 'phoney war' and he was placed in the Reserves waiting to be called up. At last, on 15 March 1940, his war began. He joined the Royal Dragoons, as a family friend was in that regiment (if he had failed to get his first choice his next was the Warwickshire or North Somerset Yeomanry). Given his love of horses it is not surprising that he chose a mounted regiment, and at the start of the war that was what they were, mounted on horses, not in vehicles or tanks.

The Royal Dragoons trace their origin back to Charles II in 1661, and the term 'dragoon' comes from the name of a musket that was used by soldiers on horseback. The regiment was more commonly known as The Royals and they had fought in many of the famous campaigns of the eighteenth and nineteenth centuries, including the Battle of Waterloo. Before the Great War they had been in India and Kenneth's father, who had been a volunteer in the Calcutta Light Horse, would certainly have known many of their officers. They returned to Europe in 1914 and fought in France. With the outbreak of the Second World War in September 1939 The Royal Dragoons were stationed at Lydda in Palestine.

His army medical gives a picture of the young Kenneth: 'Height 5' 9" and a half, Complexion "fresh", eyes brown, hair brown, weight 140 lbs (10 stone) and marks or scars nil'. He passed as 'A1'. His training now began, first with the 3rd Horsed Cavalry in Edinburgh and then to Weedon for officer cadet training. He did well, and the commanding officer reported:

An outstanding cadet in every respect who has set a fine example throughout his course; he has intelligence and great powers of leadership which have steadily developed, and which will go to make him an officer of the highest class.

He was commissioned in October 1940 as a second lieutenant and sent to Tidworth on Salisbury Plain for training with the Royal Armoured

Corps. It was to the Middle East that Second Lieutenant Evers was sent after his initial training. The coincidence would not have been lost on Kenneth that his own father had ended his time as a soldier in 1918 on horseback in Palestine, and that 21 years later here he was, at least during training, sitting astride a horse about to go out to the very same part of the world. But by the time Kenneth joined The Royals in August 1941 they were no longer mounted; centuries of tradition had ended:- though it was The Royals themselves who had pressed for change and modernisation. Their commanding officer, Lieutenant-Colonel Heyworth, wrote later:

If there was any intention of retaining our horses merely in order to carry out internal duties in the country, I knew I should find it extremely difficult to keep officers and men happy and contented. All my best officers would apply for transfer elsewhere. (*The Story of the Royal Dragoons*, 1938–45, p. 4.)

The War Office gave the regiment a choice of roles within the Royal Armoured Corps, and they chose armoured cars on the grounds that it more nearly corresponded to their traditional task of reconnaissance. As they said farewell to their horses, good news came from Egypt where General Wavell had won a victory over the occupying Italian forces. The regiment was sent to Egypt for training in how to drive and use their new armoured cars – not just driving and mechanics but also how to use the wireless, guns, and most important of all, how to navigate in a featureless desert (the men themselves claimed that the most important training of all was the quickest method to brew up a cup of tea!). Their new 'horse' was the Marmon Harrington Mark III armoured car, made in South Africa. It was big, which made it quite an easy target for the enemy, and its armoured sides were thin. Its own weapon was a rather ineffectual anti-tank rifle and, as the men joked, the only thing their guns were strong enough to pierce was another Marmon Harrington car!

In May 1940, as Kenneth started his officer training in England, the regiment were moved northwards from Palestine to the Syrian border where the Vichy French forces were becoming a threat. Their job was to patrol the desert up to the enemy's position. These patrols usually lasted about three days and then reported back on anything they had gleaned as to what the French were doing. At the end of May the squadron reached the Syrian border. Two allied divisions were to attack the French Army. The 7th Australian Division, and an Indian Brigade with two Free French brigades, were to take Damascus with the armoured cars being in the lead. The attack started on 8th June, and the fighting was fierce. By mid-July the Allied forces had occupied half of Syria, and a peace armistice was signed. The Royals had survived their first active service.

Kenneth in North Africa

In September 1940, 11 months before Kenneth finished his training, North Africa was to see fierce conflict. The Italians were allies of Germany and had moved their troops from their base in Libya across into Egypt to threaten the British forces but within two months the Italians had been forced into retreat. Embarrassed by his ally's failure, Hitler sent an ambitious young general, Erwin Rommel, to Libya to block any further British advance. Within a month he had forced the British army to retreat back to Egypt.

Kenneth disembarked at Suez on 21st August 1941 and joined 'B' Squadron in Syria. On 17th November 1941 the Eighth Army launched an attack on the Germans with the aim of relieving Tobruk. The Royal Dragoons were ordered to return to Egypt and join the Eighth Army. This was the beginning of a very intense period of desert warfare. Their job was reconnaissance, but the terrain was extremely difficult. We imagine deserts as big flat areas of sand, and if our only experience is running over a Cornish beach it doesn't seem a difficult job to drive a vehicle across. But the reality for Kenneth and his men was very different. The desert was rocky, and sudden rains could make areas muddy and almost impossible to cross without continuous stops to pull out bogged vehicles. It was also very dangerous. The Germans had dive-bombers, the Junkers 87, and every patrol would come under attack from the air. These planes flew in arrowhead formation, very close together, and then when they spotted a target they would dive low releasing their bombs a few hundred feet above the armoured cars. The armour on the vehicles would provide protection so long as the bomb didn't fall too close and whenever the patrol stopped the first job was always to quickly dig a protective bank around the cars. But often the soldiers would hardly have started digging before hearing the scream of the dive-bombers. They would throw themselves behind whatever protection they could find, emerging deafened by the explosions from the bombs.

During the morning of 10th December as they were operating in the Libyan Desert, 'B' Squadron was attacked from the air, and three men were killed. Then in the afternoon a second German attack wounded

Kenneth and his sergeant. Fortunately it was a surface wound to his back and not too serious.

The most dangerous place to be was 10 to 20 miles behind the British lines, as this is where there were always a lot of dive-bomber attacks as the German planes looked for the British headquarters. A squadron consisted of five troops; a troop had three cars, each with a crew of four: the officer, the driver, co-driver and wireless operator. Each vehicle had a wooden box that was used to stand on to see above the turret, and to sit on when driving. A fellow officer, Philip Fielden described the conditions in a book he wrote some years after (*Swings and Roundabouts*). He tells how it was extremely hot and dress was usually khaki shorts, shirt and grey beret with the eagle badge and of course desert boots. The men were always short of water, and invariably the dive-bomber' bullets hit the water containers carried on the side of the vehicle. Water was never wasted; usually each man got three mugs of tea per day and just enough for a shave. Washing only happened when based at HQ – never on patrol.

The Royals were sent to join the 4th Armoured Brigade as part of the British advance into North Africa. 'B' Squadron joined ten light tanks and anti-tank guns to harass the HQ of the German 21st Panzer Division at Bir Temrad (in Egypt, to the west of Tobruk). By December 1941 Major Herman was commanding 'B' Squadron, and they were given the job of cutting off the German escape route to the south. It was at this time that the commanding officer, Colonel Heyworth, and the second-in-command, Major Jay, were both killed. Given the danger that men were daily experiencing it's not surprising that they developed certain attitudes, and language to cope with the horrors. To *have had it* meant being killed; if a soldier cracked up mentally under the stress of the conditions it was described as *happiness,* and so a man ill from the dive bombers was *bomb-happy,* or a man suffering psychologically from being in the desert too long was *sand-happy.* To try to tame the vast desert they nicknamed places with London landmarks, Piccadilly, Knightsbridge and Oxford Circus. The men didn't boast of any achievements. At night if they did share events of the day it was always with humour and self-depreciation, if they had done something dangerous they would claim that they 'had never been so frightened in all their life', or that 'once the job had been done they had fled as fast as the armoured car could go'.

In January 1942 Kenneth and the regiment were in reserve at Msus awaiting the delivery of 30 new armoured cars when the Germans began a counter attack, and so The Royals were back in action. For the next three months they were constantly patrolling a strip of no-man's land about 80

Plate 5.5 October 1940: Kenneth is commissioned as Second Lieutenant and starts his training on Salisbury Plain to serve with the Royal Armoured Corps.

miles wide. The only relief was a week's leave in Cairo. It is to be hoped that Kenneth enjoyed his break, as soon he was to receive bad news; his father had quite unexpectedly died at his home, Hill House.

In March General Montgomery took command of the British troops in North Africa. As soon as 'Monty' took over he began transforming the British force and rebuilding its morale, which had been severely damaged by the earlier setbacks. The Royals at last had their vehicles replaced by some superior armoured cars, Daimlers and Humbers. The Humber carried a 15mm automatic gun in addition to its machine gun and had a turret with thicker armour. 'B' squadron resumed its duties. Often they had to play a cat and mouse game with the German forces, Kenneth and his fellow men being the mouse. Their job was to assess German positions, and the most effective way of doing this was to drive into an area of desert where it was suspected the enemy was positioned. If they were there the Germans would fire and so reveal their location. This was a dangerous tactic, but one that the squadron carried out for many months. In August the Germans launched an attack, but were forced back at the Battle of Alam Halfa. Montgomery built up his strength and then in October attacked Rommel at El Alamein. By January 1943 the Regiment left the open desert and entered the more enclosed hilly terrain of Western Tripolitania, and by the end of the month the British Eighth Army had captured Tripoli.

Rommel regrouped in Tunisia and started to strike at the newly arrived American First Army. In April the British were able to move out of the hilly area and make towards Bizerta and Tunis. Kenneth was injured for a second time. It was on 23rd April, when 'B' Squadron had been ordered to push forward and test the enemy's strength. As his car drove towards the German positions they came close to a cactus plantation. Hidden within was a German anti-tank gun. It opened fire destroying Kenneth's Humber and another vehicle. He and two of his men were wounded, Kenneth in his right arm. But the Africa war was almost over. Montgomery's strategy had been successful; on 15th May 1943 the Germans surrendered and a quarter of a million soldiers laid down their arms. The Royal Dragoons were sent to Homs for a period of rest, and here they remained till early September.

In November Kenneth, along with his regiment, left North Africa for Italy. In July Operation Huskey was launched by the Allies with the aim of driving the Germans out of Italy. The Italian forces put up little resistance but the Germans fell back slowly, and by the end of the year were just south of Rome. It was in Italy that Kenneth became ill with jaundice. After two years and 35 days living under such harsh desert conditions perhaps some ill health is not surprising. But at this point General Montgomery was called back to England to prepare for D-Day and the invasion of Europe. Kenneth and the regiment were called back too.

D-Day and After

The Royal Dragoons returned to England in January 1944 and the men were given leave. Rumours were rife that very soon a new front would be opened in Western Europe, and a landing in France was considered the most likely option. General Montgomery returned to plan the invasion. The Royals were increased in numbers; in March they became part of the

21st Army Group and moved to Ashford in Kent. In May Kenneth was promoted to the rank of captain. D Day took place on 6th June, and The Royals were to provide support once the bridgehead in France had been established. After an endless wait they embarked on 26th July, and landed in France to set up camp a few miles north of Tilley. At this point the Regiment consisted of 55 officers, eleven warrant officers and 718 men, with 159 armoured vehicles. But Kenneth was already there as on D-Day plus 6 he had been sent as ADC to General Dempsey. Over the next few weeks The Royals played a part in probing the German positions, but rural France, with its narrow lanes and wooded countryside, was not ideal armoured car territory. By 23rd August the regiment had reached Bernay. The French people welcomed them warmly and young Resistance fighters, like pirates with pistols stuffed in their belts, took charge of any captured German prisoners.

The push north continued and by early September they were fighting the Germans by the River Somme. On 15th September The Royals moved towards the Dutch frontier. The battle for Arnhem was one of the Allies' most famous failures, but it provided a short period of respite. On 30th September The Dragoons found billets in the outskirts of Eindhoven, the first time every man had spent a night indoors. Over the winter the regiment was to successfully hold this area. During March they prepared for the crossing of the Rhine; they were to be in charge of the flow of troops and vehicles across the river. Under shellfire from the Germans the regiment oversaw the crossing points and after five days it was done. Over the next two months The Royals pushed into Germany. By 2nd May no fewer than 10,000 German soldiers had surrendered to them alone. Though the official armistice was not signed till the 5th, in effect the war was over, as the local German commanders had already done the only thing they could do, surrender.

For Kenneth and most of his fellow soldiers the last period of their army career was spent in Denmark and Holland. On 7th May they were ordered to cross the Danish frontier, where they received a joyous welcome from civilians and officials. Their duties now were to control the disbanding of German soldiers and equipment, the repatriation of refugees, the pursuit of black-marketeers and general policing of the population. Kenneth was appointed as Adjutant in March 1945 and attached as an intelligence officer to General Montgomery's staff.

Plate 5.6 Kenneth in Denmark enjoying his passion for horses – 1946.

The war ends

Kenneth had been a good soldier and obviously enjoyed the life. The last six months of his war were spent in Denmark where he and five other officers were billeted with the Juel family in their manor house at Juelsburg on the island of Funen. Kenneth became great friends with the family, a friendship that was to last for life. He was a godfather to their daughter Anne, who was born in 1946 and was thrilled 20 or so years later to be a guest, along with the King and Queen of Denmark, at her wedding. When the war was over Kenneth applied to become a regular officer, having decided to make the army his career. He passed the selection panel with flying colours, the Brigadier who interviewed him recommending him 'very strongly'. His commanding officer wrote:

This officer . . . is quick and intelligent and has the knack of getting on with everyone. He has been Adjutant for nearly a year and has done the job admirably at a very difficult time. He was employed as LO [Liaison Officer] by the C-in-C, 21st Army Group and was entirely successful in this role. I am confident that this officer will go a long way in the army and make a first class Regular officer.

Everything looked set for his future life in the army; he had been on General Montgomery's staff and had performed well. But it was not to be. At the end of April 1946 he wrote to the Army HQ:

Recently I attended a War Office Selection Board for Regular Officers in England and while on leave after this received information that the financial position of my family and myself was not as good as I had been led to assume previously, and it was therefore considered necessary that I should not continue with my intention to remain in the Army as a regular soldier but go into my family business. I therefore request that my name be not considered for placing on this register of Candidates for Regular Commissions.

What this new information was is not known. His father had died four years earlier and so many things may have happened to the business in India during the upheavals of the war period. He was promoted during these last few months and then received permission from the War Office 'to proceed overseas . . . you will relinquish your commission . . . from 21st October 1946 . . . you will be granted the honorary rank of Major . . .'

A family tragedy

In a short period of time Kenneth experienced the deaths of many people close to him; his mother when he was 19, his father when he was 23, comrades during the war and then, just as peace had come, the tragic accidental death of his sister and her husband. Jean was three years older than Kenneth. She had married William Hasler and with their two sons, Julian and Crispin lived at the Manor House in Sissinghurst. William was an economist and had joined the Civil Service. During the war he worked at the Board of Trade and was responsible for many of the complex lend-lease agreements Britain had with her American ally. But Jean also had a career and a very significant one. She was gifted at languages, but after Finishing School it might have been expected that she would settle down to living quietly as a married woman in Kent. However, during the war she worked in the War Department and immediately after for the United Nations. An obituary of her appeared in *The Times* on June 14th 1946:

She spent some early years in India and under her father's encouragement she acquired an adventurous realism of outlook and a delightful sense of humour. She made herself first-class at modern languages, including Russian, and her ability to talk fluently to Soviet representatives in their own tongue proved on occasion a great asset. She also had a deep appreciation of art and music. The Civil Service Commission admitted her as a temporary administrative officer in 1942, and through her successful work in the Ministry of War Transport she played a large part in building up the flow of allied supplies to the Middle East and to a large part of Europe. Early this year she went to help the secretariat for the London Assembly of the United Nations, and was pressed into staying on as a personal assistant engaged in administrative duties under the head of the United Nations temporary London Office. Her promise as an administrator was impressive, in spite of her brief experience her character was visibly maturing and mellowing as she found herself.

If we ignore the rather patronising tone, a reflection of the attitudes towards women with careers and holding responsible positions it is clear that Jean was a dynamic person. As another obituary a few days later put it: 'the hackneyed adjective "unsparing" can rightly be applied to her effort [in the Ministry of War]. As I recollect she never took ones day's sick leave. Her single minded and even ruthless concentration on winning the war was a standing example' (*The Times*, 27th June). This was the start of the Cold War, when relations between the West and the Soviet Union were becoming difficult and people believed that another war, and one with nuclear weapons, was possible, even likely. The kind of job Jean was doing, her middle class background and her fluency in Russian makes her the type of person who featured in the many spy novels that have been written about this period. There is no evidence at all that Jean was other than the person described in the obituaries, but the circumstances of her death are the stuff of a spy thriller.

It was 10th June 1946, Whit Monday and a glorious hot early summer's day. William and Jean, their two sons and the young Timothy Evers (Jean's six-year-old half-brother) and the nanny were on holiday in Devon. The family were on the beach at Croyde Bay. The parents went for a swim – they didn't come back. An inquest was held ten days later in the local village:

A verdict of accidental death was returned at the inquest at Georgeham North Devon on Saturday on Mr William Julian Hasler of the Manor House, Sissinghurst, Kent who with his wife disappeared while bathing at Croyde Bay on June 10th. (*The Times*, 24th June.)

This is a very dangerous beach. A year later two Oxford under-graduates were drowned, and the mother of one organised a campaign through the letters page of *The Times* to make it safer. Many of the correspondents reported other deaths. Croyde Bay is on the west-facing coastline of North Devon and has very strong rip tides, especially at low tides, and even with a small swell they can pull a strong swimmer out. The campaign pointed to Australian beaches and how they had flags and lifeguards to prevent such tragedies. As a result Croyde Bay put in these things, but too late to save two young boys from losing their parents and Kenneth losing his sister.

In the autumn after these terrible events Kenneth married. For a short time before his marriage he lived at the Manor House in Sissinghurst – some of his correspondence is from that address – so it is possible that he was involved in sorting out some of the practical things that needed to be done after such unexpected deaths. His bride, Elizabeth, was the daughter of Eugene Cathcart-Nicholls. Her family was originally from St James in the Cape Province of South Africa, but her father had died and her mother was now living in London.

On leaving the army Kenneth went to work for one of his father's old companies, J. Thomas. Things obviously went well; his brother Hugh joined the company in 1949 and Kenneth became managing director in 1954. Kenneth and Elizabeth lived in Calcutta but here tragedy struck again. Elizabeth became ill with polio and died in 1955.

England and a family

Kenneth returned to England. He spent some time with friends and family and took a new job, this time in London with another of his father's companies, Thomas Cumberlege and Inskipp. One evening at a cocktail party he met a very attractive young woman, Felicity Ingleby-Mackenzie, and on 14th January 1956 at St James's Piccadilly they were married. After a reception at the Royal College of Surgeons the couple flew to France, then Spain and Portugal for their honeymoon.

Tea plays a very large part in Kenneth's story as his entire career after the army was in tea – as a broker. English people drink more tea than all the rest of Europe and the United States, and being such an important commodity, the tea industry has evolved expertise and systems to ensure its supply and quality. Perhaps rather tongue in cheek, in one of the many forms that Kenneth had completed during his Army days one question had asked about his professional skills; he had written 'tea taster'. As a 21 year-old he may have been joking, or perhaps his father had already taught him some of the things he would need to know. But after the Army Kenneth did became an expert in pekoe teas. But the job of broker involved far more than just having a good palate. In London tea brokers were traditionally based on the north bank of the Thames between St Paul's Cathedral and London Bridge. If today you walk across the

Millennium Bridge from the Tate Modern and look right onto the north shore, this is where Kenneth worked. During the 1950s when Kenneth started at Cumberlege and Inskipp, this area was a complex of brokers, consultants, producers, warehouse companies and buyers; in fact the whole of London's tea world, could be found in High Timber Street. The first auctions had been held on the banks of the river in 1679, when clippers loaded with chests of tea returned from China. Aside from a few years during the Second World War, auctions have been held on a weekly basis since 1864. So great were the quantities in the early 1900s that Indian teas were auctioned off on Mondays and Wednesdays, Ceylon teas on Tuesdays, and China, Java and other teas on Thursdays.

When Kenneth returned from Calcutta the auctions took place in the huge amphitheatre in Plantation House on Mincing Lane, known as the 'Street of Tea', and so packed were these auctions that it was standing room only. There were about twelve companies of brokers at this time and they did far more than simply sell the tea. They provided guidance on its growing, and Kenneth spent much of his time visiting plantations in India and Assam advising plantation managers on what was needed by the consumers. Brokers also grade teas, an art that defies quantification. There is a story told of Kenneth visiting Western Canada where he was given a blind tea tasting of ten blends. He correctly identified all ten.

Kenneth worked from London for the first years of his marriage, but Felicity did have the chance to accompany him on some of his trips. In 1958 they went to Ceylon and India and then on to Assam. They visited tea gardens. Felicity had been born in Ceylon, so it was a wonderful opportunity for her to feel that she was returning to her roots. A great event happened in 1960 with the birth of their first child, Bruce. Soon after Kenneth was asked by the company to go out to Calcutta, and the family of three made a new home in this very big and very hot city. They stayed until the end of 1963 and then returned to London setting up house in Yeoman's Row. Kenneth was keen that his son should be brought up in the country so after some searching they eventually found a large country house with gardens and paddocks at Ashampstead in Berkshire.

Another great event happened in January 1972; a second son, Angus. When it was time for Bruce to go off to school Kenneth chose Eton rather than Winchester; he thought it would provide a more rounded, and less academic, education. Both his sons were like their father in looks and sporting ability. Perhaps the only slight disappointment he may have felt was that neither shared his passion for horses. Though he encouraged them to ride it was not for them. Both had his love of soldiering and both were very active in the OTC at school. It was a terrible time for Felicity and Kenneth when as a 17 year old Bruce was accidentally shot by a fellow cadet while on a weekend exercise, and was critically ill in the Military Hospital in Aldershot. He did survive, but Kenneth more than any other must have known how close he had been to losing his son.

By 1979 the boys were away at school and so Kenneth and Felicity bought a smaller house in the village. He was very much a *home man,* and though he had membership of the Cavalry Club and White's he preferred to be in his own house after work and not sitting in a gentleman's club. He travelled up to London from Berkshire but also spent time in places that few other Western businessmen visited, places like Georgia and Russia. The Cold War was at its height and on occasions, such as one trip to Tbilisi, his movements were closely monitored and his hotel room bugged. Given that it was the Soviet Union, business negotiations involved much drinking of vodka; his trick was to take a swig of olive oil before the sessions and so maintain a good enough state not to agree foolish deals. Later in his career as he gained more expertise he was the Wednesday auctioneer at some of the sales. After Kenneth's retirement in 1982 it was not long before the tea trade changed completely. Today there are only two brokers still operating in London. With the Internet and better communications most of the tea brokers are now in the countries where the tea is produced. J. Thomas is still in existence and in fact is now the world's largest brokerage, with their headquarters in Calcutta.

Retirement

After his retirement Kenneth had the chance to play more sport. He enjoyed golf and had a ten-stroke handicap. He was a keen skier too and the family went out to the Alps each winter. Later in life he didn't shoot very much but he had Labradors, each named after an admiral, Drake, then Rodney and finally Calder, and he would take his dog to shoots as a picker-up. He always kept his love of horses and his library was dominated by books to do with horse-breeding and bloodlines. His sons remembered him as *good at holidays.* Strangely for a man who had spent so much time in India he hated hot weather and would sit in the shade under a large blue hat. He drank red wine and whisky, adored tomato ketchup and sometimes ate pheasant and snipe for breakfast! He was a hoarder who didn't throw things away, and rather bizarrely for a man who was punctual, never wore a watch. His had been stolen during

Plate 5.7 Kenneth in later life.

the war and he saw no reason to buy another. He and Felicity enjoyed their visits to Eton for the different open days and school sporting events and had every reason to be proud parents. Music was also important to him and in retirement he and Felicity went to opera in London and concerts, especially if it was Handel or Brahms.

Kenneth became ill with cancer in the late 1980s. He was well enough to attend Bruce's wedding in September 1990, and his younger brother Timothy remembers his concern, even during the last few months, to make sure that he and his mother were all right. Perhaps the last description of Kenneth should be from Tim:

My memories of Kenneth form a general impression of gentleness, courtesy and concern for others. Like most of us Evers he didn't give a great deal away . . . not very demonstrative, but caring and effective when it mattered.

His father Thomas George had carried with him a passage from a prayer by St Ignatius. Ignatius was a soldier in the Spanish army who in 1521 was injured in a battle and was close to death. He survived and in later life established the Jesuits. In the Anglican Book of Common Prayer are to be found the words that meant so much to Thomas George. Both were gentle men who achieved much, lived through some turbulent times and in their quiet way did the best for their family and their country. Kenneth may not have chosen these words to end *his story,* and today they may seem rather old fashioned, but the underpinning values of this prayer are those that guided his life and the lives of many of his generation:

> Teach us Good Lord,
> To serve Thee as Thou deservest;
> To give and not to count the cost,
> To fight and not to heed the wounds;
> To labour and not to ask for any reward,
> Save that of knowing that we do Thy will.
> Through Jesus Christ Our Lord. Amen.

CHAPTER 6

Felicity's Story

There is a photograph album that my parents kept from my earliest years. In it my father, a naval surgeon, wrote an account by each picture as if it was I recalling the event. Here are some of the things he said on my behalf at my birth in Sri Lanka or, as it was called in those days, Ceylon:

I was born in Colombo on 25th September 1930. I weighed 7lbs 4 ozs and twenty minutes after I was born I was shown to my mother and father. The latter of who had arrived in Colombo 36 hours before the Great Event from HMS *Effingham* . . .

As a naval man my father often had to be away from us on board his ship, and so a few weeks after my birth he left for Aden to meet the Duke of Gloucester. My mother and I would travel to be in port when his ship returned from these voyages. Being a doctor my father was concerned that I didn't become ill, and that I was developing in a healthy way. As you will see he kept a very close eye on my weight!

At the time of my first month my weight was 8lbs 2ozs. Soon after I was vaccinated . . . we sailed for Bombay and then continued our journey to Karachi. My grandmother, having come from Italy, met us in Bombay.

My christening took place on board my father's ship when it was in port at Karachi at the end of December 1930. A London newspaper reported the event:

. . . Felicity Jane the daughter of Commander and Mrs Ingleby-Mackenzie . . . Her father's ship is HMS *Effingham*, and the event took place on board. Although it was only two days after Christmas, they required an awning to keep off the sun from the deck where the temporary chapel was arranged. And even then the temperature was high enough.
All the crew were present in spotless white uniforms. The babe wore a priceless lace veil and cap, lent for the occasion by her grandmother, Lady Tindal-Atkinson, who went out East for the ceremony. A little rosette of the Mackenzie tartan served as a reminder of her Scot's ancestry. The ship's bell was used as a font, and Felicity's name is to be inscribed on it as a memento.

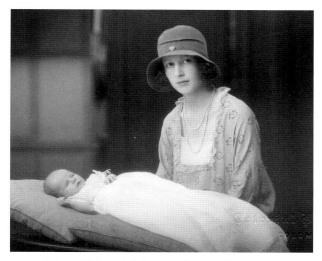

Plate 6.1 Baby Felicity with her mother Violetta – Ceylon 1930.

Sixty officers and guests attended the Admiral's cabin, where helped by her happy parents the babe cut the cake with her father's sword. The cake was suitably decorated with white sugar lifebuoys and flags. You can imagine its size, each member of the crew received a portion and it weighed fully forty pounds.

I don't know if the bell was ever inscribed or where it is now. Ten years later during the Second World War, the *Effingham* sank. She was patrolling the north Atlantic, in the Iceland Region, hunting German ships. This led her to Norway where she was attacked by a submarine, but not hit. A few days later she escorted a troop ship to the island of Bodo, just north of the Artic Circle, where she struck a large rock. This event was very unlucky indeed, because the rock was well known and marked on the ship's charts, but when the navigator had drawn the ship's passage onto the map, his pencil mark had obscured the obstacle directly in the ship's path. Fortunately no one was killed, and the wreck had to be destroyed by a British navy torpedo to ensure she didn't fall into enemy hands. All her crucial papers and equipment were removed and perhaps the bell was among the things saved. I don't know, but the remains of the ship that saw my baptism are now on the Norwegian seabed.

In the early days of my life there was a lot of travelling. Shortly after the New Year my father's ship left for Bombay and we followed on the SS *Chakla*. I slept in a cabin in my pram and was well looked after by my

Plate 6.2 HMS *Effingham* – Felicity's father's ship, where she was baptised in the ship's bell.

mother and grandmother, and with my ayah sleeping on deck alongside me. After Bombay and some time with my father we returned by passenger ship to Colombo. From the town we travelled by car to a government rest house at Trincomalie. My father wrote in the album:

I had now begun to hold a bottle, and I could nearly sit up by myself . . . my weight now was 15 lbs 8 ozs.

My grandmother was still with us when I was six months old. My father always had his camera handy and as the many photographs show he was a very proud parent. Father was still very concerned to monitor my growth. He wrote in the album:

The weighing question was very difficult . . . but Surgeon Lieut-Commander Sorley came to the rescue by weighing me in the meat scales of the RN camp . . . I weighed 16 lbs 2 ozs.

In June there was great excitement as an English nurse Nanny Bull, came to look after me. Almost the first thing she did was to take me to the Royal Naval camp with my father and mother in order that I might be weighed! This impressive ceremony took place in Commander Philip Neville's cabin in the big *Effingham* scales, witnessed by no less than the Captain Commander and two midshipmen. I weighed 20 lbs 13 ozs, which seemed to please all those present.

Plate 6.3 Surgeon – Commander Alexander Ingleby Mackenzie and
daughter Felicity – Ceylon 1931.

July came and father left with his ship for East Africa. My grandmother
was not well and so my mother had to take her to Colombo and then see
her off by ship for England. My first birthday came and my mother
organised a lovely cake, and I got a wireless telegram of greetings from my
father. During this time my mother would travel down from our house at
Trincomalie to see my father when his ship came into port, and on one
occasion even went as far as Calcutta to be with him for a short while. So
there were quite long periods when my nanny looked after me.

In May 1932 we boarded the SS *Ormonde* and sailed for England,
arriving at Southampton in June. We travelled to Ryde on the Isle of
Wight to stay with my father's parents (Dr and Mrs Kenneth Ingleby-
Mackenzie). A new nanny, the wonderful Nanny Galpin, arrived to look

Plate 6.4 Felicity's grandmother Lady Tindal-Atkinson. She came out to Ceylon to visit the new baby. Here she is staying at Admiralty House and writing letters home.

after me. She stayed with our family till I was 18 and then returned some years later to look after my son Bruce. That summer we did lots of different things: I rode a donkey for the first time and while visiting London saw Princess Elizabeth in the park and waved. In the summer I played an important part in the church fete.

In September 1932 after three and a half years at sea, my father's ship returned to England and berthed in Portsmouth Dockyard. Hundreds of people came to welcome her home, including my grandfather who had come over from Ryde. We had a marvellous autumn as a family together, and in December Father went down to Devon to take up his new appointment at the Royal Naval College at Dartmouth. We joined him later and moved into a house next door to the hospital and alongside the River Dart. My mother loved the garden, and as a newspaper article reported:

Mrs Ingleby-Mackenzie is devoted to her garden and whatever the weather may be seen in Wellington boots, with a hose, watering the flower beds. She is cousin to clever Miss Peggy Ashcroft. Perhaps the most fascinating member of the Devonshire household is Felicity-Jane, the tiny daughter of the home, who is not quite three and was born in the East . . .

About this time I fell down and broke my arm. I had to wear a sling and was X-rayed once a week in the hospital. I continued making a great rate of growth, much to my father's pleasure, and when Admiral Fullerton inspected the College in July he noted to my parents how much I had grown since he had last seen me at Portsmouth. A momentous event happened in September. My mother gave birth to a baby boy. In the family he was called Colin, but his full name was Alexander Colin David Ingleby-Mackenzie. My father was quick to record his weight: 8lbs! In fact my brother's birth is my very earliest memory. I can recall being taken by Nanny into my mother's bedroom to see him for the first time and asking

Plate 6.5 Back in England, circa 1936. Felicity and mother with her younger brother Colin, older half brother Angus and two Dandy Dinmont terriers.

very pointedly when he was going home! Needless to say he stayed and from that point I had to share my parents with this interloper.

We left Dartmouth in January 1935 when I had just turned four, as Father had been appointed to HMS *Resolution*. But my life could have come to an end at this point, as a few days before we left, Colin and I were nearly killed. Our Nanny and I were walking along a country lane with Colin in his pram, when a car travelling far too fast hit the handle of the pram and poor Colin was thrown up into the air and into the ditch. Nanny quickly gathered up her charges and took us to recover into a nearby cottage, and fortunately we were not hurt. The driver, a certain Mrs Kate Pope, had to go to court and she was fined £4 for driving without due care and attention. Colin and I survived, and so there is more story to tell.

We lived in Paignton after Father left for sea but we did spend some time in London. In July 1935 I did my bit for National Baby Week by donating a purse, with its contents, to the Duchess of York at a garden party in St. James's Palace. Later in the year we moved to Malta but peace in the world was becoming fragile. Italy invaded Abysinnia (Ethiopia). Father's ship was sent to Egypt to keep an eye on the political situation and so, after just six weeks on the island, we had to return to England where we lived in Glebe Place in Chelsea. In January King George V died and Colin and I wore black armbands. Mummy took me to see the funeral at the cinema, there being very few televisions in the 1930s. We led very active lives during these last few years before the war. I started to learn French and outside school Colin and I performed at Christmas in the *Merry Masque of Our Lady in London Town* – we were angels but at Easter Colin got promoted to acting as the Christ child. We were also taken to many of the big national events like the Military Tournament at Olympia, the Trooping of the Colour and the Children's Day of Remembrance at Ranelagh Gardens.

In December 1936 King Edward VIII abdicated and in April we stayed in London for the coronation of George VI. But it was a sad summer, as in July my grandmother, Granny Tindal, died. In September Father retired from the Navy to become Secretary of the Union Club in Carlton House Terrace. Our parents bought a house in Drayton Gardens and this became our family home until 1952. I was now at school with the nuns of the Assumption in Kensington. One of my mother's interests was showing Dandie Dinmont terriers, and she won a prize at the Kennel Club Show for her dog Alpine Andrew. My Grannie Tindall had also kept this breed, as had my grandfather Judge Longstaffe, so we knew the breed well.

Plate 6.6 Felicity donating a charitable purse to the Duchess of York (soon to become Queen and future Queen Mother) July 1935.

It was obvious that the political events in Europe were getting dangerous and the probability of war with Germany more likely. Daddy rejoined the Navy but for a while life went on as normal. Our holiday that year was at Sheerness so that we could be near Father whose ship the *Resolution* was berthed close by and Colin had his fifth birthday on board. We often visited Twyford, to the west of London, during this period to stay with Aunt Lucy, my mother's sister, and Uncle Hal.

The war comes

Of course in that summer of 1939 we didn't know how close we were to the start of the Second World War. Things became serious when Germany invaded Poland, and then on Sunday 3rd September war was declared. I remember coming out of church to find firemen in helmets, as there was an immediate fear that German planes would soon start dropping bombs on our towns. We couldn't stay in London because of the danger so we moved to Twyford to stay with our aunt and uncle. My mother was a VAD, the Voluntary Aid Detachment, and was summoned to take up a post at the Royal Berkshire Hospital. Later in the month, on my ninth birthday, I went off to boarding school at St Mary's at Ascot. I enjoyed life at school. I don't remember too much about my time at the Assumption Convent in Kensington Square but I was very happy at Ascot, and when my father got leave from the *Resolution* he came to see me. I enjoyed all the subjects, with the exception of maths. I played the piano, sang in the choir and liked gymnastics, hockey, netball and tennis. I was good at swimming as I had learned at the age of four when we lived in Malta, and we were lucky that St Mary's had a big pool. We still managed to have holidays and even the occasional shopping trip to town. But the air raids on London became really bad and we were very fortunate to have our house in the country.

In July 1941 my mother became Commandant of the British Red Cross. Some bombs fell on Ascot but our school was not hit. Daddy was appointed to Dartmouth again, but then it was very badly damaged by German bomber planes and the college had to move up to Cheshire. My parents bought a house in Wargrave and Father was sent off to sea again. He was appointed to HMS *Hood*, a very famous ship that was sunk by the Germans just six weeks after Father was transferred in April 1941 to a hospital ship, the HMS *Vita*. The Hood was in action with the battleship *Bismarck* on 24th May at the Battle of Denmark Strait and was so badly damaged that she sank. After service on the *Vita* Father was sent to Ceylon to join the staff of Lord Mountbatten. He came home in 1944 and decided that I should leave St Mary's and attend another school. I think he believed it had too great a Catholic influence on me and it is amusing now in later life, when I occasionally accompany friends to a Roman Catholic service to see their amazement that an Anglican can recite the Hail Mary! I was very happy at St Mary's and decidedly didn't want to leave, but children in those days did not have a voice in such matters. I had gone to Ascot at age nine and I was now 14 and the form captain, so a sizeable part of my life and friendships were at that school

By this time the threat of air raids had stopped so it appeared safe for us to return. I passed the entrance exam to Queen's College School in Harley Street, but a new danger started – the doodlebugs. These were self-propelled bombs that were fired from France and dropped down in

London exploding on impact. They made a funny droning noise like an insect, hence their nickname, but when the sound stopped it meant that the missile was dropping to earth and within 15 seconds would hit the ground and explode. More than two thousand of them landed on London and over six thousand Londoners died as a result. So I didn't go to Queen's College but to Hampden House in Great Missenden, Buckinghamshire. After I had settled I enjoyed my time there too. There was no hockey, only lacrosse, which I didn't enjoy, but I made some more good friends, many of whom I still have today.

The war ends

The war in Europe ended in May 1945. I was at boarding school and for weeks we had been listening on the radio, or wireless as we called it in those days, to the progress the Allied troops were making as they headed for Berlin. We had a map and marked where they were with little flags. Then at last the great news came – the war in Europe was over. We were given a day's holiday and then a long weekend so we could all return home to celebrate with our familes. In August Japan surrendered and the war really was at an end. I was on holiday and living at home in London. On the evening of the announcement we joined the crowds outside the gates of Buckingham Palace and called for the King and Queen, and of course Winston Churchill, to come out onto the balcony. Suddenly there they were and how we shouted! We heard later that the two Princesses had, unknown to the crowd, slipped out of the Palace and joined us. They were accompanied by two detectives and four Guards officers, one of who was our great friend James Denny.

Slowly a more normal life resumed. I left school in 1947 and became a student at the House of Citizenship in London. This as its name suggests was an educational institution with the purpose of giving young ladies both a sense of good citizenship and skills in typing and shorthand but it was in the following year when I became 18 that life became very busy and exciting. I 'came out' as a debutante. I made my official debut at the Queen Charlotte's Ball in April, and my parents gave me a party at the Savoy in May. I was presented at Buckingham Palace on 12th May and then life consisted of very many parties. It was party after party with 50 to 100 guests at each. There were parties at hotels, in London houses and weekends at country mansions. Few young men had cars in those days so we all travelled down by train to these wonderful places. Most of the girls were 17 or 18 like me, while the men were a little older being at university

Plate 6.7 Felicity in her 'deb' year – 1948.

or doing their National Service in the forces. It was a spring and summer of college balls at Oxford and Cambridge, a cricket match at Eton and Harrow, and even the rural Royal Agricultural College was on our list. I was doing what my mother and future mother-in-law had done before, they too had 'come out' and I still have photographs of them dressed in their wonderful ballgowns.

At the same time my brother was also enjoying life to the full. He was a good sportsman like our father. He was a superb cricketer at Eton. After the war when competitions between schools resumed he was the hero of the match at Lords between Eton and Harrow. He hit the winning four to give victory to Eton. As the newspapers reported:

A small figure brought a roar from the crowd and dashed Harrow's hopes with a triumphant four in the Eton and Harrow match at Lords last week.

He was 15 year old Colin Ingleby-Mackenzie . . . as far as is known the youngest boy to play for Eton in this famous match . . .

On the ground at Lords he appeared small among his teammates, all three or four years older than himself.

He proved that he was well up with them, however, by his fine show at the end of the match when he retired with a score of 24 not out.

My mother very modestly said at the time that she could not take any of the credit for Colin's talent at the game; that was down to his Father and Colin's early days in Kensington Gardens when he spent all his time practising. 'Vicarage garden tennis and swimming are just about my mark'.

In 1950 I went to Egypt and stayed with family friends. The husband was the naval attaché at the British Embassy in Cairo. This was great fun and my first time as an independent adult overseas. After a number of weeks partying at the different embassies I left to see something of the neighbouring places. With a friend I flew across to Cyprus and then travelled through Italy and France. Back in London I got a job with Rufford Travel Service.

The Coronation

A great event happened in June 1953, the Coronation of Princess Elizabeth in Westminster Abbey. The whole country took part in this, one way or another, but my parents were very lucky indeed to be there in the Abbey itself. There was huge excitement – a lovely young Queen ascending the throne after the grim austerity of the war years. Decorations went up everywhere, stands were erected in the centre of London and buildings were repaired and painted along the route that the Queen's procession was to take. Excitement is hardly the word to describe the feelings in our household. We were now living in South Terrace and Mother and Father had been invited to be present in the Abbey, and my father was to be part of the procession, wearing his magnificent naval uniform and sword. In preparation he took long walks every weekend to ensure that he would be fit enough.

I was very lucky because Father got me two tickets for the final rehearsal of the Coronation ceremony in the Abbey. It was performed exactly as on the day with the exception that the Duke of Norfolk stood in for the Princess – she was having a last practice at the Palace. The big day arrived; it dawned damp and chilly though we hardly noticed. I watched the procession from a window in the Haymarket. I had to be there by 6 am, a very early start, but we got both breakfast and lunch, with champagne being poured for us all the time! My parents also had to be in the Abbey early and while they could see it at first hand I, like the rest of the nation,

Plate 6.8 Felicity's parents – Surgeon Vice-Admiral Sir Alexander
Ingleby-Mackenzie and Lady Ingleby-Mackenzie at the
Queen's Coronation, 1953.

watched it on television. Then came the Procession through the streets
and I felt so proud to see Father march by close to the new Queen's coach;
it was magnificent with so much colour and the music from all the
military bands.

When the procession had passed we somehow had to get home through
the thousands and thousands of people celebrating in the streets. But the
day was far from being over. We all went to the Coronation Dinner at the
Dorchester in Park Lane. We had been invited by American friends who
had come over from Chicago especially. It was a great evening and I
tumbled into bed at 4 am – I had been up for 24 hours!

Marriage and India

I met Kenneth in 1955 at a cocktail party and in January the following year we married at St James's in Piccadilly. We flew off on our honeymoon to Paris, and then made our way to Portugal and Spain. Returning to London we set up home in Yeoman's Row, just off Brompton Road, and lived there for the next four years. Kenneth, like his father, was a tea broker and after his war service had been based in Calcutta. During the first four years of our marriage he had a job in London with Thomas Cumberledge and Inskip but I did get a chance to travel with him. In 1958 Kenneth and I took a short trip to Ceylon and India via Beirut and then on to Assam. We flew up from Calcutta in a noisy and very terrifying Dakota. Kenneth was visiting tea gardens. It was like being in a Somerset Maugham novel; there were only certain gardens where I could stay, as tea planters tended to get drunk on the occasions when they got a chance to have a break at the club. In March 1960 an exciting event happened, the birth of Bruce. Soon afterwards Kenneth was asked to go back to Calcutta; he went out first to set up home and I followed with baby Bruce and Nanny Gelpin, who to my great delight had rejoined our family.

We went by sea. It took three weeks and was very much like an extended cruising holiday. We arrived in Bombay and then flew across India to Calcutta. Our first family home was a flat in Elgin Road. India is a hot place and the coastal area is very hot indeed, especially during April. In the hot season of 1961 Bruce, Nanny and I moved to Ooty. This is in the hills of southern India and because it is higher up the climate is much more bearable. We stayed at the Ooty Club and I can remember that they had a pack of hounds that hunted jackals but when we stayed it was a very quiet time. After two years Kenneth got a four-month leave back in England. A sad event had happened in January 1961 with the death of my father. I flew back and supported my mother at his memorial service. By this time my brother Colin had become captain of the Hampshire Cricket Team and they went on to win the national county title, but unfortunately Father died before he could see this great triumph.

In 1962 we returned to India for another two-year term. We had a delightful house. I led the life expected of a European wife: I played golf and tennis and swam at the Tollygunge Club. We had plenty of help in the house: there was Nanny of course but also nine Indian staff – the butler or *khitmughar* who was in charge of the running of the house; the under butler or *chokra;* the cook; the valet, who was always referred to as the bearer; two drivers, one for Kenneth and one for me; *mali* or gardener; the *dhobi* who washed our clothes, and the sweeper. It may seem like a lot of servants but you have to remember that in those days we didn't have the range of electrical appliances such as washing machines or sophisticated vacuum cleaners, and there was also an expectation that a European family would be a provider of employment for many local people.

Return to England

We came back in December 1963. Though planes flew regularly between India and London it was more fun, and a gentler way of easing the return, to take the three-week boat trip. This we did on the *Iberia,* leaving it at Naples to fly back to London where we spent Christmas. In January we travelled to the Alpine resort of Klosters and rented a chalet for three months. The idea was to have some serious skiing but I broke my arm and Kenneth became unwell, perhaps not too surprising when you compare the climate of India to that of Switzerland in winter. In the spring we set up home again in Yeoman's Row and Bruce, who was nearly four, started school. His first taste of education was at Garden House in Sloane Square. This was an old fashioned school and it's probably true to say that Bruce had been allowed to run wild in India. Either the school would have to adapt to Bruce or Bruce to the school. At the end of each day the children lined up to say good-bye to their teacher; the girls made a small curtsy and the boys doffed their caps. This was not to Bruce's liking and he refused to take it off. He was sent back up the line of classmates to try a second time. It took many attempts before Bruce got out through the school gates.

Kenneth was keen that Bruce should not be brought up in a city and so we looked for a house in the country to spend weekends. Eventually we found Field House in the Berkshire village of Ashampstead. It was a big house with many bedrooms and four bathrooms, four acres of garden and a gardener's cottage – as friends joked – 'the Evers have a country cottage with nine bedrooms'. After a few years we decided to make Field House our main family home, and from 1968 Kenneth commuted up to his office by train. At five Bruce started as a day boy at Hill House School and then at eight he went as a boarder to Heatherdown in Ascot. He was very good at sport, becoming the *victor ludorum* and captain of rugby. It was here that he became friends with a fellow pupil, Prince Andrew, and I quite regularly drove him to parties at Windsor Castle and Buckingham Palace. Nanny stayed on after Bruce left for school, but in 1972 she got married. By then she had known our family for forty years and was 60. It was very sad losing her but more than 30 years later when she was in her 90s I regularly went down to Brighton to spend the day with her talking about old times.

Another great event happened in 1972, when Angus was born. It was probably quite a surprise for 12 year-old Bruce to have a younger brother. A new nanny came – Nanny McKernon. She was not a young woman and in fact Angus was to be her last baby before she retired. Bruce went to Eton and Angus started at the village school when he was three. At five he attended St Andrew's pre-prep school in Pangbourne and then at eight he became a boarder at Horris Hill in Newbury. We had many happy family holidays. I remember one in Italy with our friends the Pease family. We rented a villa with a swimming pool and Angus was feeling particularly lively that holiday. In fact so lively that our friends gave him the name of 'Gadfly' as he was in the habit of splashing everybody who wanted to relax by the pool. This nickname stuck with the Pease family and they would even send him birthday cards addressed using that name. Fortunately the teachers at his boarding school had the good sense to keep the envelope away from his fellow pupils. Neither of our sons were interested in horses, and given both Kenneth's passion for riding and their paternal grand-fathers genius at racing, it appears that some interests are not simply carried in the genes. About this time a very horrific event took place. Bruce, who was a keen member of the school Army Cadets, was away at a weekend exercise. A friend was playing with a rifle and accidentally shot Bruce in the back. He was rushed to the Military Hospital in Aldershot and was critically ill. Kenneth and I went down to see him and tried to make sense of what had happened. He did recover but it was a very traumatic event.

We moved from Field House in 1979; both boys were away at school and we bought a smaller house in the village. Blorenge House had just five bedrooms and one acre of garden so was much more manageable. By now Kenneth was a consultant advising on tea production and quality. This involved him travelling up to London and some trips to exotic places like Moscow. The day after Angus's 13th birthday he followed in his brother's footsteps and went to Eton. Of course Bruce had long since left school by then. Angus was in David Evans house. We were proud of him as he worked very hard at his school subjects and was a good athlete. He could not emulate his uncle's skills at cricket but he was a very good sprinter winning many national junior championships, and was gifted at the jumping events, winning national schoolboy competitions in the long

Plate 6.9 Felicity and Bruce with the newly baptised Angus.

jump. He became an Oppidan Scholar, for academic achievement, and so eligible to wear *stick-ups.* He was very keen on the Army Cadets and was head of his corps – an interest he maintained in later life with a commission in the Territorial Army.

Angus had a gap year after Eton working at a mission school in India and then some travelling in Australia. On his return in 1990 he went to Durham University. But the following year was a tragic one; Kenneth died from cancer. He had just lived long enough to see Bruce and Marie-Ann married in the previous September – an event that made us both very happy. After his death I sold Blorenge House and moved to Goring, and here I have been ever since. In fact it is the longest I have lived in any one place.

Plate 6.10 Angus Evers – in the garden of Field House in Ashampstead
with his first bike.

Goring on Thames

I chose Goring because I had friends living in this very pretty village alongside the Thames. It's not far from where I had spent much of my married life, and with a small railway station it is convenient for London. I worship at the local Anglican Church of St Thomas where I help to do the church flowers, and support lots of the village groups. Early on I became a member of the Amenities Association, and we try our best to maintain the things that are good about Goring and to make it an even better place. For many years I have been a supporter of the Arthritis Association. I am very fortunate not to suffer from the disease though my mother did, and I know how much this condition can affect people's lives. I have always loved art, and one of my joys is membership of NADFAS – the National Association of Decorative and Fine Arts Society. I have been an active member for a number of years, and each month we have lectures and visits to galleries and places of interest. More recently I have joined the U3A, the University of the Third Age, so you can see I am doing my best to keep the brain cells active. I have always loved travel and been fortunate enough to have lived or visited many exciting places, of course Sri Lanka where I was born and India where Kenneth and I lived, but also Italy, Spain, Egypt, Crete, the Baltic and the Black Sea.

Throughout my life I have been very lucky in making friends easily and so have a network of people I visit and spend time with. Of course there are some who are particularly close and who I have known from schooldays. One is Eve Phillips who I first met in 1942 when our brothers were best friends at their prep school. I met her again in 1948 when we were both debs and it was with her that I went to Cairo in 1950–51. She is godmother to Bruce. Another close friend is Anne Naumann who I also first met in 1948 (and whose mother had been at school with my mother in Leeds) and she is a godmother to Angus. A school friend from Hampden is Ann Dent, and I have spent many happy holidays with her in Cornwall. I met Rosie Kindersley at the House of Citizenship and I still see her regularly. One person who has been incredibly kind is Sue Adams. She has taken me on some wonderful holidays and helped me in so many ways. Our parents were friends before the war but we didn't meet till we were both in Calcutta, and she is another godparent to Angus.

It was a very special phone call that I got from Angus when he rang to ask if he could come and visit me and bring a friend. They came and I met for the first time a young woman who I immediately liked whose name was Morag. She brought me flowers and was charming. They stayed on a number of weekends and I gradually got to know my future daughter-in-law. When they moved into a flat in Islington I realised that this was more than a passing friendship, Angus had always said he would never marry before the age of 30. On his 30th birthday we had a small celebration with Bruce and Marie-Ann. A few more months later he and Morag went on holiday to Slovenia. There up a mountain Angus had proposed and Morag accepted. It was a wonderful April wedding. I shall always remember the beautiful cherry blossom in the quad at Magdalen College. They looked a splendid couple and so happy in the magnificent setting of the college chapel. We had a reception at the college and dinner at the Old Bank Hotel in the High Street with close family and ushers – all old friends that Angus had made at school or university. I eventually went to bed a happy and proud mother but also with some sadness that Kenneth was not with us to share this wonderful day.

A few months later they visited me in Goring. I was sitting alone with Morag and told her how well she looked, she giggled and I started to suspect that I might hear some very good news in the near future. Not long after Angus announced at a family gathering that Morag was expecting a baby the following April. I first saw Alexander when he came out of hospital. I had waited a long time for a grandchild, and there was this wonderful white bundle! It was not long after that we heard that Morag was going to have another baby. I first saw Felix when he was a few days old. I arrived at the house and Alexander took me by the hand and led me to the cot – he pointed and said 'baby'. It has been a great joy to me to get to know the two boys. When they were pre-school I had the opportunity to go with them on three family holidays to Crete. Max and Alyson came too, so it was a time to get to know my new extended family much better.

My life has been in three, distinct parts: before marriage, then my life with Kenneth, and my years as a widow in Goring. I have always enjoyed novels and poetry. A few years ago I was staying with a cousin in Norfolk and met an artist friend of hers – Marcia Gibson-Watt. She had just illustrated a book called *The Four Graces and Other Prayers to Celebrate Radnor 2000 AD*. As the title suggests it is a collection of prayers and reflections. One of the readings in the book I already knew; I guess I must have first heard it read at a funeral. It's by Elizabeth Craven and captures so many of my feelings. It is a celebration of life; the love of family and friends, music at night and the eyes of dogs, but at the same time not ducking the fact that life, and all people's lives have sadness and difficult periods. I think I would rather like it to be read at my funeral:

I thank thee God, that I have lived in this great world and know its many joys;
The song of birds, the strong sweet scent of hay and cooling breezes in the
    secret dusk,
The flaming sunsets at the close of day, hills, and the lonely heather-covered
    moors,
Music at night and moonlight on the sea, the beat of waves upon the rocky
    shore
And wild white spray, flung high in ecstasy; the faithful eyes of dogs, and
    treasured books,
The love of kin and fellowship of friends, and all that makes life dear and
    beautiful.
I thank thee too, that there has come to me a little sorrow and sometimes
    defeat.
A little heartache and the loneliness that comes with parting and the word
    'Goodbye'.
Dawn breaking after weary hours of pain, when I discovered that night's
    gloom must yield.

And morning light breaks through to me again. Because of these and other
    blessings poured
Unasked upon my wondering head, because I know there is yet to come
An even richer and more glorious life, and most of all because thine only Son
Once sacrificed life's loveliness for me; I thank thee God that I have lived.

CHAPTER 7

Max's Story

One of my earliest memories was the family move to Buckingham when for 18 months we lived on the edge of the small village of Maids Moreton. We had a large house – well, big when you are only four, and certainly grander than the house we had before in a suburb of Leicester. The garden at the back was just the right size for a small child; I could sit inside the wooden train my father had made for me and push it along with my feet or play with my pedal car and create my own pathways around the lawn and fruit trees. The house, which was called Ashburnham, was bordered by a field, and beyond that an avenue of beech trees. It was here that I first experienced the country and country people. Even now, 60 years later, I remember the thrill of being invited by the lady next door to go with her to collect the eggs from her chicken house across the road. She let me search through each nesting box and place the still warm eggs in her bucket.

It was in Maids Moreton that I started school, a short walk along a field path from our house to the village. The first morning my mother took me, but after that I told her that my friend Rosemary, who was slightly older than me, would bring me home each day. I wasn't prepared for school in the way that Morag and Conrad, or Alexander and Felix, were prepared. Children in the 1950s didn't go to nursery, and I can't recall being taken to any event that involved other children before starting school, and as I had no brothers or sisters this was my first experience of being with others of my own age. Everything was new, from learning the names of the numbers – and I had big problems with remembering the name of the funny squiggle that was eight – to mastering the alphabet, and being in one large room with 20 other children.

I liked school but I hated warm milk: in winter the free bottle that we got during the morning break was placed on the coke boiler in the centre of the classroom to unfreeze the milk that had almost turned solid. But when it was warm the straw went soggy and I just could not bear that texture in my mouth. I also had a problem pronouncing certain words. I couldn't say school, it came out as *stool,* and later when we moved back to

Plate 7.1 Max at his first school in the village of Maids Moreton,
Buckinghamshire, 1952.

Leicester and I went to a larger school that had a balcony running above
the hall my little tongue always produced the word *baconey*.

During this time in Buckingham I had the freedom to roam that few
children today experience, well, if they do their parents will be considered
negligent. I rode my pedal car down to the police station and I walked
along the avenue of trees with its mysterious high wall and locked garden
gate, desperately wanting to know what was on the other side – all this was
before I had been influenced by children's stories such as the *Secret
Garden*. On one occasion I was the hero of the town's weekly cattle
market as I was able to encourage a bull to go into the right cattle pen. My
mother had taken me to see the animals but on this morning a young bull
had got frightened and was refusing to move. The men spotted me and
my bright red blazer – my mother always dressed me in rather distinctive
outfits – and as bulls were believed to hate this colour and would charge

Plate 7.2 A wooden train made by Walter, in the garden of
Ashburnham House, 1952.

any red material they asked me to go and stand on the far side of the pen. It worked! The bull raced in and I proudly received praise for my bravery.

Before Buckingham I recall just a few happenings, and all were when I was four. My very first memory was on my fourth birthday when my mother organised a party. I think this was the only birthday party that I had until I shared one with Alyson's sister on my 21st. It was not that my mother didn't care, she was loving and within her means generous, but those from her generation and class just did not invite others into their home. They worked hard, kept to the rules and minded their own business. The only other occasion when my mother invited a child to tea was five or six years later when a neighbour's husband died suddenly one morning. My mother collected their son from school and looked after him till his mother could return from hospital and break the news. I don't think I was a totally angelic child, as at my fourth birthday party I recall chasing a screaming guest upstairs with a balloon when I discovered he was terrified of the noise it would make if it burst.

We returned to Leicester when I was six and moved back into a house in the same street. I realise now that my mother must have been very unhappy in Buckingham away from the places and people she knew. She had always lived in Leicester and her identity was bound up in her friends. The word *friends* is probably too strong as neither my father nor mother had people that could be called confidants, but my mother did have a network of people she knew and who knew her. A rewarding trip out of the house was one that had involved meeting a number of these acquaintances and hearing their family news. So in 1953, the year of the Queen's Coronation, we moved back to a house only a few hundred yards away from the one we had left. Like many others we bought our first television at that time in order to watch the ceremony, and I can remember going into the garden at one point to hear the gun salute being fired a few miles away in Victoria Park.

I started at a new school, Avenue Road Junior School. It was a ten-minute walk away and I was soon walking there each day on my own. I had started mid-term and I remember the first day sitting at a small table with two or three other children who were finishing the buildings of a farm they had been making from card. They must have been on the project for a few weeks so it was too late for me to take part. The boy next to me had made a wonderful Dutch barn, and it seemed to me the most desirable thing I had ever encountered. Perhaps going to agricultural college 13 years later was all about trying to find the barn that I had been denied.

One consequence of my first schooling being in Buckinghamshire was the way I spoke. What Leicester people heard was a posh accent, and I certainly spoke differently to the other children. Apart from anything else it made it harder for me to understand spelling as I became confused between the pronunciation I heard around me, which was different from the way that I pronounced words. Simple things like grass and pass led me to believe that an 'r' needed to be placed after the 'a' to comply with how I was saying them. In junior school Mr Green would be sarcastic over these mistakes, with the result that I gave up on trying to master the silly spelling rules that made no sense.

Not having any brothers or sisters led me to become independent and self-contained, and probably lonely. I say probably lonely because during childhood I didn't have a sense of being 'alone' as my parents were there in the background and I got on with entertaining myself. Parents did not play with their children in the 50s. The only exceptions that I can remember are as a small child on the beach when I was helped to make castles, and in the winter when my father would take me sledging. We had cold winters, and snow always came within days of the New Year. Wrapped up we would go in the car to Houghton-on-the-Hill and my Father, using his feet and hands, would carve out a St Moritz bobsled-run down the steep slope, just stopping dangerously short of the hedge at the bottom. These trips were never very long, as my fingers and toes would get cold, I would cry and then we would go home.

I could do almost anything I wanted in the garden of our new Leicester house. I climbed the apple tree, had a den in a secret corner behind the garage, and a special route that ran over the top of the shed dropping down under the privet hedge to a place where I had my secret treasure box buried. In this I kept coins, shells and cigarette cards, and would regularly dig it up to inspect my valuables. I was a well-behaved child. This is not surprising, as I had no need to be badly behaved. With no siblings I had no rivals and as much freedom as I knew what to do with. By eight or nine I would cycle out of town and explore. I remember one hot summer's day when I was walking on the golf course to the east of the city. There was a thunderstorm, and knowing it wasn't safe to shelter under trees I decided to run the few miles to my grandmother's house in Knighton. I arrived there very wet and very cold. She lit a fire and I dried out. By then she was in her 70s and living alone. I was always ambivalent about her house. I loved the canaries in Mr Pilbrow's aviary next door; I was fascinated by the dark wooden grandfathers' clock that struck the hours with a scary sound that echoed over the house in a way that no clock in our house could ever achieve, and I half loved and half feared the damp kitchen and even cooler scullery. Grandmother was the only one to use the word 'scullery' in our family. She didn't have a fridge, so meat and butter were kept on the stone shelves in the walk-in scullery, while her bottle of milk was kept cool by standing it in a bucket of water in the back yard. Over the top was draped a cloth that was kept moist, and as the water evaporated the cloth was cooled. No food was ever wasted. On the shelf above the kitchen table would be a row of cups – in one some congealed gravy left over from the previous day, a few peas in the second and cold potatoes in the third, all to be used in the next cooked meal.

She spent most of her time in the back parlour, the front one only used at Christmas. On the wall was a copper plate with an engraved poem called 'Home Sweet Home'. Even as a young child I realised that the verse was sentimental and something that my parents would never have allowed to hang on their walls. But I knew she had struggled to keep her family together after my Grandfather had been killed in 1917 and in a way this plate was her medal for getting through those years. I got on well with her. She was a no-nonsense woman who smiled a lot and worked hard. One day she told me how she had come to be in Leicester. Brought up on the Packington Hall estate in Warwickshire, she had left school at twelve. An aunt worked as a housekeeper in Leicester and the 'mistress' was looking for a maid. Grandma was dressed in her best clothes and an old hat of her mother's and put on the train. Aunty Bertha met her at Leicester station and her first words were, 'My God where did you get that hat? Take it off now before the Mistress sees you in it!' So Grandma entered service in Stoneygate. The gardener had an assistant, young Herbert Green, and after a while they walked out. On the same golf course where 43 years later young Max fled from the thunderstorm, an innocent Annie Wall conceived Jessie Green.

Even in her 70s she rode her old bike to rich people's houses to do their cleaning or baby-sit their children. I didn't see her very often when I was very young as she and my mother frequently fell out, and my father never liked her, but in my later teens after my parents separated I saw her more frequently. When my passion was shooting I would take her a pheasant, which she would pluck and then a few days later we'd sit down at the kitchen table and drink sherry with our very special meal.

Secondary school

In the last year at junior school we took the 'Eleven Plus', an exam that determined whether you went on to a secondary modern and a working-class job, or to grammar school and a middle class one. Very few at Avenue Road went on to a grammar school. I neither passed nor failed, I was placed on the border. In Leicester there was one school called an 'intermediary'. Moat School selected children who fell into this in-between category. In September 1958, dressed in my black blazer with its red castle badge, surrounded by the 'moat', I started secondary school.

Moat did not even make the pretence of providing a rounded education. It had just one aim: to show the four city grammar schools that Moat boys could get as good, if not better, GCE results (General Certificate of Education), and it did just that! From day one we had daily, weekly and term tests, annual exams, mock GCE exams and detentions if you failed to reach 75%. No subject or activity appeared on the school timetable if it didn't relate to the exam syllabus or was compulsory like sport under the Education Act. The culture of the school was thus very clear and within its own terms very successful. From Year One to Year Five we were on a narrow public examination track. As pupils we were hard-working and single minded with the sole aim of achieving good exam results. The school was disciplined but in a fair and enlightened way, and I never saw or experienced any bullying from teachers or classmates. The school philosophy was encapsulated by Mr Davis the French teacher from Wales, when he stood in front of the class, obviously disappointed with our efforts and shouted 'You are throwing away this opportunity. Why I know boys who would cut off their right arms to be in your place!' We were not cynical when he said this; we really believed there were 12-year-olds in the Rhondda who would face amputation to sit at our desks. Only many years later did I understand that teachers like Mr Davis had just a few years before been in the Second World War and were motivated by a heartfelt commitment to helping others to be socially mobile. The grammar schools and our intermediary school did enable bright working class children to do just that.

The school was successful and most of us got good results. In my final year, ten of us equalled the best that had been achieved at the city's grammar schools and our names and results appeared in the *Leicester Mercury*. We didn't leave the Fifth Year well educated but we could pass exams.

It was 1963 and in the world outside school and home many big events had taken place like the Cuban Missile Crisis and the fear that we had been close to a global nuclear war, but most of these things passed me by almost unnoticed. A few years before leaving Moat we had moved to a village six or seven miles south of the city. My father had designed his ideal house and after searching for some time found a building plot in a field on the edge of Great Glen. The garden was not big but it was quite dramatic, being on a high bank overlooking the River Sense. I became a friend and helper of the retired farm worker who lived next door. Mr Dewsbury had a smallholding with pigsties and hen houses, and a vegetable garden that was so magnificent its appearance could have been lifted from the pages of a gardening magazine. It was George Dewsbury who taught me how to keep poultry, to talk to pigs (you always started with a friendly *chug chug chug*) and how to dig a vegetable plot correctly so that the manure was at the bottom of a perfectly straight trench and with not a sign of a weed poking through.

The farmer who had been Mr Dewsbury's employer was the same landowner who my father had bought the building plot from. Mr Wooster was like a character from a Hardy novel. I was with my father the first time he drove to the farm to enquire whether Mr Wooster would be interested in selling some land. As we pulled up outside the farmhouse a small, weather worn man came out to see who we were. I had never been as fearful of an adult as I was of this strange man approaching our car. He wore clothes that had gone out of fashion 50 years before and my eyes were fixed on the leather spats covering his lower legs. He carried a great leather whip curled up in his hand. Everything about his manner said –

'clear off'. We already knew that Mr Wooster belonged to a strict religious sect and did not receive visitors or discuss business on Sundays. This was a Saturday, but we got out of the car with no expectation of success. But Mr Wooster turned out to be a very reasonable and almost affable man. He sold my father a piece of field and in the years that followed allowed me to wander over the farm with my shotgun. I even went to work on the farm for a short while before going off to agricultural college.

Moving into the country set my life on a certain track that it otherwise would not have taken. It wasn't simply my interest in farming or botany – I became quite expert at recognising the flora of Leicestershire – but being able to wander in the lanes and fields gave me a way of coping with the unpleasant things of life. Walking in the country has remained the most important way I have coped with anxieties and stress. Soon after we moved life did become difficult.

During the last two years at Moat I had travelled each day by bus into Leicester, but when I came to enter the Sixth Form it seemed the right time to attend a school in the county. Guthlaxton was a comprehensive (Leicestershire was one of the first places in the country to introduce non streamed schools). I liked my new teachers and got on well with the other pupils. I enjoyed being able to try some new sports, as at Moat they had been considered a distraction, and I found that I was good at pole vaulting. I had developed some skill in our garden, as the only way for me to get across the river was to take a long, strong branch and vault across. Guthlaxton had poles and even an indoor pole-vaulting pit, so I could train throughout the winter. In my final year at the school I became the County Schoolboy Champion breaking the county record and my elbow all in the same jump. The legacy of this is that since the age of 17 I have one shorter arm, something I am self-conscious about. But though I liked my new school it was not a happy time. My parents' relationship got steadily worse. Jessie didn't like being out of the city and spent more and more evenings away. I had been aware from about the age of ten that some of these friends were men of my father's age and that my mother did not want me to talk about this. Father's job took him away alternate weeks and after a big row my mother left. I stayed. I didn't make a decision to remain with my father any more than I consciously decided not to go with my mother: the house was where I lived and my mother had left the house.

The practical consequence was that from the age of 16 I looked after myself for much of the time. My father went away as before and I managed on school lunches (which I thought were wonderful), some simple things that I could cook and the occasional meal in other people's homes. In the summer holidays I started up my own business as a freelance gardener. I had had two earlier businesses; at the age of eight I had collected wooden orange boxes from greengrocers' shops, chopped them up and sold firewood at one shilling a bucket. Then in Great Glen under Mr Dewsbury's guidance I had my poultry enterprise. Through my mother's whist friends I sold eggs, but I soon discovered that the demand was much greater than my hens could supply so I bought more from a local farm and sold them on at a good profit. But in the summer of 1964 I advertised my services in the *Leicester Mercury,* as a reliable gardener charging just five shillings an hour to do maintenance work. My first customer was the local vicar. In a confidential tone he explained that he already had two men cutting the grass in the churchyard but as both were in their 70s he wanted a younger, more energetic person to actually do the 'heavy stuff'.

One of these two older men was Mr Mott and we became great friends. Like Mr Dewsbury he had been a farm labourer. He and his wife lived in an end of row cottage at the edge of the village. It was Mr Mott who encouraged me to keep a ferret, and together we caught rabbits in the fields opposite his house. Mrs Mott's rabbit stew was one of the meals that supplemented school dinners and when I shot a pheasant it went either to Grandma or the Motts but either way I got another meal. There was one thing that always fascinated me about Mr Mott; he smoked shag. Sometimes I would be sent to the village shop to buy him an ounce. Shag was sold in little greased packets, inside was a stick of black, hard tobacco. There was a ritual to observe before it could be smoked. Mr Mott would take out his small penknife, carefully open the blade and slice off about a quarter of an inch. Then, laying it in the palm of his left hand, he rubbed it until it was finely flaked. Only when it was *just right* could it be placed in the pipe and the match struck. Working one day with Mr Mott in the churchyard cutting a hedge I got my first wasp sting, and within hours my left arm had swollen to twice its size. It was the day of my 17th birthday and I still have the mark of that sting more than 40 years later.

Into farming

Initially I did well academically at my new school, especially in history, and my history master encouraged me to consider applying for Oxbridge entry, but by the final sixth form year I had become confused, and probably quite lonely. The countryside was my comfort and security, and so I returned to the idea of working in farming. I was studying the wrong type of A levels (history, English and divinity) to read agriculture at university, so I applied to the Royal Agricultural College. On a snowy January day my Father drove me to Cirencester for the interview. He dropped me off at the entrance to a long driveway and I trudged through the falling flakes to the imposing old manor house entrance. The interview consisted of tea and jam tarts and a very informal chat with the Principal in his study. A butler brought in the tea tray and it all felt very grand. I was offered a place there and then – 'But what grades do I need to get?' I asked. 'Oh none, we'll take you. Sit them if you want to but there is a place here whether you get them or not'.

I did pass a couple of these superfluous to needs A levels and then worked for a year on a dairy farm a few miles away from Great Glen to gain some practical experience before going to Cirencester. It is only now after researching the Peberdy family history that I realise I was working in fields that my great, great grandfather Manoah would have known, as the farm bordered Thurnby where he had lived in the middle period of his life. In September 1967 I bought my first car and started at college. We didn't do practical work at the Royal Agricultural College, perhaps rather surprising for farmers-to-be, but the Royal was not for the manually inclined but for those who would return home to run their family 'estates' or manage the estates of wealthy people. My fellow students included the Marquis of Hartington (the heir to the Duke of Devonshire), a viscount and many 'honourables'. Such a disparity in backgrounds between the students who had titles and thousands of acres, and the ones like me was not a problem, as the two groups had virtually no contact. The rich ones did not attend lectures but drove their sports cars up to London while the rest of us worked hard to ensure we passed the exams and hopefully get a job at the end.

Cirencester and the Cotswolds were very different from Leicestershire. I immediately felt at home on the limestone soils. The college had a pack of beagles and in the winter I followed them on foot at the different meetings across Gloucestershire. Before college I had hunted with the Westerby Bassett Hounds and on occasion rode to hounds with the Quorn. In the 60s there were no anti-hunting activists, and in fact no debate as to the rights and wrongs of the sport. I just loved being able to go into woods and valleys that would normally be inaccessible. In my second year I again encountered the Williams family who had run the stables in Leicestershire where I had learned to ride. They had moved a few miles south of Cirencester and opened new stables in the grounds of a large house at Purton. So I took up riding again and cultivated my first real garden. The house had a large and neglected walled vegetable garden. It was huge and in Victorian times no doubt had a half a dozen men and boys maintaining the borders and greenhouses. But the Williamses said I could have the use of the garden rent-free and sell produce to the people coming to ride. I was never able to cultivate more than a small part of the garden, but I did enjoy being the master of my own world behind the walls, and of my brick greenhouse with its defunct coke boiler and great water butts.

It was through riding horses from Purton that I came to know the Marlborough Downs and to be excited by the pre-Roman burial sites and causeway camps. Neither the Cotswolds nor the little hills of Leicestershire had the wide skies and great open coombes of this countryside. I remember the awe that I felt the first time I drove on the road from Swindon southwards to Marlborough, and being almost in fear of the bigness of the landscape ahead of me. I started to explore the strange bumps, and mounds that seemed to be present in every direction – Barbary Castle, Wayland's Smithy long barrow, Silbury Hill and Avebury. I felt totally at home here, though it was to be another 15 years before I actually lived on the downlands.

During this time I did have one other interest, and that was learning to parachute. I became the captain of the grandly named Royal Agricultural College Sky Diving Club. A misnamed society as nobody ever actually *skydived;* what we did was to jump out of a plane on a static line that after a few yards pulled out the cord holding the chute together and automatically released the canopy. But given the many hours we had to journey to the aerodrome in Hampshire and the fact that as novices we could only jump on days with virtually no wind or clouds, we did well in two years to get through the training and make some jumps. I did eight, the most of anybody, and so well deserved my position as captain!

Alyson Garnett

I finished college in 1969. By now my father had sold the house in Great Glen and bought a menswear business in Tamworth. I hated the town, and loathed even more the dark depressing flat that he lived in above the shop. I stayed only once and never went back. Instead I went to live with Grandma in Knighton. It was then that I met Alyson again. We had both been in the VI Form at Guthlaxton with history and English as our common subjects; in fact Conrad is named *Conrad* because one of our set books was Joseph's Conrad's novel *Nostromo*. Alyson was finishing her final year at Durham University and I visited her at her college. Oh, it was so cold that far north!

We started to see each other often. I applied to do a biology course in Wolverhampton, mainly to get a higher qualification as at the Royal we graduated with membership of the RAC and a national diploma but not a degree. Alyson applied to Wolverhampton Social Services to become a trainee childcare officer. So in the summer we moved from Leicester. At first she lived in a flat with a school friend who was also starting training as a social worker and I rented the top part of a house close by. Within a week I realised I had made a mistake trying to study biology. Fortunately my application to the County Council for a grant got mislaid and so I found that I couldn't pay the fees or keep myself as a student, so a new career direction was needed. Alyson had always wanted to work overseas. She had applied to VSO (Voluntary Service Overseas) and I had a vague idea that I'd like to be an agricultural adviser in a developing country (or 'undeveloped country' as they were referred to then). As a teenager I had seen a television programme about a colonial officer in Kenya going about giving good advice to poor farmers and I could imagine myself doing that with flair. We decided to marry and also to apply to VSO. I needed temporary work while we went through the selection process and advertised in the local paper for a job; within a few weeks I was working for Sun Life of Canada as an insurance salesman.

We married on a Wednesday in December 1969. All the Garnett daughters married on Wednesday, not, as may have been the case with Chinese families, because of a belief that mid week is an auspicious time, but because it was half day closing in Mr Garnett's shop and so a wedding on that day meant less business lost. It snowed a rather half hearted snow, but it was a memorable day as all our friends were there and even Mr Garnett came, though he had threatened to stay away if Alyson insisted on wearing white knee length boots with her shocking pink mini dress.

A few months later in June we went to Switzerland as part of the preparation for being volunteers overseas. We joined an international work camp of ten young people building a road in the Alps for 'poor Swiss farmers'. We hadn't been aware that there were any poor Swiss people at all, let alone farmers, but we were assured that they were deserving and they did need a road to help them get their animals up to the summer pastures. We lived in a hay barn above the cows and washed out in the field in the icy cold water trough. A Swiss roadman was our boss and he introduced us to the combinations of chocolate and apple and chocolate and cheese, perhaps not very revolutionary but quite shocking in its newness for two youngsters from Leicester. The work camp was cut short by a week because one of our group, a young Frenchman, fired up by his experience of the 1968 Paris student protests, had persuaded us to walk to the end of the proposed road to see the 'poor farmers'. When we got to the end there were no farmers, just a hotel, a hotel owned by the mayor of the canton who had made the initial request for volunteers! We went on strike and though the project coordinator came down from Zurich to reassure us that there really were deserving farmers living quite close, our French leader told us not to believe the capitalists and so we downed tools and went home.

During these early months of our marriage Alyson was working for Social Services. She would come back each day to our top floor flat in Showell Lane above Mr and Mrs Dumphy, and tell me all about the horrors she had seen on the large council estates. If not horrors, then incidents, like the time a mother had complained of the insult she had experienced at Alyson's hands because she had been left a note written in red ink. I had got my job as an insurance salesman as the result of the advert I placed in the *Wolverhampton Express and Star* – 'Educated young man, with driving licence, is looking for a post'. My original draft had said 'anything considered' but the nice lady at the newspaper office told me that wasn't an advisable form of words. I got five replies. I can't remember two of them but one was for a post as a manager of a garage (I have no mechanical aptitude at all), one for a job as a manager of an amusement arcade in Birmingham, and one to join Mr Ronald Milhench's sales team at Sun Life of Canada. I chose this as it sounded the most respectable. It was a respectable job but for a most unrespectable person. I learnt a lot about selling and communication from a master, and during those few months before we went off on VSO it was good experience and very well paid. Milhench was *just about* honest when I worked for him, but a few years later he was under suspicion of murdering his wife her body having been found in their submerged car in a pond on Cannock Chase. A little later he was arrested, not for murder, but for forging the Prime Minister Harold Wilson's signature on a fraudulent land deal, and for that he ended up in Winston Prison. Considering that he and his wife had first met as cornet players in the Salvation Army their lives had taken some unexpected twists.

Nigeria

Going to Nigeria in 1970 was a very significant event for both of us and set our careers in a certain direction. Also from this point in my story the *I* increasingly becomes *we* as after our marriage in 1969 most of the significant things that happened, were shared experiences. It was intended that we would teach at an isolated state secondary school, and stay for two years. We lasted one year, and though we did teach for some of the time, there were long periods when the school didn't want its teachers to teach. Like the three weeks when we and the other staff sat around while the pupils made mud bricks for a teacher's house. After that, there was the week waiting for the children to finish clearing the bush to make a sports field. Why didn't we muck in and help? Because manual work was considered too demeaning for teachers to do, so we kicked our heels till lessons could resume. Then there was a riot. The head teacher called in armed police to restore control, and they removed the barricades the children had built around the school. The riot had been about respect, or rather the feelings among the older pupils that the younger children were not showing them enough, and should prostrate themselves when meeting a senior child. The younger ones, not surprisingly, didn't agree, and said that only very old people got this sort of outward show, not kids barely older than themselves. Once order was restored there was punishment: a public flogging of the six deemed to be the riot's ringleaders. Alyson and I had argued against this but all the Nigerian staff were in agreement that severe beatings were needed. All the pupils were seated in a large semicircle in front of the main building and the six were held down by their arms and legs across wooden benches. Each teacher took it in turn to run up and strike a bamboo cane across the child's buttocks; six strokes for each of the ringleaders. We were asked to take up canes but refused. There were no more discipline issues after this, so who was right? In Nigerian culture beatings were part of life, but we were certainly not going to support such cruel punishment.

As white people we were novelties. Nigeria had gained independence only a few years before and then there was a terrible civil war between the Western Nigerians and those living in Biafra, in the east. The war had ended only a few months before our arrival and there were still the remains of a burnt out tank on the road into the village. Not many Europeans were in the area. For the farmers living a few miles into the bush we were often the first white people they had seen, and Alyson's long, blonde hair was especially intriguing for children, who would rush up to touch her head. We didn't learn any Yoruba except the word *ay ebo*. Women and kids would excitedly shout these words from the side of the road as we passed by on our motorcycle. It translated as 'peeled-one' – as our black skin had been removed to reveal the whiteness below.

We were very young, and just too inexperienced to respond in a mature way to the challenge of this situation. We felt isolated. There was an Irish Catholic priest living close by, Father Paddy Keely, but he was away a lot of the time visiting parishes in the swamp, so we only had his advice and support when he was around. The school was pleased that we were there, but what they wanted was the status of two white teachers; we didn't have to teach or contribute in any way other than by our presence on the staff. If we had been older and wiser we would have carved out a niche, perhaps a small project among the local farming communities. I did try to start up a school garden, and it went well till one night grasshoppers invaded and stripped everything bare. That disaster was also partly a result of my inexperience, because I had used techniques and crop varieties that were suitable for the environment in England, but which were totally wrong for a tropical situation.

The heat, the isolation, the corruption, the aggressiveness of the Yoruba and the pointlessness of what we were doing, or rather not doing, reached its nadir one hot night about six months after our arrival. We always went to bed early. It was dark by seven, and the school's generator often stopped shortly after nightfall, leaving us in candlelight or trying to read by a paraffin lamp. Somerset Maugham captured so well the claustrophobia of the rainforest. It seemed as if the trees had pulled up their roots and were pushing at the walls of our bungalow. The wet heat took away any remaining energy, and the night noises were so loud that conversations had to compete with the clicking, whirling and screech of the forest insects. So we retreated early each evening to the relative safety and comfort of our mosquito netted bed. Being on the edge of a swamp there were huge numbers of flying bugs, and in the dark snakes would come in from the garden and coil around the beams. If we had to go to the loo in the dark we learned to walk in a particular way – keeping the soles down on the floor and sliding our feet outwards. This way any toads that had invaded would not make a squashy mess on the bedroom floor.

On this particular steamy night in April we were woken by the sound of drums in the forest about half a mile away. We knew it was the sound of a traditional religious gathering, or as Father Keely called it – a juju ceremony. We had heard this type of sound before but not so close, and these drums were getting louder and nearer. Then we heard a bullroarer. This is a shaped piece of wood that is spun very fast on a cord. It makes the most horrible sound, a sound like a dog being tortured to death. We could hear voices and louder drumming and we realised that a group of people had surrounded our bungalow and were just yards from our windows. Why had they come? Why us? Did they mean to harm us? Should we try and run from the house to the garage and hope we could start our motorbike and ride off before they caught us? Or were we safer staying put and keeping quiet? We stayed, and after a while the drumming, the bullroarer and the people moved back into the trees, leaving us very frightened. Next day we learned that far from being threatening, the village people had come to drive away any evil spirits from around our house. Cholera was known to be in the country and spreading towards our area, and this ceremony had been intended to protect us from the disease. If only we had known that before going to bed.

That Easter we were adventurous. We put our Honda 90 motorcycle on the train northwards to Kano and went to the edge of the Sahara. Then over a week we drove back in 200-mile stages, staying at government resthouses or with other VSOs. It was very hot, very, very dusty, and very difficult to find fuel. On one stage of our journey the distance between petrol stations was 140 miles, and as our bike's tank only held enough to cover 120 miles we ran out and had to negotiate with the driver of a mammy wagon to buy just enough fuel to get us to the next filling station. Spokes in the wheels would break almost every hour, and we crossed the River Niger missing almost half of them in the back wheel. Luckily we found a cycle repair stall by the side of the road, and a young boy managed to replace enough spokes for us to continue onto Ibadan where we could get a full set.

What we didn't know, but came to suspect as we bounced along these dusty highways, was that Alyson was pregnant. A visit to a doctor gave us confirmation but also the warning that Aly must avoid malaria as she could lose the baby if she became sick. As we lived on the edge of a swamp where almost every person got fever on a regular basis, we decided not to take the risk and gave notice to the school that we would return to England at the end of the academic year. So Morag's early growth came, not from the traditional ingredients that little girls are made from, sugar and spice but from yams, cassava and peppered snails.

But one event happened before our return that did come to have significance. Given the unexpected news of our forthcoming parenthood, Aly and I needed to read up about babies. One Saturday we drove the 50 miles northwards to Ondo, our closest town with a bookshop. The shop had just one book about children. It was not about prenatal care or childbirth but jumped right forward instead to child rearing. This sole book had the simple title *How to Raise a Brighter Child*. Normally we would never have bought a book with such a pretentious title but given our 100-mile trip and the long evenings ahead we really had no option. Over the next six months this book was read, studied and re-read many times over. When Morag was born the following January her little cold nursery in Berkshire was adorned from Day One with mobiles hanging from the ceiling, classical music playing softly in the background, and home made books with sandpaper to provide tactile stimulation. In fact every suggestion in *How to Raise a Brighter Child* was followed to the letter. Thus her path to Magdalen College began in that little shop in Nigeria.

Return to England

We flew back to London in the summer. Mr Garnett was due to meet us at Gatwick but the plane was diverted to Heathrow, so we got a coach to Leicester and encountered our first culture shock. During the time away the currency had been decimalised. I stood in front of the bus driver with a handful of strange money – whatever was this peculiar multisided silver thing? It turned out to be a 50 pence piece; a coin had replaced the ten-shilling note, and we had become like first time visitors to England.

Our priority was to earn some money. We moved in with Aly's parents and I worked as a gardener in the Wigston Parks Department while Alyson became a temporary childcare officer. Two big adventures lay ahead: the birth of Morag – and as there were no scanning machines in 1972 we did not know whether the baby was a boy or a girl, and starting as post-graduate students at Reading University. Aly was to study Theoretical Sociology for a diploma and then hopefully a master's degree; and I a diploma in Agricultural Extension. This was a subject that nobody has ever heard of but which is really about how to help farmers receive advice. We had no financial support for either the fees or the living expenses but being just 23 and naive we didn't think this would be much of a problem.

In the autumn we said goodbye to the Garnetts and rented a small house called East Cottage on the beautiful Ridges at Finchampstead in

Berkshire. That autumn was bliss; we had a cottage in the country and a garden. Just a little distance away were acres of pinewoods, and because we had so little money we decided to live as far as possible off the land. We invested in a field guide to mushrooms and armed with this little book set off in the hope of filling our basket with free breakfasts. One species had white flesh, and the guide assured us that this type was edible, though its pink-fleshed relative was deadly poisonous, however sometimes the white one could be pink and sometimes the pink one could be white. We put the book away and turned our efforts to digging the garden ready for the bumper crops we'd live on next year.

The rent was £12 per week. I applied for unemployment benefit on the grounds that though I appeared to be a student I was available for work if an employer should jump out and drag me into an available job. My benefit was a grand £17 per week, so we had £5 to live on. But it did work out, and the optimism of youth was well founded. We had saved enough from our summer jobs, and with the generous handouts from parents (well, we were about to give them a grandchild) we got by.

One very cold winter's day Aly went into labour and an ambulance drove us in the early hours to the Royal Berks Hospital, where later in the day Morag Louise was born at 3.50 p.m. We were both very happy. Life did get more complicated in the weeks to come with the realisation of the responsibility we now had for this new life, but the following year was a memorable one. I have such fond memories of pushing Morag in her pram along the lanes of Finchampstead and playing with her in the garden. Some of the photographs taken at this time show her standing on wobbly legs under the cottage apple tree.

A less happy experience came a little later. Aly was pregnant again but after an afternoon walk on Watership Down in Hampshire she began to be aware that all was not well. Later that day she had a miscarriage. The doctor came and sent for an ambulance. After a day in hospital she was back, and we buried our little tiny son or daughter in the garden. We didn't know whether our baby was a boy or girl so we gave him or her a name that would suit – Rowan. Only Aly can describe how she felt but as for me the grief was very great. I have never experienced the death of a child that we have got to know but Rowan was a being with a life, even if that life was not experienced outside of Alyson's womb. Since then I have always felt strongly about abortion and really cannot imagine any circumstance when it would be right to terminate a pregnancy. Some children are born into the world not being wanted, some with a disability, but the onus is on the rest of us to provide the support that enables all children to have the fullest life that is possible whatever these disadvantages may be.

Aly became pregnant again and we moved house to a village 20 miles west of Reading called Inkpen. The country around was magnificent. We rented a large house called Ambleside, which was beside Inkpen Common and just a short walk from the northern escarpment of the Downs. At the highest point overlooking the village was a long barrow, on which was erected Coombe Gibbet. This was the first time we had lived on chalk soils; I remember Aly's father visiting us, and when he saw all the chalk and flint stones in the bare winter fields he wouldn't believe that crops could be grown in them. In the Spring Aly went into labour and as the sun rose over Savernake Forest we drove to the little hospital on the edge of Marlborough, where Midwife Hadyn was waiting. It emerged she was a keen birdwatcher and her conversation was more about goldfinches than contractions (or 'pains' to use the language of nurses and doctors in 1974). My main job during the labour was to distract Nurse Hadyn so that Aly could get on with childbirth without the ornithology. Joy, Conrad arrived.

By the time Conrad was born we had finished the diploma and master's courses. I had been fortunate to be approached by a government training body to extend the research I was doing about farm workers in the Basingstoke area and they offered to pay me a full academic salary to study the reasons so many young farm workers were leaving the government's Apprenticeship Scheme. An additional incentive was that I could submit the research for a PhD, and so for the next four years I followed a sample of 800 new farm entrants and monitored their progress. It was interesting and as I had a large budget I could employ Guinness Market Researchers to conduct regular interviews across the country with my young people. A sad aspect was that three of the 800 died; all aged 17, all male, and all in motorcycle accidents.

Morag's interest in biology started in Inkpen. On the days that Aly was away at university I was in charge. We would walk through a small wood to get to the post office and during these trips the plants and fungi intrigued Morag. Every parent likes to boast of their child's brilliance and my story is how at three she was given a routine development test by the GP. He showed her a collection of pictures and asked her to name them. She named them all with one exception, and over this one she hesitated. 'That's a mushroom' said the doctor; 'Yes I knew it was a fungus but I wasn't sure it was a mushroom' replied our little girl.

I did my first long walk from Inkpen. On clear days when I pushed Morag and Conrad out in the buggy I could see a distant hill in the west with a circular copse of beech trees on its crown. I guessed it was 15 miles away and eventually found it marked on the map as Eastern Hill. One Saturday I walked along field paths and after six hours arrived at the top. Aly picked me up and this was the start of a number of long downland walks. My next was the 44 miles from Streatly to Avebury along the Ridgeway. I did it non-stop, starting at 10 a.m. and finishing at 4 the next morning. And yes, Aly and the kids came and picked me up from a lay by close to Silbury Hill before dawn had broken. After that, twenty-mile walks to Stonehenge and Salisbury were hardly a challenge.

The fact that I had a well-paid job meant we could buy our first house. We drew circles around Reading and started to look through estate agents lists. It was Alyson who found Gytha Cottage in a small hamlet eight or nine miles south west of Hungerford. We moved in November 1974, renaming the house Rowan Tree Cottage after our lost baby. The influence of *How to Raise a Brighter Child* was still present in our family. As Morag approached four I began to teach her to read using the *Ladybird Key Word Reading Scheme*. Her response was incredible and I could hardly get to the shop to buy the next in the series (there were 36 in total) before she was ready to absorb the new book. By four and a half she had completed the set and had the reading age of a 12-year-old. She started school at the state primary in the neighbouring village and soon became a favourite of the two teachers.

I was very much part of the local community during this initial five years in Wilton. I ran a whist drive for the older people, an interest acquired from my mother; was elected to the parish council, and the chair of the village fete. I even stood in the Wiltshire County Council elections as a Labour Party candidate. I didn't win, well, no Labour person had won in this part of the county even at the landslide Labour victory after the war. But I did get 30% of the vote. I had canvassed every house and farm in the ten villages in the division. I had even managed to get the Foreign Secretary, Dr David Owen, who by good fortune was on our local electoral register, to be my nominator and to give a glowing endorsement of my quite remarkable qualities. This was astonishing as he had only met me the once, and that was when I went to his weekend retreat with my agent to ask him to support me, but it helped that I had drafted myself, a glowing endorsement and he thought it sounded just right.

The negative consequence of my standing was that some of our Conservative neighbours showed their disapproval by withdrawing favours, the most important of which was the wonderful and immense outdoor swimming pool at Mrs Heard's house. It seemed most unfair that our children should be punished for the wrongdoing of their father.

I finished the research for the ATB in 1978 and submitted my PhD thesis. Getting a higher degree put to rest any lingering sense of childhood failure. I no longer had to prove anything academically to anyone. In the autumn we moved to Oxford for a short period so that Aly could get ready to do fieldwork for her doctorate at the university in social anthropology. Conrad started at nursery in Headington and Morag went to the Windmill School where her teacher was the wonderful Miss Bratt, who lined them up at the end of each day in the playground and kissed each child goodbye.

Papua New Guinea

We had not intended to go to PNG; our original plan was to spend a few years on the Solomon Islands so that Aly could do her anthropology fieldwork. But we discovered from our reading that children on the Solomons had a high incidence of chest complaints, and as we had some notion that our two would be prone to chesty things we decided to look at other potential islands in the South Pacific. It was by chance that we ended up on East New Britain. One evening we were at a party at Alyson's college, St Anthony's, and met a couple who had just returned from New Guinea. They made it sound exotic. On returning home I was flicking through the pages of the *Farmers Weekly* when I spotted an advertisement for a lecturer in agricultural extension at Vudal Agricultural College on the PNG island of East New Britain. Given the conversation earlier in the evening I decided to apply. A few months later we were there and living in the heat of a tropical rainforest.

New Britain was a large island with mountains that were almost impossible to cross. Most people lived on the coastal plain on the eastern side or worked on the oil palm plantations over to the west, with the mountain ranges keeping the two apart. Vudal College was in the east, about an hour's drive from the one town.

It was very hot, very humid (95% relative humidity by midday), but the college had electricity and some other modern facilities. We had a large bungalow that was raised up about eight feet above the ground on stilts. This was mainly to give protection from the very frequent earth tremors that shook our beds and tipped the crockery to the floor but the design also helped to keep the house cooler as air could circulate below.

Plate 7.3 Rabaul Harbour, Papua New Guinea 1980. Alyson and Max doing a 'barbie'. Within a few years the harbour was covered by ash and destroyed when the nearby volcano erupted.

We had electricity that worked most of the time and piped water that was collected off the roof into a large storage tank. Morag and Conrad went to a superb international primary school a few miles away in Keravat. There were two teachers, both young Australians, and just 23 pupils. Between them these two teachers were gifted in sport, music, drama and all the normal academic subjects. Morag and Conrad enjoyed their two and a half years at the school, and when they returned to Wiltshire they were well ahead of their English peers.

Alyson found a village about eight miles away that seemed a promising community where she could try to get permission to stay and get to know the people. It was officially called Napapar Five, the name given to it by the Australian colonial administration, but more correctly known as Bitagunan. Slowly over the first year of our stay she paid regular visits. Eventually the village elders gave permission for her to stay overnight and then for extended periods. Bernard and Martha were chosen by the village to host Aly. They were a respected couple in their middle age, and as most of their children were working away in the capital they had some room for another person in their little palm house. Bernard was the Catholic catechist and Martha the leader of the Legion of Mary. For the next 18 months Aly lived with them during the week. It was a tough existence for a European, no bathrooms or even running water, no electricity and no privacy at all. The villagers belonged to the Tolai people and she learned both Melanesian Pidgin and the Tolai language.

It was a very active life for all of us. Aly would get back to the college most weekends and so was leading a double life of village woman and expatriate wife. There was quite a large population of foreign workers, mainly from Australia, New Zealand and the UK, working at either the agricultural college, the Keravat Agricultural Research Station or the nearby High School. The expatriate club was the place where we all met, along with the swimming pool and the French Café in Rabaul. As we had children we very quickly made friends with other young parents, and those friendships have been maintained for more than 30 years.

After a year I was promoted to Deputy Principal. It was a challenging job trying to hold together a very large staff with very different back-grounds. Among the academic staff we had six or seven nationalities, and among the support staff of cooks, gardeners, farm workers and drivers we had dozens of different New Guinea tribal groups and, of course, languages. Traditionally these tribal groups did not interact, with the consequence that the basis of social networks was the loyalty and responsibility you had to those from your own group. In pidgin this was expressed as who was your *wantok* – literally the obligations you had to those who talked your language, the same *one talk*.

We had three suicides among the students during our time at the college. These young people were caught between two worlds: on one side the western world with its focus on the individual, and on the other their traditional culture with the priority it gave to fulfilling social obligations to members of the extended family and *wantok* group. Some young students just couldn't square this circle. We also had a riot during which the gardeners and farm workers surrounded the administration building dressed in traditional clothes and armed with bows and arrows; they were not playing games but were very angry. They believed, quite wrongly, that a lecturer had tried to kidnap and murder one of the agricultural labourers. The lecturer was from a coastal tribe in Milne Bay; the labourer and most of those surrounding the buildings were from Highland tribal groups. The incident had happened at a pay-Friday party held out in the bush. The labourer had fallen asleep in the back of a parked pick-up truck and awoke when the lecturer drove it away. The man jumped off and ran back through the forest to his fellow partygoers, shouting that he had been taken away to be killed. My response was to go and talk with the angry labourers but the Principal, who was a Highland man himself, said that the only safe thing to do was to rush the lecturer and his family to Rabaul airport and fly them off the island. Within three hours that is what happened. He never returned.

There were many times when differences in the interpretation of events occurred between the foreign expatriate staff and the nationals. On another occasion a female student freaked out because a bottle in her room had fallen and broken, releasing the spirit that had been placed inside by her boyfriend back in her home village. The spirit was there to keep a watch on her behaviour and now that it had escaped she was terrified. By good chance a national staff member from a coastal tribe went to deal with the disturbance. I am sure that a European would have explained in a very rational way that there was nothing in the bottle and that she should just calm down, but the national lecturer took a different approach. He told her that he had great powers himself and she was to go out of the room. He then went and got another bottle and went into her bedroom. Coming out with the bottle tightly sealed, he told her: 'Here is the spirit, safe inside a new bottle'. What he did and what he said was not a tactic to calm down a hysterical student. He believed in the presence of the watching spirit and that he had the power to return it to another bottle. A few years later when Aly was reading a book about health in Melanesia the author was explaining the importance of 'place sickness' and the role of spirits as causes of illness – the author was the PNG Minister of Health.

It was an exciting three years. Every few months I would take a party of trainee extension officers 'on patrol'. This involved living in a remote village for a week and trying to help the local farmers grow better crops or eat an improved diet. Even today when I hear a cock crow, especially in the early morning, I am taken back to that time. Then there was sea fishing: to go out in a canoe or small motorboat after the tuna was exciting while bottom fishing at night was scary. To catch tuna involved going right out into the open sea and watching the horizon for sea birds diving; that usually indicated big schools of leaping tuna and we would manoeuvre the boat so that our long trailing lines with baited hooks would sweep through the centre of the schools. If lucky you got a bite, and after a sudden jerk on the line you struggled to haul the six or more pound fish over the boat's side. Night fishing could be frightening. Sitting in the dark, a baited hook was lowered to the sea floor and then, gently holding the line you concentrated hard to feel even the slightest of tugs on the bait – then a quick pull and hopefully the fish was hooked. But then you had to get the line and fish to the surface before the circling sharks took it from you. One night we were concentrating so hard on trying to outwit the sharks that we didn't notice the change of weather behind us. Soon the wind started to blow and we had to start the engine and head as fast as we could for the shore. We were on a part of the island's coast that none of us knew and as we tried to make our way in the dark through the rapidly swelling waves the propeller hit a reef and stopped. We managed to paddle the boat safely onto a sandy beach but like Robinson Crusoe we were marooned. Luckily there was a grass hut on the edge of the forest where we could take shelter for the night. The biting insects swarmed around us as we lay on the bamboo floor and none of us got much sleep. When we did wake, there in the rafters was a rusty file and in another beam a six-inch nail. After many hours' work we replaced the damaged

Plate 7.4 Max and Conrad examining young cocoa trees on an Australian owned plantation.

shear pin with our home-made replica, and once the storm had passed we got back to Vudal.

I had a contract for three years, and we always knew that we'd stay no longer than this as by then Morag would be ten and moving on to a secondary school. Though the local international school was excellent we did not want to send her to an international secondary school, as this would have meant Morag boarding in either Port Moresby or Queensland. My work was getting stressful and I realized that I was ready to move on. One morning I awoke from a wonderfully reassuring dream; it involved an old-fashioned single-decker bus that was going along a country lane. I knew in the dream that the destination of the bus was *happiness*. As it got closer I could read the sign at the front above the driver's window – it said *Salisbury*. I felt it was time to go back to our cottage in Wiltshire. Aly needed more time for her research, so in May 1982 I returned to England with Morag and Conrad and four months later Alyson joined us back in Rowan Tree Cottage.

Wilton and Oxford

While we had been away two friends, Robert and Lesley Wheeler, had rented the cottage. When they moved out, or to be more accurate, when we evicted them – an agreed strategy to enable them to get a council house – Morag, Conrad and I settled ourselves into Wiltshire life. It was a beautiful May. The sun shone, the Pope visited Britain, it was the World Cup, *Fame* was on television and Morag and Conrad started back at Grafton Primary. I cooked and gardened and we lived on our savings. Fortunately we were well off as I had earned a lot as Deputy Principal, and with little tax and a very strong PNG currency we had a big wad of banknotes to keep us going. I went *green* at least 20 years ahead of the majority and decided that a car was an unnecessary use of resources. Instead I bought a new bike with child's seat. When Conrad got toothache we cycled the 16 mile round trip along forest tracks to the dentist in Marlborough. In August Alyson returned safely and I started to look for a job. As a temporary measure I returned to the university as a tutor and cycled each day to Bedwyn to catch the train into Reading. But I needed the challenge of something different.

I set a target of 85 job applications and told myself that if I received 84 rejections I wouldn't get fed up, not until till rejection 85. In fact I got offered a job after the third, but turned it down as it paid less money then

I had been getting in PNG. This was very foolish reasoning, as I soon came to understand that I was very unlikely ever to get a job as well paid as I had been as an expatriate on a government contract. I didn't get another offer till number 66, and that was for Christian Aid as their area organizer in Oxford.

It was also necessary to make a decision about which secondary school Morag was to attend. She was in the final months at the village school, and if we stayed in the state system she would go to Pewsey Comprehensive. We had no anti-comprehensive school attitudes but wanted Morag to be stretched, and certainly all the educational research at the time indicated that girls in mixed classes did poorly in the sciences because of the bias of science teachers who encouraged boys at the expense of girls. Another possibility was Oxford High School, an independent girls-only school that topped all the national exam result tables. One Friday afternoon in Spring Morag and I drove to Oxford and stayed overnight at a hotel in Summertown. Next morning we joined the throng of middle-class parents and their daughters in Belbroughton Road. As I stood there I was convinced I had made a terrible mistake – how could I put my little girl through this terrible ordeal? What would it do to her self-confidence if she failed miserably? Even if she passed today's written exam the next stage involved her being interviewed by the head teacher, and from that smaller group the intake would be selected. No, I thought, as I waited for her to return, we had made a bad decision to apply.

On Monday morning the Head telephoned me at work. Morag had done brilliantly well and had come third! An interview was not needed and they would give her an assisted place. We were proud of her and of course proud of ourselves for making such a wise decision to apply.

I took the job with Christian Aid and we bought a house in Oxford, just a short walk from Oxford High and close to Bishop Kirk Middle School which Conrad was to attend. It was a very sad day for me when we left Rowan Tree Cottage. I had been very much part of the community and felt totally at home on the chalk land in a way I didn't in other parts of the country. Aly was happy to be moving to a city that was more intellectually alive and of course Morag had the excitement of a new school. But Conrad also felt sad at going. He had made good friends in the village and enjoyed the freedom to roam the fields and woods. But I had a new job and a whole set of new things to learn and our Edwardian house had to be converted into something resembling a modern 1980s home.

We lived in Lonsdale Road for the next 13 years, from 1983 to 1996.

Conrad didn't enjoy Bishop Kirk; it was very different from the village school, and even more different from an international school of 23 children on a Pacific island. But he made lots of friends and got through middle school and then Cherwell without any major trauma. Morag worked steadily and did well academically.

This period was a busy one. We all had good health and Aly and I both had jobs that stretched us. Alyson became a lecturer at the Open University and drove the 40 miles to Milton Keynes. The title of her job was a misnomer, as lecturers at the OU didn't *lecture* as such but wrote materials for the distant learning courses, her subject being health and well-being. As the Christian Aid organizer I worked long but irregular hours. At the core of the job were 177 Christian Aid groups in the three counties of Oxfordshire, Berkshire and Buckinghamshire. I was out visiting the groups in the evenings and preaching in churches on Sundays, but the job changed quite dramatically when within a year of starting there was a famine in Ethiopia. There had been many before but this was more catastrophic in terms of how many people were without food, and also much worse because there was a civil war taking place in the north of the country. The rains had not come and the sorghum crop had failed. It was the province of Tigray where the deaths were at their highest and it was here that the people had been kept deliberately poor by those in power to ensure that they would not cause trouble to the ruling regime.

I was asked to take a big bag of money, £300,000 in notes, from the Sudanese town of Kassala on the western edge of the Eritrean desert and travel down to the lowlands of Tigray where I would be able to buy grain from local merchants and get it taken to the places where the famine victims were camped. The challenge to achieve this was the conflict. As far as the Ethiopian government was concerned these starving people were the enemy; they were Tigrayans and it was the Tigray People's Liberation Front (TPLF) who were fighting the Ethiopian Army to gain some form of autonomy. So the Army wasn't going to let a British charity, albeit one with a humanitarian intent, go and give food to the enemy. So if I was to be successful I had to work through the local humanitarian organization (REST – The Relief Society of Tigray) but travel undercover and with a sizeable bodyguard. This was real boy's own stuff!

I flew to Khartoum and then travelled by local bus to Kassala. Here I was put up in a TPLF compound and the money, which was waiting for me in a bank, was exchanged on the black market into Ethiopian Birr. We had to wait for intelligence reports as to the Ethiopian Army's movements, but after a few days we got the message that now was the time to go. Under cover of darkness we set off – me, the money and 50 young TPLF soldiers – in a convoy of trucks across the desert. It was very hot and very dusty and the level of dust was always high as my truck had to be in the middle of the convoy to ensure that if there was a mine on the road it would be detonated by the first truck, not the one carrying the money! When daylight came we stopped under the cover of any shrubs and trees that were around and pulled sheets over the trucks to hide them from the air. On the second day, as I rested under my truck, two Ethiopian Air Force MiG fighters screamed a few hundred feet above. They had obviously seen our tracks but did not see us. At that point I did ask myself, like Laurel and Hardy, how I had got in this fine mess.

After a few more days we reached the lowlands area and I started to buy grain and arrange for it to be carried to the camps. My bag of cash got lighter, and I could start the second part of the job, to look at other ways British aid agencies could help the people. The reason Christian Aid had asked me (beside my obvious aptitude as an action man in dangerous situations) was that I was an agriculturalist and could assess what might be done to help prevent another famine. I visited farms and saw the terrible erosion of the mountain areas and began to identify small-scale projects that could be funded once the immediate effects of the famine had been tackled. After a few weeks I set off back on another convoy to Sudan. I had lost eight kilograms in weight and was very pleased to sleep in a bed again when I reached Khartoum. Back in England there was a spate of interviews for radio, and Conrad came with me to the BBC's head-quarters. He played 'spot the stars' as we walked the corridors, and after an article appeared in the *Oxford Times* Morag's art teacher Mr Crisp referred to her as the 'explorer's daughter'.

Over the next year the famine got worse and the entire world became aware of the terrible situation. Bob Geldof organized the Live Aid Concert and my work in the UK became almost entirely centred on Ethiopia. I was much in demand for even more radio and television interviews and talks to Christian Aid groups and schools, and I wrote a small book, *Tigray: Ethiopia's Untold Story* that sold a fair number of copies.

That should have been the end of the story but 26 years later it dramatically hit the headlines again. As I was writing this chapter in March 2010, the BBC World Service broadcast a documentary claiming that much of the aid given to Ethiopia during the 1984/85 famine had been taken by the TPLF to buy guns. Their evidence was an Ethiopian government minister who had fallen out with the Prime Minister (the

Plate 7.5 The convoy travelled at night for safety and hid during the day
in whatever shrub it could find. Eritrea 1984.

former head of the TPLF) and fled into exile in the Netherlands. He claimed that during the famine he had been instructed to disguise himself as a merchant and pretend to sell grain to Max Peberdy and then use the money to purchase weapons in the Middle East. He said that the photograph in *Tigray: Ethiopia's Untold Story* of a merchant was him, and that the REST official was also a senior TPLF fighter. As for the grain, the sacks at the front were sorghum but those at the back were filled with sand. The BBC also interviewed the former head of the CIA in Ethiopia who had written a report at the time suggesting that much of the aid money was being diverted by the anti-government forces to buy arms.

For a week the story was on Radio Four and in the newspapers, and the picture of me counting out the money to the merchant was the second most visited place on the BBC website. Bob Geldof who had been the inspiration for Band Aid and Live Aid became involved, as the ex-Minister also claimed that 95% of all the aid money given during the famine had gone astray. Geldof made a formal complaint to the BBC about the documentary and its spurious claims. Eventually as with all news the story slipped away. What was the truth? The claim that most of

Plate 7.6 Max counting out some of the £300,000 in aid money to purchase grain from a merchant – Tigray, 1984.

the aid went to buy arms is certainly nonsense, but whether some of the £300,000 that I carried was taken by the TPLF I have no way of knowing. We followed good 'aid practice' and did everything in our power to ensure it was used by the local humanitarian organization and not the TPLF, and it would have been both tragic and immoral if a group of Ethiopians, for whatever reasons, had diverted help from tens of thousands of people facing starvation.

The time came when Morag had to make a decision about which university she would choose. Three were in the running: Oxford, Cambridge and Durham. Alyson and I were in favour of Cambridge, mainly because it wasn't Oxford and we thought it would be good for her to live away from her parents and in a new place. Durham's Trevelyan College was where Alyson had been an undergraduate. Morag went for an interview with the Principal of Trevelyan and they were very keen to have her, as she would be the first daughter of a former student to attend. However Morag's choice was Oxford's Magdalen College. She did superbly well at Oxford, getting a First in Biology and winning a Demi-Fellowship award. We must surely have been the proudest of parents in June 1993 as we sat in the Sheldonian Theatre on her graduation day.

Plate 7.7 Morag Peberdy leaning on the sign for Peberdys Creek in New South Wales, 1994.

Conrad was not happy at the Cherwell and didn't do well in his A levels. When he left the Sixth Form he became a chauffeur to a child psychiatrist who could no longer drive because of her poor health. He enjoyed the job and it gave him the confidence to plan a year travelling the world. We waved goodbye as he set off for Los Angeles, New Zealand, Australia, Fiji and Thailand. Halfway through this year Aly and I had our 25th Wedding Anniversary (1969–1994) and to celebrate we took a trip to New Zealand, meeting up with Conrad in Auckland and then with Morag who joined us in Sydney. The four of us travelled northwards to Brisbane and stayed with Australian friends we had known from PNG. After a week or so enjoying the sun in Queensland we hired a car and set off on the inland road through New South Wales back to Sydney. It took three days; halfway we passed over a small river and Morag and Conrad both shouted to me to stop the car – 'didn't you see the name?'. I reversed to the signboard, which read *Peberdys Creek*. We got the camera out and posed proudly in front of our river. Later when we stopped in the next town we looked in the telephone directory and found a column of Peberdys. Was the John Peberdy transported from Saddington in 1828 for stealing a lamb the father of this clan? Or was it Thomas Peberdy who had got four years for larceny?

It was very sad to say goodbye to Conrad in Sydney. Morag returned home but Conrad was to continue his travels. We had a last meal together on the waterfront in Sydney Harbour; close by a Chinese man was playing a melancholic song on a Chinese violin. To hear that instrument today takes me back to the loss I was feeling on that afternoon as we left him to go to the airport. But some months later he did arrive back in Oxford. I got a telephone call one morning to say he had arrived in England and would be home within hours – what joy, and even greater happiness when he walked in the door just minutes later. As a joke he had phoned from the end of the street and then ran to number 77.

He was determined to retake his A-levels and go to university. He enrolled at an A-level college and worked hard and got good enough grades to study urban development at the West of England University in Bristol. He was a little older than most of the other students and this suited him well; it gave him confidence and a certain authority. He also worked much harder than most of the other students and got a good degree. Aly and I were very proud parents at the degree awards in Bristol Cathedral.

Alyson was an activist in the Peace Movement; Greenham Common and Upper Heyford were two air-force bases quite close to Oxford, and they became focal points for protest as both sites had American nuclear bombers stationed. On one occasion she was arrested along with some Catholic priests and nuns (and Conrad) for threatening to cut the perimeter fence and was taken to the police station. They were all released after a short time and a photograph appeared in the *Oxford Times* of them being carted off. That birthday I bought her a new pair of bolt cutters. Shortly after this Aly became a member of the Movement for the Ordination of Women (MOW). They were campaigning for the legislation in the Anglican Church to be changed to enable women to become priests. Eventually she became the Vice Moderator and a member of General Synod. One very memorable day in 1992 all three Houses of the Synod voted with sufficient numbers for the legislation to be passed

Plate 7.8 Visiting rural development projects in Andhra Pradesh, India 1985.

and the process was put in place for women to be ordained. It wasn't a total shock when Aly told me that she was going to apply for ordination herself, and shortly, afterwards she started training part time on the Oxford Ministry course.

I left Christian Aid and joined the training team in Oxfam, which was the largest of the British non-government agencies, supporting development work in more than 70 countries. It was an exciting job that took me all over the globe. I ran courses for Oxfam staff in Africa, Latin America, Asia and the Middle East. Some of the jobs and places were very enjoyable and almost like being on holiday: running a workshop in Bali, facilitating a meeting in the Troodos Mountains of Cyprus, lying by the pool in Mexico and training at a Safari Lodge in Kenya. But there were also many challenging situations, such as the time I was training Palestinian groups in the West Bank just days before the Gulf War, or being at a refugee camp in Northern Uganda that involved travelling through storm clouds in a little plane with the pilot leading us in prayers; or working in an Albanian town during a riot with the office door bolted and cars barricading the street just outside to give us some protection from the gun carrying mob.

Plate 7.9 Working in the West Bank, October 1990. Standing on the Mount of Temptations looking across to the Jordan Valley.

In my non-work time I developed a passion that for a few years became almost an obsession, hang gliding. I had frequently dreamed of drifting over the countryside. I always awoke very happy after this dream but a dream it remained until one afternoon I saw on television a children's TV presenter launching himself off the Blorenge Mountain in Wales and landing in the centre of Abergavenny. I knew that I must do that. I enrolled at a hang-gliding school on the Marlborough Downs and along with nine others started the six-month training. It was all that I had imagined. Slowly we progressed to launching ourselves off little hills, then cliffs on the Gower Peninsula and finally proper big mountains. My comrades and I did what we had seen the TV presenter do, taking off from the Blorenge, flying over the top of 50,000 volt cables, then hovering above the houses of Abergavenny and landing on the park in the heart of the town. What an adrenaline rush and what a huge sense of comradeship. We had all done it, all survived, and without one broken bone.

Hang gliding was both frightening and exhilarating, and though much time was spent sitting on hills waiting for the wind to get stronger or weaker this was more than compensated for by the time in the air, even if it was only a matter of minutes. I have a memory of flying above the southern escarpment of the Marlborough Downs; I was a few hundred feet above the face of the hill and as I flew along a kestrel followed me just below my wings. Along and back we went until finally he tired of my company and went off searching for voles in the fields below. Eventually, after almost three years of flying, the inevitable happened – I crashed. The accident happened in Wales. I was flying from the top of a mountain when the wind strength dropped and I was unable to land back on top. I circled the valley below for a landing site. I found a flat area but could not tell which way the wind was blowing along the valley. Like a plane, a hang glider must take off and land into wind. I guessed the wind direction and got it wrong; as my feet touched the ground the wind slammed the glider and me into the earth. I managed to get out of the wreckage and unstrap my harness. The good news was my back was fine, but the grating of bone in my mangled right arm indicated that I needed a hospital. Fortunately a man out walking with his daughter called an ambulance and I was taken to the Prince of Wales Hospital in Merthyr Tydfil. As I was stretchered in to A&E the duty nurse heard my accent and bent over and said: 'we say to you English, come to Wales for a break'. Oh how I laughed. I spent ten days in the men's ward getting used to a metal bar and six screws holding my arm together. I really enjoyed my time with the other patients. They were miners and lorry drivers, and after their initial suspicion of the foreigner in bed three they were very friendly. When the nurse switched off the lights at night we partied, even ordering Indian takeaways to be delivered secretly to the ward. I was sad when the day came for me to be discharged. It took me about a year to get enough strength back in the arm to hang glide again, but within a few weeks I had two more accidents, not serious, but the last one did a lot of costly damage to the glider. After five accidents I thought it was time to put my surplus energy into something safer.

My father became ill in the winter of 1990. He was diagnosed with lymphoma. I travelled up to Leicester frequently to see him and support Barbara. The way I responded to his cancer was to learn all about the illness, but I made the mistake of assuming that this was also the way he would respond. It wasn't, and he did not want to talk about being ill and even less to know about lymphoma. I realise now that I was not sensitive enough to the way he wanted to handle his illness. I went with him to meetings with consultants, and like most people under stress he often came away not fully remembering or understanding what the doctor had

Plate 7.10 Hang gliding over Tan Hill on the Marlborough Downs, Wiltshire.

said. So I did perform a useful support in explaining what he had been told. Eventually the consultant told me when my father was not in the room that he had about two weeks to live. Barbara was wonderful; she was strong and yet so kind. My father had been given a precious gift when he married for the second time. On the day he died Barbara and I visited him in hospital. It was mid morning but he lay in bed unshaved. We were both upset by this lack of care and a nurse came straight away to make amends for the neglect. He smiled at us and was not in pain or distressed. We went back to their house for lunch but as soon as we arrived the phone rang to tell us he had just died.

By a strange coincidence my mother's partner Maurice was also a cancer patient in the same hospital. My mother never referred to Walter and so neither did I, and thus she was unaware that during his last days Walter was just a floor above Maurice. A few weeks later Maurice died. He was a kind and unassuming man who got on with life and accepted whatever it brought. A few years earlier he had won quite a lot of money in a competition. He just put it into a savings account and carried on as before. Within two years of Maurice's death Jessie was taken ill with advanced breast cancer. She was always a fighter and not a person to feel sorry for herself. During her last weeks she cooked, played cards and visited friends as she always had done. On Valentine's Day (1993) I went

Plate 7.11 Jessie Peberdy the year before her death in 1993.

to see her in hospital and took her a card. She was in good spirits and could walk around the ward with me. The next day Aly travelled up to Leicester to visit and arrived just after she had died. That night Aly and I slept in her little bungalow and started to sort through her things. Opening her sewing machine we saw a bundle of notes, a thousand pounds. Like my grandmother she never quite trusted banks.

The cottage

Twynham Cottage now enters my story, and it plays an important part. Two things had happened that led us to buy what essentially was a weekend-cottage. One was my decision to stop flying and conserve life and limb. This meant I needed to direct my out-of-work energy towards a new project, and renovating an old property seemed a good idea. Secondly, the inheritance from my mother gave us enough money to look for a country home. My mother was never well off but her share of my grandmother's house plus the money she inherited from Maurice was quite a reasonable amount in 1993.

I had come to love the Vale of Pewsey. Hour after hour of sitting on Milk Hill beside my hang glider waiting for the wind to do something had given me plenty of opportunity to view all the Vale's little hillocks and folds and to watch the clouds spilling over the northern face of Salisbury Plain. My search for a house started and finished in the dozen or so villages that make up the Vale and the immediate area. Tywnham Cottage was almost the first property I went to see, and I knew at once this was the one. It was an old cob walled and thatched house beside the river Avon. It was very run down. Nobody had lived in it for at least a year; the front doors (there were two) would not open without a mighty pull, as the ceilings were lined with boards and some of these had dropped. It's not quite true to say nobody had lived there for a long time, as squatters had moved in and torn off much of the original walling panels to make a fire in the hearth. But as the estate agents say – the house had potential. Because of the poor condition we bought it for very little and therefore had enough to start the repairs. Luckily for us, the building recession of the early 1990s meant that our friend Robert had virtually no other building jobs so he threw himself into the renovations with great enthusiasm. Within two hours of us buying the house he was knocking down the fireplace with a sledgehammer, assuring me that behind those bricks would be an old inglenook fireplace. And he was right. Not just an original hearth but also a bread oven. Then he started on the floor. This was earth with 200-year-old bricks simply laid on top.

On he went, repairing and replacing. Within six months the cottage was habitable and I slept overnight for the first time. To sleep at Twynham is to sleep in another land. On a summer evening with the window open, the rush of the Avon through the sluice gates as it makes its way to the sea appears to come from behind the cottage, yet commonsense insists that the river is in front. But the house sits snugly into a chalk face that is higher than even the chimney pot, and so the river sounds are collected by the chalk wall behind and echoed gently into the bedroom.

Robert made many discoveries. First, embedded in the mud walls was an old clay tobacco pipe that had obviously been part of the rubbish in the midden used to add bulk to the chalk cob. On the bowl of the pipe was a set of maker's initials -- TW. I sent the bowl to Devizes Museum, and back came a letter telling me that the initials were those of Thomas Widdowes, who was a pipe maker in Marlborough around 1710 to 1720. Assuming that the pipe had been used for a few years before being discarded in the rubbish pit, it suggested that the house was probably built around the mid to late 1700s. Robert's next discovery was a leather boot hidden in the roof in the thatch. Off this went to the Clarke's Shoe Museum and another letter came back with the information that the style was called a 'Balmoral Boot', and it dated from the mid 1850s. It was interesting, they said, because it was a *concealed boot*. Cottagers placed a shoe or a boot in the thatch to ward off the devil. Roofs and windows are vulnerable to the entry of evil and so country people placed a piece of human clothing, especially something that had taken the shape of the person, in the roof as a powerful force to stop the devil from coming in. There were about 150 examples of houses with these concealed items on the Clarke's Museum list and now there was 151.

My first job was to create a garden by the river. It had been neglected and was waste ground, overgrown and with just one apple tree. My neighbour at the Mill House taught me to use a mechanical brush cutter and I got the undergrowth into something resembling a grassy area. Then came the fence. I spent days jointing posts and rails and then attaching round headed wooden slats that I had specially made at a sawmill in Oxford-shire. Then came the beech hedge; 100 saplings were planted in the winter and 98 survived, bursting into splendid bud in the following May.

I joined the Bulford Conservation Group and acted as a volunteer warden, monitoring the archaeological sites on the Ministry of Defence land behind the cottage. Almost every field had a significant earthwork and most parts of a field would reveal pottery from the Bronze Age, the Iron Age, the Roman period and even some medieval glazed sherds. It was so exciting just to walk out and discover barrows and trackways and middens, all within an hour's walk. I got a permit to enter the artillery training impact area (when the army was not firing!), and this was both thrilling and scary. I would be the only person walking in these uncultivated areas. The Army had taken over this part of the Plain in the mid 1890s and since then nature had been left to its own devices. But it was also a dangerous place; I had been given training by the Army as part of the process to get a permit, so I knew what not to touch, but after one experience when I found myself in a valley picking my footsteps very, very carefully around shell casings and other bits of metal ordnance, I decided that on balance impact-area archaeology held about the same level of danger as hang gliding – and for good reasons I had given that up.

After a few years we bought the 1.6 acre plantation next to the cottage. I had not planned to be a woodland owner but once I started to work in the wood, cutting pathways, coppicing the sycamores, planting hedges and

Plate 7.12 Twynham Cottage, Coombe in Wiltshire.

making a secluded sunbathing area, I could not imagine how any one could possibly say they *were alive* without being the steward of a thousand trees. Over the next ten years I created a woodland garden, something that is very different from the vegetable and flower gardening I had done before. The timescale is longer, and the things one is planting, tending and cutting are very much bigger and heavier! So I had to learn a different way of thinking and a new set of skills, from using a chainsaw to log splitting and pest control. When nurturing young trees almost everything on four legs is a pest – deer, rabbits, goats, horses, moles and badgers. Along with managing the wood we doubled the size of the cottage by adding an extension, and then a conservatory where we could sit on sunny cold days and watch the wildlife in the chalk pit. Morag and Angus brought Alexander and Felix in the summer and Conrad also spent a lot of time working in the wood.

The cottage is a magical place. Even a one-day stay restores the spirit, cures colds, hangovers, an upset stomach, broken legs and almost anything else that might be in need of repair.

Windsor 1996

Alyson was ordained in Oxford Cathedral in September 1996 and the Bishop placed her in Windsor Parish as a curate, an incumbent in training. A house came with the job, but for a short period I stayed part of the week in the house in Lonsdale Road and the rest with Aly. We had both made big changes in the direction of our lives. I decided that this was a good time for me to do something different and to be more courageous. I left Oxfam after ten years and launched myself as an independent trainer and development adviser. It was risky because I was almost 50 and if I failed at self-employment it would be difficult to find another job. But taking a new direction just seemed *right,* and I was pretty certain that I could be successful as my own boss.

I worked as a freelancer in the development charity sector. It involved a lot of overseas travel but usually only for a few days or weeks at a time. In total I worked in 41 countries and ran training, consultancies or evaluations in Africa, Asia, Europe and the Middle East. After a trip a period at the cottage was always a time to regain energy. I remember coming back on one occasion in the summer. We had a wonderful Wiltshire milkman called John. I doubt if John had ever been far from the county but he always asked how things were: 'how is abroad, is it getting better?'. I assured him that it was – 'Oh I am pleased' he replied.

In 1999 Aly completed her curacy and started to apply for jobs as a vicar. She wanted a parish with a diversity of people, and ideally with a cross-cultural mix. Few places in Oxford Diocese could offer this so she looked towards London. In the summer she was licensed as the vicar of St Saviours, Brockley Hill in south-east London. Neither of us had ever lived in London and generally it is young people who move into the capital and middle aged ones who go in the other direction, but we did it the opposite way. The vicarage was very large and Conrad came over to help paint and decorate. By July we were established in our new home.

London 1999

Being a vicar meant much greater responsibility for Alyson, and living in a very diverse parish, with a range of cultural and social backgrounds, was certainly challenging for both of us. For me there was a new role: I was the vicar's husband, which as a concept was still a novelty for most of the congregation, and they had to get accustomed to leadership being in the hands of a woman. I was very conscious that I needed to support church activities enthusiastically but not take on leadership roles. Getting the balance right was not always easy but I at least could ensure I wasn't appointed to any official bodies like the Parochial Church Council as that would give husband and wife too much power. The parish perceived me only in terms of being the vicar's spouse. I was still working hard as a development consultant, but for the congregation I was just Max, Alyson's husband who did good works overseas.

The turn of the Millennium came. We are not party people and neither of our parents had celebrated New Year, so at midnight as the new century was born Aly and I stood on Blythe Hill Fields above the vicarage and looked out at the fireworks blazing across the night sky over the Thames. Though we were not in among the thousands of revellers we felt we shared the hopes for what the next thousand years would bring.

Because Aly worked so hard, and as a priest she was always on call, we tried to take at least two holidays each year in a warm place. Usually it was the Canary Islands in January to recover from all the Christmas services, and Greece in the summer. I have always loved the sun; from the age of 15 or so I needed to be outside and to feel the warm rays. Alyson's mother had the same compulsion and when inside at a family meal both of us would be glancing through the window to see if we were missing anything. On Lanzarote I found an almost perfect beach; a long sandy bay sheltered by cliffs from the cooler north winds and only an hour's walk from where we were staying. But the first time we went we discovered that most of the sun worshippers on the beach were naturists. Though a little hesitant to go the whole hog I was soon won over to the ultimate sun experience. To feel the sun on one's skin, especially after dreary winter months, and to swim and walk free of clothing, was blissful. Soon my main criterion for choosing a holiday destination was whether it had good naturist beaches. Aly had never shared my passion for the sun but she would spend half of the day with me, and half doing things that she preferred.

In April 2003 a wonderful event took place, Morag and Angus married. The service was in the chapel at Magdalen College, and then a year later an even more wonderful event took place Alexander Luke Mackenzie Evers was born. By chance we were walking outside the Wittington Hospital in North London just minutes after the birth and thus were able to rush in almost immediately (well, the hospital was only 12 miles from our home and coincidences happen). The exhausted parents were a little surprised by how soon we had arrived but they were very happy to show off their first-born son.

The fact that Alexander was a 'he' and not a 'she' was a surprise to me as I had been convinced that the bump was a girl. So convinced in fact that I had a working title for this new granddaughter; Honeysuckle. I had recently heard the name from a television drama in which the lead actress was Honeysuckle Weeks. The name seemed just right for Miss Evers. A year later when Angus's uncle, Colin Ingleby-Mackenzie, died there was a memorial service in St Paul's Cathedral. Hundreds of sports people, politicians and actors filled the pews and *The Times* published a list of those who had attended. Among the family members was Honeysuckle Weeks! My choice of name was not bizarre. One year, nine months and seven days after Alexander's birth Felix Oliver Max Evers arrived. This time we impatiently waited quite a few hours before rushing to see him.

Alyson and I have always had jobs that gave us the flexibility to spend a lot of time with Alexander and Felix. During the time before they reached school age we enjoyed being 'in charge' for the day and taking

Plate 7.13 A proud grandfather with Alexander – Crete 2008.

them to their favourite places: Waterlow Park with its children's playground, ducks and café selling gingerbread men; Whittington Park and its water fountains that could be started by little feet stamping very hard on specially marked pads; Foxham Gardens with the pirate boat, and Dalmeny Park and its terribly frightening bear that hid in the bushes. We were in awe of their ability to learn language – just how does a two year old understand that *wave* is what you do when you say goodbye, and *wave* is what knocks your sand castle down after it's just been completed? We've watched as the brothers have learnt to adjust to each other's existence and slowly move from mere acceptance to cooperating in joint ventures. We have been very fortunate, and know what a gift it is, to be able to enjoy the two best grandchildren in the whole of Tufnell Park.

This is my story – but how to finish? My account has been about the things I've done and the places where I've lived or worked, so in one way it's like an extended household census return with a few births, deaths and marriages thrown in. So my story has been much more about facts and events than feelings or personality. But there is a poem by Edward Thomas that I want read at my funeral that touches another dimension. Thomas was Welsh by background but brought up in London. Like my maternal grandfather he died in France in 1917. He wrote many poems, some about my most loved county of Wiltshire, but the one that reaches out and touches the inner me was inspired by a train journey he made from London to Worcestershire. It was June, a hot afternoon, and the steam engine stopped at a village station on the Oxfordshire border. I picture him sitting alone in an eight-seater carriage with the window pulled down. It's peaceful; other than the gentle hiss of the idling engine there is hardly any sound, as nobody gets on and nobody gets off. But then a bird sings, and for the poet this fragile song carries the voices of all the birds in Oxfordshire and Gloucestershire.

Very, very occasionally I have felt this oneness that Thomas captures in his poem. When Conrad was about a year old Alyson drove the children to visit Aunt Freda in Trowbridge. She dropped me off at the edge of Pewsey Vale so that I could walk across the hills to Devizes. It was Easter Sunday, and as I crossed a small brick bridge over a stream I rested and looked down into the flowing water. For just a few seconds my whole being felt warmth, and all that I was, and all that the little river was, were one. So at my funeral and when my ashes are scattered on Knapp Hill I'd like this poem to be part of the farewell:

Adlestrop

Yes, I remember Adlestrop —
The name, because one afternoon
Of heat the express train drew up there
Unwontedly. It was late June.

The steam hissed. Someone cleared his throat,
No one left and no one came
On this bare platform. What I saw
Was Adlestrop — only the name.

And willows, willow herb, and grass,
And meadowsweet, and haycocks dry,
No whit less still and lonely fair
Than the high cloudlets in the sky.

And for that minute a blackbird sang
Close by, and round him, mistier,
Farther and farther, all the birds
Of Oxfordshire and Gloucestershire.

CHAPTER 8

Alyson's Story

As is the case for Alexander and Felix, the house I knew as home for the first few years of my life is not the one in which I spent most of my childhood. We moved when I was four. I was born in January 1948 the third and last child of Ethel and Ernie Garnett, who lived in the house attached to my grandfather's newsagent shop at 59 Blaby Road, South Wigston. The hospital in Leicester where I was born also saw the birth of Max five months earlier, but it was another 16 years before we met. I had two sisters: Carol, aged 10, and Elizabeth, aged 3. My parents were both in their early forties when I was born. Ethel adored babies so I was made a great fuss of especially as I had followed a number of miscarriages. Ethel claimed that it was the doctor's insistence that she drink Guinness every night before my birth that had made me such a bonny child. I tend to think her habit bred into me a great liking for alcohol.

Plate 8.1 Alyson – the first photograph.

I don't remember my bedroom but I do recall the wonderful playroom I shared with my sisters. We called it Scrobie Island and though we had far fewer toys than children today there was a big dolls' house and lots of space for our imaginations to explore. I also remember the back yard with its two small flowerbeds (great for making mud pies) and a long shed in which the cats lived and in which the miracle of kitten birth happened. Both the shed and Scrobie Island were places of excitement and even magic to me.

Occasionally I found my way into the shop to win my grandfather's attention. He always wore a navy, striped suit with waistcoat, smoked a pipe, and wore a gold watch on a chain in his top pocket. My father also worked in the shop, which sold newspapers, cigarettes and sweets from two huge high counters. Our neighbour on one side was the Ritz Cinema, and the other Cully's Grocery Shop.

In my fourth year we moved into a real house, 164 Saffron Road, with a long garden and as neighbours other houses, not businesses. This was about a mile away from the shop where my father continued to spend long hours that became even longer after my grandfather died from throat cancer. I felt very sad when my grandfather died, especially as I wasn't allowed to go and say goodbye at his funeral. This was still a time when it was unwisely believed that children should not be spoken to about death, even when someone very close died.

The first big public event I remember was the Coronation of Princess Elizabeth as Queen in 1953 when I was just five. We watched it on our newly purchased very small black and white television, though a much stronger memory is of the red, white and blue spotted T-shirt I was given to wear, and the union jack flags bought for us to wave and even hang from the windows of our home. I also remember being encouraged to keep a scrapbook of the royal family by cutting out photos from newspapers. I began school when I was five, and after a short spell at the local primary school I managed to persuade my parents to let me attend the same school as my older sister Elizabeth and cousin Margaret. Margaret's mother, Norah, was my father's sister and Margaret's parents' marriage had ended when Margaret was a few months old. Norah earned a living by working with my father in the shop and Margaret spent much of her time with my family. Margaret was about a year younger than Elizabeth and they did most things together. The school they attended was fee paying and two bus-rides away. I hated missing out on anything Elisabeth and Margaret did and made a great fuss until allowed to join them. We wore brown uniforms with a gold and brown striped tie and a

Plate 8.2 Hiding among the rocks

hat with a badge on it. I was very proud of the uniform but rather good at losing my hat by leaving it on the bus.

To my eldest sister Carol I was something of a plaything and she loved doing things to my hair and dressing me up. It was her job to take me to dancing classes (ballet and tap). After a while I began to rebel against her and our relationship deteriorated. My mother was keen that we should all

Plate 8.3 At the seaside with older sister Elizabeth (left) and cousin Margaret (the monkeys are not relatives).

learn to swim, as a young relative of hers had died from drowning in the
sea at Caernarfon, North Wales. We went to swimming lessons at an
indoor pool reached by bus, and later in summer holidays to the outdoor
pool reached by bus and a very long walk. Although I was never very
sporty, like a lot of young girls I begged to have riding lessons which for a
while I did with Elizabeth and Margaret. As Elizabeth and Margaret were
best friends as well as cousins I needed a best friend of my own. This was
Trudy who lived a few houses away and was about my age. I'm not sure
what age we were (about ten I think) when we were allowed to go off
together by bus on Saturday mornings to ballroom dance classes in
Leicester, after which we would treat ourselves to ice-cream sodas at a
large Italian café called Bruciannis.

My mother returned to work as a teacher when I was eight. I regret to
say I greatly resented not having her at my beck and call, especially if I had
a day off school through illness or her term dates differed from mine. She
paid someone to do cleaning but all the other housework and cooking,
including a full lunch every day, was done by her. This must have been
very stressful indeed, though at the time this did not enter my mind. In
the summer holidays as well as sometimes going swimming we would take
ourselves off to the park next to the biscuit factory (I always associate the
smell of biscuits with swings and slides) or for a nature walk through the
fields, picking cowslips and blackberries or collecting frog-spawn,
depending on the season. We also normally had a week or two by the
sea, driven there by my father who would never be able to stay for the
whole time because of the newsagent's business. The nearest seaside was
Skegness in Lincolnshire but we sometimes ventured to Wales (my
mother's home) and later down to the south coast.

My first trip abroad was with my aunt Freda (my mother's sister), who
had married late and had no children of her own. She was an ideal aunt,
full of stories and imagination. When she came to visit us she would
invent wonderful accounts of her life and adventures as a warden in a
women's prison (she was in fact a teacher), and even turn up disguised as
someone else! She also had time to give her nieces individual attention. I
was 11 or 12, I think, when it was my turn to be taken on holiday by
Freda and her husband George. We travelled to Italy by coach, a very sick-
making experience I would prefer to forget, and visited Assisi, Pisa,
Florence, and Rome. Apart from the coach travel I loved the excitement
of Italy, including the sharpness of fresh lemon juice drinks, the shock of
being served fish with their heads on and the awful smell of the street
markets (rubbish rotting in the heat). After this trip my career aspirations

Plate 8.4 At Guide camp with friend Elizabeth Jessop
and holding on to Cindy.

changed from being a hairdresser or teacher of ballet or horse riding to the dizzy heights of working in a travel agency so I could continue to learn about new places. I never achieved this ambition but the underlying curiosity was later expressed in studying anthropology and, with Max, living and working in Nigeria and New Guinea.

At the age of 11 and a half I moved to a more local state secondary school, South Wigston High. This was mainly because the 11 plus test showed I would benefit from a more academic education. So the brown uniform changed to navy blue and the two bus rides were replaced by a 20-minute walk. For the first two years I blossomed, relishing French and Latin and doing well in everything except maths.

After three years my year moved on to yet another school, Guthlaxton Comprehensive, and the blue uniform was replaced by purple and gold. This was a massive school with over 1,000 pupils. Its size daunted me as did the constant change of classrooms and teachers (even in my 60s I still sometimes have nightmares about being in the wrong place at the wrong time, having done the wrong homework!) The rationale for the size of the school was that it meant all subjects could be studied and all levels of ability catered for in an inclusive and equal way, but for shy children (I was very shy) it was all too big and impersonal. Whilst I did all right in my GCSE exams (taken at 16) at the final A levels I only did well in English

Literature, got a fairly poor grade in French and failed History. Thankfully I still managed to get a place at Durham University which, with its collegiate system, was a much happier experience.

Neither of my sisters had gone to university so just being given a place felt a great achievement, which in some ways created a rift between us. Trevelyan College was brand new, and the first intake of 100 was in temporary accommodation for a year before the building to the south of the city was completed and ready. Durham I quickly fell in love with. The wonderful Norman cathedral, river and weir formed the heart of the city, and the walk (sometimes run) along the wooded riverbank to lectures was a peaceful start to the day. During the first week there was a visit to Hadrian's Wall, and en route the rugged nature of the countryside became apparent. Some of my neighbours in college had incomprehensible Geordie accents I had never heard before. My immediate neighbours, Janet from Wigan and Charlotte from Banbury, became lifelong friends. In the second year at Trevelyan I was elected vice president of the college undergraduates, which brought interesting responsibilities including having to tell the Bursar what the students thought about the college food (most people lived in college). Looking back, the requirement to live in meant there was no pressure to learn to cook or budget, but at the time most students enjoyed the comfort.

I had originally applied to read Psychology, as I wanted to understand people more. In Durham the approach was very scientific, requiring an ability in maths I didn't have. So at the end of the first year, having failed the statistics exam I changed to a general degree in Theology, Sociology and Politics. An interest in theology had started when I was still at school and had read a book that was perhaps the first theology to hit the headlines in the popular press. Called *Honest to God* and written by John Robinson when Bishop of Woolwich in South London, it made thinking about the nature of God and the words, concepts and images we use to do so immensely exciting in contrast to the fixed and oppressive concepts I had encountered in church.

The question of what to do after university eventually loomed and, after missing the deadline for applications to Voluntary Service Overseas (VSO) because of a late reference I applied for and accepted a post in Wolverhampton as a trainee social worker. An old school friend, Andrea, followed suit and we were also joined in Wolverhampton by Max. Max and I married at St Thomas' Church, South Wigston on the 17th December 1969 some three months after arriving in Wolverhampton, and set up home in a flat on the rural edge of this very urban, industrialised area. My work base was in Bilston (where my grandmother had lived after leaving Wales). Being a trainee social worker meant being thrown into the deep-end of practical social work for a year before being sponsored to return to university for professional training. The work included arranging adoptions, checking up on children in foster care and on families deemed to be at risk especially where the police had found young children left at home without an adult. I still remember one sad situation where children had been left tied to the furniture whilst their father went to the pub for a drink. The mother had walked out of the family and he simply could not cope with work and childcare on his own. My role was to do spot checks, because if he continued to leave them alone they would need to be taken into care. I knew if I was in his situation I would probably not have coped either: I hated my police-like role, which did not include helping him find additional help so they could all stay together. The frustration of this helped me decide to leave social work, at least for a while, and not pursue the professional training.

Instead Max and I applied together for VSO, this time in advance of the deadline. As part of the preparation we went on an international work camp in Switzerland. The project was building a road to what we were told was an isolated community in the Alps. The work was physically hard and the living conditions basic; we slept in a barn to the sound of cowbells and washed in cold water in the open air. The highlight of the workday was dynamite-blasting the rock and running for cover, followed by eating apple and chocolate and bread for our picnic lunches. It seemed odd that a relatively rich country should need this project, so one day we walked up to the top of the planned road to understand more. To our surprise we found not the homes of poor farmers but a new hotel owned by the head of the local council which had requested the project. Whilst this did not put us off working overseas as volunteers it did make us ask hard questions. Eventually we headed off for Nigeria as teachers for two years. Our travel was paid for and we received free housing and a subsistence wage.

Nigeria

For most Europeans their first time in Nigeria is quite a culture shock, and so it was for us too. The size and loudness of Lagos and the absence of many of the social rules we take for granted is quite disorienting. Cars and lorries drive anywhere they can, including on the pavement, and almost every transaction whether in a bank or airport requires a bribe. This coupled with the damp heat can lead to a very short temper as I discovered in myself when I stormed out of a bank having thrown a torn up form at the assistant who was wanting a bribe before opening an account for us. Our first night was spent at the house of a British Council official before being taken to Ode Irele where the school was. Since the house at the school wasn't ready for us we lodged with the only other European in the 'town', Paddy Keeley, an eccentric, warm hearted, Irish priest who had developed very strange habits having been on his own for so long. His housemate was a big chimpanzee who came unannounced to welcome us (his owner only appeared some days later). The house was very basic; cooking was done on a wood fire outside. Covering the bathroom floor at night was a sea of toads which were difficult to avoid in the dark! Thankfully our own home tended to have only soldier ants, snakes and lizards as uninvited pets. There was intermittent electricity from the school generator, a calor gas cooker and a kerosene powered fridge standing in pots of water to keep the ants out. Our transport was a 90cc motorbike (quite small and slow) which had to carry both of us plus bags. Not surprisingly, especially on the very bumpy mud roads, the spokes frequently broke and the wheels buckled from hitting potholes.

At the school my job was to teach French and English. We were the first white teachers at this school so we were objects of curiosity, which meant people would come and stare at us through the mosquito netting that counted as windows (even when we were in bed). The previous French teacher had come from the Ivory Coast and his accent and grammar were very different from the European French I had learned, so it was difficult for me and the students to get on the same wavelength. The students came in all ages (a few were older than us) and from many different language groups. Some days there was nothing to do because all the students were busy making mud bricks for a new school building. So it could feel that time was passing very slowly. Our major diversion was the occasional weekend or holiday time trip to Ibadan, though on one holiday we got as far as Kano in Northern Nigeria, and on another to the neighbouring French West African countries of Togo and Dahomey. Where possible we stayed with other volunteers or in some kind of hostel, as our pay was quite basic.

In his chapter Max has written about the memorable night when we were alone on the campus and, without warning, were suddenly surrounded by people performing a ceremony meant to protect the area from cholera (we were storing the anti cholera vaccine in our fridge at the time). The episode was very frightening. Since discovering that this was all intended as preventative medicine I was determined to understand more about cultural concepts of illness and eventually embarked on a doctorate about this. Throughout the ages people have used whatever they can to ward off illness and to heal; only recently has this involved the kind of beliefs and medicine we now use in modern western medicine.

We had intended to stay for two years but because we were not well used and rather lonely one year was enough. I became pregnant with Morag and we wanted to return home in good time for the birth. So Morag can see herself as initially made from Nigerian foodstuffs such as sweet potato and taro even though she has the UK as her country of birth.

The arrival of Morag and Conrad

Back in England, after a spell staying with my parents, Max and I embarked on further study at Reading University living in a rented house at Finchampstead. Feeling rather unqualified to get a job back home I had enrolled for a part-time course in Sociology. Morag was born in the Royal Berkshire Hospital in Reading on 13th January 1972, just days before my 23rd birthday. After a few days we returned from the heat of the hospital to the cold of the cottage (no central heating). Max who had read books about child rearing, had rigged up a thermostat on the heater in Morag's nursery which unfortunately did not work, so on the first night home the poor baby almost expired from over heat and dehydration! Compared to our Nigerian house the cottage was well equipped, but still there was no washing machine so the nappy washing seemed endless. Morag's after-noon sleep was my main study period and one day a week Max took care of her whilst I went to Reading. Whenever possible this would involve going for walks and having lessons en route about the local plants and animals. Finchampstead is surrounded by woods and we had many hours pushing the pram through the beech trees and picking wild mushrooms. I enjoyed playing with my lovely little girl and seeing her develop so quickly. She was very bright and so aware of what she saw around her.

As neither Max nor I had a grant, money was short. So paying for a babysitter or childcare was out of the question. In the summer holiday we both found temporary work in Leicester, expecting my mother, by then in her mid 60s to look after Morag for us (but in the way we wanted). Looking back I am rather ashamed of this.

When Morag was about a year old I had a miscarriage. This was a very sad time: grieving the loss of a child one hasn't met and will never know I

Plate 8.5 In grandma Ethel's garden – Conrad and Morag
helping Alyson to weed the border.

found complex and very painful. We called the child Rowan (a name that would fit either a girl or boy) and buried her/him in the garden of the cottage. Our second child, Conrad, was born in May 1974 after we had moved to Inkpen in Berkshire to a larger and more rural house backing on to open common. Again this was rented. By then Max was earning and so money was not quite so tight. It wasn't until 1976 that I had a paid post (part-time) teaching Sociology on a Bachelor in Education degree course at a college near Reading. When Conrad was a few months old we bought a small house which we named Rowan Tree Cottage. It was in the village of Wilton, Wiltshire. Conrad, who had been a good sleeper, decided he did not like this change and spent the whole of the first night there screaming. As a baby Conrad's nickname was Biff, a name earned when a very small baby because of the way his little hands seemed to be hitting the air and, sometimes, himself.

Wilton was a picturesque little village with no facilities other than a pub and a small shop (which soon closed down). The nearest large village was Great Bedwyn, some two miles away. This had a baker, a small super-market and a railway station from which Max and I could reach Reading. It also had a Citroen garage and so it made sense for our car to be a Citroen. The most basic and characterful model, the 2CV, had been developed for French farmers; the canvas roof could be rolled back to allow for farm implements to be carried across the fields. By normal standards it was not a comfortable family car but despite its smallness we managed to pack into it all manner of camping equipment as well as four people, clothes, toys and so on. This was the car I used to commute into Oxford for a year's course in Social Anthropology to develop my interest in beliefs about health and illness, the subject of my MA dissertation at Reading. I was rather unprepared for the smugness of Oxford and its sense that it was the academic centre of the world. After completing this one-year course I won a grant to do a research degree. We decided to move to Oxford renting a house in Headington so that we could all be together more. Conrad attended a nearby nursery and Morag the local primary school, Windmill. Max and I began to consider possible places for my fieldwork. The initial plan was the Solomon Islands but having met some people extremely enthusiastic about Papua New Guinea where they had been working we decided to find out more. In fact Max quickly saw a post advertised and applied for it: so it was that we prepared to head for East New Britain, Max going ahead and the children and I following soon after. It was a very long and tiring journey with two young children in tow. We went first to Hong Kong, then on to Port Moresby and finally in a small plane to Rabaul, New Britain. En route to Rabaul we were offloaded at a very tiny airport where we walked across the tarmac to a waiting room with no fans or cold drinks, exhausted but with Conrad clutching Dougal, his enormous magic Roundabout dog, before finally being allowed back on a plane and flying to Rabaul airport.

Papua New Guinea

Once we had recovered from the shock of the heat and humidity things began to fall into place with the children quickly settling into the small two teacher international school a short drive away. We made some very good friends through the school, many of whom we still remain in contact with. The only practical problem for me was the slowness in receiving permission to work in a village on anthropological research. Quite reasonably applications to do research were vetted by the university and government, checking references etc and seeking assurance that the work would help and not exploit local people. At the time, there was a sense that anthropologists took away local knowledge, using it for their own ends. My own application had been carefully framed with these sensitivities in mind, but in fact I never got the required permit: my application must have got lost somewhere in the bureaucracy. It was impossible to begin the research I had planned or even learn the Tolai language, though I was able to get a grasp of Melanesian Pidgin (a lingua franca developed by European traders and which most people used to communicate with 'outsiders'). So eventually, having worked for over six months at the college at which Max was teaching, I decided nothing would be lost by trying to go ahead without the permit. The college already had some contacts in nearby villages and using these I began to visit Bitagunan (meaning in the Tolai language the last place or furthest place in their area).

 Bitagunan (administratively known also as Napapar 5) lay off the road to Rabaul about 14 kilometres from Vudal College. It was basically a clearing in the forest and was home for about a 100 or so people. The simple houses, made from bamboo but often with corrugated iron roofing, were scattered over a fairly big area. The largest and only community building was the mud block church: most meetings were held out in the open. I took with me to an open air meeting of village elders a Tolai speaking friend from Vudal to explain I wanted permission to stay in the village to learn both the language and about the way they lived, rather like the anthropologist Scarlett Epstein had done in another Tolai village. I'm not sure how well my friend translated the request as, to my dismay, the answer was that I could come and *visit* them once a fortnight. It began to feel as though I would never be able to get started. But to the rescue came one of the most respected of the village women, Ia Pitini (Martha). As I dejectedly made my way out of the village Martha was standing by the roadside waiting for me. When you come back, she said, you will stay in my house and become my sister. Here was an invitation I couldn't afford to reject, even though it was very far from the textbook way of getting permission to work as an anthropologist.

Martha was a wonderful and unusual person. Orphaned when young she had been brought up by German nuns. Her only languages were Tolai and some pidgin and she could neither read nor write. Mother of several children, the youngest being Lucy aged 12, she was married to Bernard, the village catechist. As the catechist's wife she was the informal leader of the village women. The whole village was Roman Catholic and so she was known and respected by everyone. This uniformity of religious allegiance was a result of the German Colonial policy of allowing only one Christian missionary group to go into an area. A line had been drawn down the island: one side was Catholic and the other Protestant. In this way families

Plate 8.6 Papua New Guinea 1980: Martha has a poorly throat and is having a consultation.

and villages were not divided amongst themselves. I soon discovered that the role of a catechist (and his wife) was important, as the German priest had care of an enormous number of villages and churches and so delegated much of the work, including sometimes the Sunday Mass, to the catechists.

Martha had a very positive view of European women and so was a great friend. I shared a sleeping room with her daughter Lucy and ate with the family. Occasionally she came to visit me at the college and tried our food, including once a cheese sandwich which made her very ill, as she had not had milk since a child and was unable to digest it. Dividing my time between two homes and, in particular, two languages was difficult and I recall having to give my head a few hours to readjust when returning to Max and the children as the two worlds were so different. When the children had come with me to the village their fair hair and skin had been a great source of fascination and soon people were crowding and touching them in a way that meant they were reluctant to return to the village afterwards.

The focus of my research was the relationship between indigenous and Western beliefs and practices relating to health and illness, and whilst it was intended to result in an academic thesis it was also one that might have useful practical implications. In Keravat, a few kilometres along the main road, there was a government run health centre which I knew villagers used, and there were also two hospitals within reach, a government one in Rabaul and a mission hospital at Vunapope. I also knew villagers practised traditional medicine and had lots of traditional beliefs and explanations about causes and cures of illness. My question was, how did the two systems relate: were they in competition? Did they each apply to different kinds of illness? Was there a generational difference with youngsters who had been to school rejecting more traditional ways or what? A Western-focussed model of social and economic development tends to assume that people need to be educated out of a pre-scientific way of looking at the world before they can access the practical benefits of, say, scientific medicine. But perhaps this is not necessarily the case. Moreover, there are hidden benefits of indigenous beliefs that mean their destruction may have unwelcome consequences. It soon became apparent that the villagers took a largely pragmatic approach to the use of different kinds of health care and would try anything they felt might stand a chance of working. For most ailments they would first try what was easiest and cheapest, whether herbal medicines from the forest or 'borrowed' from my own stock of modern medicines. If things turned serious they would try both the traditional 'specialists' who needed payment and one of the hospitals. The incoherence of the two very different belief systems was irrelevant. Highly educated Tolai were equally pragmatic, though more careful about who they talked to about this. Almost everyone believed in the power of sorcery, in other words that the evil intentions of one person could cause the death of another by direct or indirect means.

Discovering the outlines of all this was relatively easy, but documenting the detail when it came to the knowledge held by traditional specialists was amazingly difficult. Initially I thought this was due to my slowness in learning the Tolai language, but there was an even bigger problem. 'Knowledge is power' and this was definitely the view of the specialists. Innumerable times I would arrange to be taken to meet a traditional medicine specialist only to find he could not make it after all. At one point I was told that they would willingly speak about these matters with my husband but not with me: it was men's knowledge. Since Max spoke no Tolai this clearly was impossible, but it may have been an excuse anyway. Of course the women I met were able to tell me about certain simple herbal remedies but as they explained they did not know about the strong stuff! The word for strong, *ongor* also meant power (both physical and spiritual).

For a few months I joined forces with another British anthropologist, Christine Bradley, working in a much more urban Tolai area. Together we did a comparative study of decision making about family size and family planning for a national conference and book. This was interesting and productive but at the end I was still faced with the problem of how to find enough information for my DPhil thesis. Meanwhile Martha was doing a good job teaching me to be her sister, taking me off with her to the market, visiting the sick so she could sprinkle holy water over them, and to church. At one point she was admitted to hospital and I went along to ensure she got food. In the hospitals all non-medical care is done by family who camp out in the grounds of the hospital, though I was allowed to sleep on a mat by her bed! Going to church was one of her favourite activities and she was an impressively genuine and good person. At first I went with her as an anthropological observer but soon found myself wanting to take part in the Mass, feeling my observer stance was cutting me off from something really important. During a visit to the village by the Archbishop, a Belgian priest who had

Plate 8.7 Rabaul Harbour – Morag, Alyson and Conrad.

previously been in Latin America, I explained to him I was Anglican by background but would very much like to be able to receive Communion in the village (in the UK this crossing of church, this 'inter-communion', is not permitted in the Roman Catholic Church). 'Then what is stopping you?' he said with a smile. I was very moved by this welcome and the awareness that church rules should never be an end in themselves.

In between periods in the village I was back in Vudal with Max, Morag, Conrad, Paddington the dog and Kina the cat. Morag and Conrad settled well, enjoying school and the friends they made there. Many of the children lived on the coast at a Theological College, and we were sometimes invited over there for a swim in the shallow warm sea and a meal. On one particularly memorable Christmas the Australian couple who had invited us and another family were unwell so we were left to finish of and serve lunch. Quite unaware that the other visiting family was vegetarian, Max filled the children's plates with turkey which they happily devoured before there was time to discover they were meant only to have vegetables. Some other school friends lived at a plantation, and one day when the rain was heavy and the river flooded we couldn't cross it to pick up Morag and Conrad, so they stayed the night with their Australian friends at the plantation. This family would sometimes meet us all at a social club in Keravat which had a bar and showed films. Another favourite family haunt was the swimming pool at Rabaul. We usually combined a swim there with a shopping trip to the supermarket and a toasted sandwich at the air-conditioned Café de Paris, in town. The experience of air-conditioning was a rare and valued luxury. On the way from and to Vudal poor Morag and Conrad rattled around in the back of our little Suzuki jeep with just a foam cushion each to shield them from the horrendously bumpy roads. Despite these rocky rides and their mother's absences, both Morag and Conrad remember their three years in Papua New Guinea with great affection. Morag formed a strong friendship with Sally and Ian, the English couple who lived in the house next to ours at Vudal. Ian had never been out of the UK before, so his first foray abroad was a big one. Certainly these three years were for us all an excellent education in international living. The syllabus the children followed at school was that of New South Wales and they returned to the UK with a detailed knowledge of geography and history from this perspective, as well as some Australian words very casually used in everyday conversation over there but seen as swear words in the UK.

Conrad discovered this to his dismay when back at school in England he told the teacher his pen was 'buggered up', a phrase commonly used in Australia and PNG to mean broken. The UK teacher was appalled! Instead of receiving sympathy he was sent to the head teacher's office as a punishment for bad language.

Part way through our time in PNG, having reconnected with the Church through Matha I was casually reading the weekly English language national paper, the *Papua New Guinea Times* when I saw a full page article by the Anglican Archbishop of PNG arguing that any women ordained priest would not be recognised or allowed in PNG. The main reason seemed to be that sometimes women became pregnant. To my amazement I was speechless with anger. A few months before, whilst we were on leave in the UK, I had attended a meeting in Durham led by an American woman priest. The effect was very powerful so I guess it was the dissonance between this and the views I had read which so shocked me. When words returned after a couple of days I penned a letter to the paper. It was published the next week. Here is the main part of the letter (bigmen is the pidgin term for powerful, important, men):

Bigmen and Pregnant priests

Dear Editor,

The women's page recently featured Archbishop David Hand's reasons for opposing the ordination of women to the priesthood. When I read the article I was filled with sadness and anger. Jesus valued women so why does not the Anglican church? The Archbishop asserts that 'Priests must be male because Jesus was male.' Archbishop, Jesus was many things; he was Jewish, the son of a carpenter, and of a certain blood type. Do you insist that all priests share all of these characteristics? On what grounds have you decided that maleness is essential when racial and social origins are not? 'What happens if a woman priest gets pregnant?' asks the Archbishop. Does he ask the same question of women teachers, typists and doctors? The answer is that all being well she has a baby. Then she and the father rear that child in the way that most suits their personalities and life style. There is no great problem as long as fathers face their responsibilities. If a woman priest becomes pregnant she probably becomes a better priest and her parishioners benefit from the widening of her experience. Archbishop do not fear pregnant priests. Embrace them. The alternative is to lead your church into the beautiful museum of extinct male cults.

Back in England

When we returned to England in 1982 I wanted to renew my member-ship of the Church of England (which did not then ordain women) but could only do so in conscience by also joining the movement for the ordination of women (MOW). MOW was led by Margaret Webster, the wife of the Dean of St Paul's Cathedral in London. My interest and involvement grew apace, organising a conference, editing a book, researching and publishing a study of lay people's experience of women ministers and becoming national vice-moderator of the movement.

We had returned with many good and memorable experiences but ready to get back to family and friends. Max and the children led the way home, with me spending a couple of months in the village trying to get enough information for my thesis and fending off many kind offers of more 'civilised' hospitality. Back in the UK we spent almost a year in our little cottage in Wilton, with Morag and Conrad attending the school in the next village and all of us 'managing' without a car. Max had temporary work at Reading University and I was trying to write up what I could of my research. When Max finally got a more permanent job it was with Christian Aid in Oxford. Morag was at the stage of needing to move to Secondary School and the local one in Wiltshire would have failed to stretch her enough, so it was yet again time to move. Initially it was to Abingdon, where there was a house that went with Max's job, but as Morag had won a scholarship for an Oxford school it made best sense for us to buy a house in Oxford within walking distance of her school there. Thus began the years based in Lonsdale Road. Conrad found the transition from a small village in which he was well known and could roam freely through the lanes and fields very painful. No one knew him in Oxford and his freedom was seriously curtailed. At his new school, Bishop Kirk, there was some bullying and at one point he developed a leg injury that seemed to have no physical cause. To find out if he actually could move his leg without pain the enterprising GP took us all out for the day in his canal boat. Conrad was happily seated on deck until passing through a lock he managed to fall in. Noble Max dived in after him amidst the swirling lock water, and the doctor and I hung over the side of the boat fishing out Conrad and then Max minus his precious spectacles. To our amazement the doctor insisted on completing the trip with our two extremely wet and shivering passengers. Surprisingly neither Max nor Conrad developed pneumonia and Conrad's leg recovered.

Our cottage at Wilton had been quite close to Greenham Common, the site of an American nuclear airbase. The morality of nuclear arms was something I questioned and seeing this camp so near brought home to me the need to protest against the government's compliance with the US's willingness to threaten to use nuclear weapons and to make our country a potential target. Some months after our return to England there was a big demonstration in which people came and encircled the base with a human chain. My old school friend Andrea travelled over from Wales and as a family we joined the action. The number of people was impressive. In Oxford I joined a group supporting the Greenham Common women's peace camp, taking food and moral support to the women who were living there in order to draw attention to the nuclear base. Friends I made in the support group included Angela West from Oxford who together with some Roman Catholic Dominicans led Christian liturgies at the Greenham camp gates and was planning a course for lay people to equip them to preach at these services. When living in Oxford I joined a two-year course and was assigned an individual tutor, Prof Rowan Williams, who later became Archbishop of Canterbury. After graduating from the course I became one of the management group keeping it going for others.

It was time to begin earning again, and I got a couple of temporary jobs, one at Oxfam, which needed extra staff to respond to requests for information about their relief and development work, and another teaching A-level Sociology in Wantage. The first job was quite easy though a little repetitive, and the second quite a challenge because of the sixth formers' 'interest us if you can and we bet you can't' approach. So it was a relief to be appointed as research officer to the community paediatrician at the Radcliffe Infirmary, working on services for children with disabilities. I had argued my suitability not on the grounds of Conrad's leg but because of my interest in ideas about health and illness and previous social work experience. The research involved visiting and interviewing families in their homes, analysing the interviews and making policy recommendations. Unlike the policing role of social work in Wolverhampton, this was aiming to make very practical changes which would be much more effective in helping families struggling with very difficult situations. On the basis of this work I was appointed Research Fellow at the Open University in Milton Keynes where I remained for ten largely stimulating years, commuting back and forth on an almost daily basis.

The Open University was the first and most experienced and respected distance-teaching university. Set up in the 1960s, its initial aim was to open up university level education to those who had missed out, many because their families could not afford it or because their own expectations had been low. Students could join at any age and without any previous qualifications. Introductory courses were available to help students learn how to study and write essays and because the determination of part-time, mature, students is so high a great deal was achieved. At first I was entirely involved in research, not teaching, evaluating a course for professionals, carers and families on mental handicap (later called learning difficulty). Then I began to advise on course design and eventually moved over into course production in the School of Health and Social Welfare. Writing OU courses is a very collaborative and stimulating enterprise. The first course was entitled 'Death and Dying', written mainly for health care workers at all levels it was aiming to make more widely available the expertise of palliative care so far restricted mainly to hospices. The pioneer St Christopher's Hospice in Sydenham was a major partner in the course and when I visited to make audio recordings of some of the patients and families I had no inkling that I would eventually live a mile away. OU courses are made up of workbooks accompanied by audiotapes and TV programmes, as well as tutorials in regional centres. Although the face-to-face teaching was not part of my job I chose to do this too in order to see how it all worked in practice. The students were very impressive. Some we tutored by phone or email, as they were overseas. It was difficult not to get involved in their lives. For one (and this story has been repeated many times), the wife of a soldier in Germany, the experience of study, the doors it opened and the confidence it gave her was something that both brought her great joy and broke her marriage. Her husband simply could not accept the happy and independent person she had become.

Although we lived in North Oxford, after a while I joined the vibrant and very mixed ecumenical church on Blackbird Leys to the south of the city having found North Oxford Christianity a bit too cosy and abstract. Blackbird Leys was a council estate built for the workers at the Cowley car works. The media had labelled it a dangerous place and it was a favourite site for car theft and 'joy-riding' amongst disaffected youngsters. So the focus of the church was to help improve individual and community self image. For a while I was involved in the debt counselling and advice centre begun by the church. When the vicar left it proved very difficult to replace him. I began to feel how much I would enjoy being in that role in that place and so a period of reviewing my life began. I was adamant I did not wish to be ordained, but simply wanted to do the job as a lay minister. So a process of what the church calls 'vocational discernment' began. I was accepted for training part-time, following the same course as those to be ordained. This was a three-year course run for three hours one evening a week, with essays and residential weekends. The tutors were mainly drawn from the three residential theological colleges in Oxford, so the standard was high. Combining this kind of course with a demanding full time job is always difficult, but for me a particular difficulty was the fact that some of the students and the Principal saw my views as too challenging. After two years I took a break and then returned to complete the course. On completion all of my fellow students were ordained and when I saw this in the cathedral the tears flowed, and eventually I too asked to be considered for ordination. A couple of tough interviews later this was agreed and it was decided that I would finish my work at the Open University, seek a full-time parish post and then be ordained.

Ordination and Windsor

I had said I was drawn to a multi-racial fairly urban parish (rather like Blackbird Leys!). The director of ordinands asked me to go and look at the churches run by the Team Rector of Windsor. I asked what would happen if this didn't seem right. The response was 'This is all we are offering you'. So I went to meet the Rector, Jeffery Whale, a gentle man with liberal views, and we got on well enough. Then there was an informal interview with some lay people and then with the other clergy, Jonathan and Andrew. All agreed I would go there as curate in the team of five churches. So at the end of September 1996 I was ordained deacon in Oxford cathedral and went to live in Windsor in a rented house near the barracks. It was quite small, so for the first year Max divided his time between Windsor and Oxford where his office was.

At Windsor I gained a breadth of experience I could not have had elsewhere and though it was not at all what I would have chosen I was determined to make the most of it. I was their first female clergyperson but most people were welcoming and warm towards me. For a few I represented everything they did not want and some made this very clear by completely avoiding me. One Christmas the MP (Conservative, as would be expected in Windsor) walked out of church when I was preaching, telling his wife, who was a regular member of the church, never to bring his son there again! There was also a woman in the choir at the parish church who always refused to shake my hand at the peace. And

Plate 8.8 September 1997 – in the grounds of Windsor Parish Church
after Alyson's ordination as priest.

of course when I was ordained priest a number of people would not receive Communion from me. I decided to treat most of them as frightened and in need of reassurance so made great efforts to be pleasant and polite, when I really wanted to tell them they were rigid and unchristian. The effort of trying to win everyone over was great. During the first year I was expected to assist at all of the five churches but it was difficult to get to know people this way and it was also difficult to remember what to do where as each church was very different. So in the second year after negotiation I was mainly in the same two churches as Jeffery, and then in the third was given day-to-day responsibility for one church, All Saints.

Jeffery had never before had a curate and was daunted to have one of my age. Much of my learning was by osmosis (not the best way for me to

Plate 8.9 April 2005: Aunt Freda's 100th Birthday Party in Trowbridge Civic Hall. The Queen's telegram is proudly on display.

learn), as he didn't really teach me anything! I just followed him around for a bit and then was told to get on with it. Jeffery and his family were very musical and so my lack of singing voice was something he could not understand. Despite this they adopted me as one of the family. It was during my time at Windsor that there were signs of our own family growing. Morag introduced us to Angus! Max and I were having a short break at our cottage in Wiltshire when Morag said a friend of hers would be passing through Salisbury so we could all meet up there. We did so at the garden café of the Fisherton Mill in Fisherton Street. On sale there are local crafts, and now in the garden of the home of Alexander and Felix stands a lovely heron bought from the Fisherton Mill. I think this was the first boyfriend we had been officially introduced to in this way so we knew this was serious. Then sometime later Morag phoned us when she and Angus were holidaying in Slovenia to say they were planning to marry. This meant it was definitely time to meet Angus's mother Felicity. The wedding took place in April 2003 on a beautiful but rather cold spring day in Oxford, at Magdalen College where Morag had been an undergraduate. Accompanying Conrad at the wedding was his partner Carla. Carla's parents were from Jamaica and had moved to Bristol before the birth of their three daughters. Her mother Joyce had been a midwife in Bristol for very many years and was by now delivering the babies of babies she had delivered. Her father had worked on oil rigs off the coast of Aberdeen as a welder but was now retired because of damage to his eyes. Apart from three years at Durham University and a short time in Oxford Carla has spent all her life in Bristol so when my very elderly aunt on first meeting her asked if she was getting used to the English weather what could she reply other than 'I was born here'.

Conrad's graduation ceremony in Bristol Cathedral was a great occasion and a great achievement. Despite leaving school with no A levels Conrad had ignored his mother's advice to avoid future disappointment by following a more practical, non-academic, route. Instead he re-sat his exams at a tutorial college, got help with his dyslexia and had not only been accepted for a degree course at Bristol but had also completed it to a high level, getting an upper second. I was delighted to say many times that my advice had been completely wrong!

Plate 8.10 Morag and Angus are married – April 2003. Below the cherry blossom in Magdalen College stands the bride's proud father, mother and brother.

A London Parish

Towards the end of my three years at Windsor I was seriously looking for a move. The only post suggested in Oxford diocese was a tiny Afro-Caribbean Anglo-Catholic church stuck behind an Asian housing estate in Slough. The congregation did not want a woman priest, but I was all they were being offered. Moreover the Bishop felt I could persuade the church to let go of their building and move to a shop front site in the main street. Only someone driven and quite ruthless would have been able to deal with the church members' dislike of a vicar who pushed them into this and I certainly did not have the required toughness of skin. So I politely declined and began to look at the adverts in the church press. The first job I applied for was in South London and to my surprise I was shortlisted. It was fairly unusual to move diocese for a first post but it was worth a try. I mainly just expected the interview to be helpful experience. To my amazement of the four candidates it was I who was offered the post. The area was Forest Hill, near Lewisham, and the church St Saviour's. I soon discovered, that there are very many St Saviour's in South London, including a large Roman Catholic Church in the centre of Lewisham: people have often turned up at my church for a funeral that was actually taking place at the other.

Getting the large Victorian vicarage decorated and carpeted and the garden accessible was a mammoth job. Conrad had just finished his degree and looking for work so was keen to earn some money and so he did much of the work with Max. A coach load of Windsor people came over to my licensing as vicar of the living of Brockley Hill, St Saviour (the official title) as well as old friends from Oxford and a few friends we had made in Papua New Guinea.

There was much to discover about this part of South London. The heavy traffic and screaming sirens of ambulances, fire engines and police cars were the most unattractive features. But the ease of access to central London, a lovely Victorian vicarage and garden and surprisingly good walks to places such a Greenwich and Crystal Palace gave lots of pleasure. The parish was quite compact and very mixed socially and ethnically. Some people had been members of this church all their lives whilst others were relatively new and often transient students or immigrants. Those who had grown up in the area had very long memories: I recall Frances Paice taking me by the hand, and showing me where the altar used to be and expressing her profound dismay that it had been moved. She spoke as though the move had taken place the previous week but it had in fact happened over 20 years before. In her mind all the previous vicars, whether alive or dead, were still very much present; she had no problem with the doctrine of the Communion of the Saints! Frances and her sister Doreen had run the Sunday school for many years and even in their 80s and 90s regularly read the lesson and led the prayers at our main services. Every year at the carol service Frances insisted on being the one to read the story of the angel telling Mary she was to have God's child, and each time she read it as though she were Mary. Frances died unexpectedly in hospital during the first carol service she had ever missed and at about the time of that particular reading.

There was already quite a large staff team; another priest, Ray, who had grown up in the parish and told me people wondered why he could not have been appointed vicar, a retired barrister, Alan, who was a licensed Reader (so could preach), another Reader, Keith, who was a school teacher and did not accept women priests, and a pastoral assistant Adeline, who was from Sierra Leone and quite a matriarch in that community. The previous vicar who had been very popular, had gone with his wife, (she was also ordained and had worked voluntarily in the parish) to be missionaries in Kenya. People told me that it was only Keith who had a problem with women clergy; everyone else had accepted the vicar's wife. But it became clear to me that whilst people had been comfortable with her they were not used to a woman in charge so all was not plain sailing.

After less than a year I was asked by the Bishop to look after two neighbouring parishes, St Augustine's and St George's, whose own vicars had just retired. Being too green to bargain him down I agreed. St Augustine's had a small congregation who were struggling to maintain a church built on a hill that kept shifting and causing cracks to appear suddenly in the walls. For a small congregation this was a heavy financial responsibility and eventually, to the Bishop's dismay, they decided to close. St George's was in the process of building a new church and would eventually appoint its own vicar. Having oversight of three parishes and running around covering the services of three churches was a stressful experience, which only ended when I gave the two additional parishes back to the Bishop. Never assume your employer has your best interests at heart.

Even when being responsible for only one parish a vicar's job is six days a week and definitely not 9 to 5. There is however considerable variety within each day which may involve, say, visiting a bereaved person to discuss a funeral, sorting out a disagreement between different groups using the church hall, making a sandwich for a homeless person who has come to the door, preparing Sunday's sermon, visiting a sick parishioner in hospital, answering phone calls, checking and invariably rewriting the minutes of the PCC (church council) meeting, drafting a rota and then attending a school Governors meeting.

Around the time Alexander was conceived I signed up for a part-time MA in Theology at Kings College London, mainly to keep my ageing mind alert. When I told her, Morag was as surprised by this news as I was by hers. She had been looking forward to my help at the very time I was filling up my one day off. Of course Max was very keen to be involved with his new grandson so, in fact, I did the MA and took my turn with Alexander and then Felix. Living only an hour and a quarter away from the young Evers family was a great bonus and we soon became very familiar with the train and underground journey to Archway and then to Tufnell Park.

Of course our involvement with Alexander and then Felix was in a support role to their parents and nanny. After Alexander was born Morag took a year off her work at the city law firm Herbert Smith. When she went back to work she hired a very good New Zealand nanny, Carla, who kept a diary each day of what Alexander had eaten and done so his parents could feel very much part of his development. Alexander was very fond of her and there are some photos of him dressing up in her boots. We had a joke that when an adult he would have a special liking for women who wear black (which his nanny did) and speak with a New Zealand accent. Because Carla worked long days she usually had most of Friday off and this was when Max and I came to play. After Felix was born and Morag returned to work a new nanny arrived. This was Jadranka from Serbia. She too was greatly loved by the children. Jadranka was artistic so both Alexander and Felix had fun with her making models and learning how to draw and paint. They also sometimes met her husband Dimitri, and a favourite game was to capture him. Although he was quite tall somehow the boys always won this game! For Max and me there were still lots of opportunities to see the boys, usually on Fridays when the nanny had already worked four long days and so was due to finish at lunch time or earlier. Both Alexander and Felix enjoyed occasional visits to the vicarage and before they moved to Tufnell Park especially liked the very many stairs found in an old Victorian house. They called it Nanny's house to distinguish it from Grandpa's cottage where they sometimes stayed too.

In the summer of 2009 they first stayed at the cottage without their parents (but with their grandparents!) Favourite adventures there included, hunting for dinosaur bones, paddling in the stream and flying kites in the field above the Bailey bridge. For both Max and me living close enough to see Alexander and Felix regularly has been a great delight for us. Things we might otherwise have missed, such as Alexander's complete fascination with motorbikes at one stage and Felix's skill at jigsaw puzzles at another, stay with us even though they themselves have probably forgotten. Certainly a number of my parishioners have taken a great interest in the boys and one, Marje, never forgets a birthday or Christmas.

Over ten years at St Saviour's the congregation had changed considerably. A number of the older people who had been there all their lives died (including Doreen and Frances Paice in 2009 and 2010 respectively). A large part of my task was to encourage older and newer members and the various ethnic groups to see themselves as one community. On Sundays there were definitely more black than white faces in church. Many African-Caribbeans had moved to London, often in response to requests from the British Government and those who had joined St Saviours now had children and grandchildren who had always known south London as their home. Also at St Saviours we had a good number of people originally from West Africa, mainly Nigeria, Sierra Leone or Ghana. The Nigerians were largely from the Yoruba speaking area which was where Max and I had taught in the early 70s and where Morag had been conceived. When I visited Jane, one of our Nigerian members, following the death of her husband, I was, to my surprise, able to understand the shout of the small girl who opened the door. 'Aibo' she called to her grandmother, meaning, literally 'peeled one' (a white person who has had their black skin peeled away).

After seven years in post clergy can take a short (six-week) sabbatical. So in my eighth year this is what I did, going to Jerusalem for a month. I had never been there before. I stayed at Tantur, in south Jerusalem, at an ecumenical centre run by Roman Catholics. Tantur aimed to bring together Christians of all traditions and backgrounds and also to meet with people from all the major faith traditions in the area, especially Jews and Moslems. A Jewish colleague with whom I worked closely at the Open University had a house in Jerusalem as well as one in London and is often there for the major religious festivals. Jeanne and her doctor husband, David, invited me to stay for a festival that involved trying to stay awake all night studying the Torah (Scriptures) and then at dawn gathering at the Western Wall of the Temple to pray. I didn't manage to stay awake for the whole night but we were awake to walk to the Western Wall at dawn. Part of what I had seen around Jerusalem I was unable to discuss with Jeanne. Tantur was very near the checkpoint to Bethlehem. The Jewish and Palestinian areas were divided by a huge wall, which Israel argued protected them from Palestinian terrorists but which also clearly humiliated and impoverished the Palestinians as well as cutting into land that was theirs by international agreement. I came away from Jerusalem with a heavy heart; the enormous injuries suffered by the Jewish people under Hitler were now in some ways being repeated by them on the Palestinians. Certainly Palestinian Christians in Bethlehem, the birthplace of Jesus and so in a sense of Christianity, are increasingly moving overseas because life has been made so difficult for them.

Where will I spend my next sabbatical? Now 63, I remain very keen to discover more about this beautifully varied world, of which I have seen just a little. I have no desire to retire yet, so who knows what opportunities there will be during the next seven years (I do have to retire at 70). New doors open and whenever we have the courage to step through we discover something new both about ourselves and about God. George Herbert put this so well:

> Love bade me welcome: yet my soul drew back,
>   Guiltie of dust and sinne.
> But quick-ey'd Love, observing me grow slack
>   From my first entrance in,
> Drew nearer to me, sweetly questioning.
>   If I lack'd any thing.
>
> A guest I answer'd, worthy to be here:
>   Love said, You shall be he.
> I the unkinde, ungratefull? Ah my deare,
>   I cannot look on thee.
> Love took my hand, and smiling did reply,
>   Who made the eyes but I ?
>
> Truth Lord, but I have marr'd them: let my shame
>   Go where it doth deserve.
> And know you not, sayes Love, who bore the blame?
>   My deare, then I will serve.
> You must sit down, sayes Love, and taste my meat:
>   So I did sit and eat.
>   *LOVE* George Herbert

CHAPTER 9

Conclusion

And the end of all our exploring
Will be to arrive where we started
And know the place for the first time.

These words from T. S. Eliot's poem *Little Gidding* describe our feelings as we finished our research into the lives of the seven generations and came to write about the things we had learned.

We started out knowing very little – very little even about our own grandparents let alone the ones who had lived a hundred years before. But it was curiosity, and a sense that it was important to understand the influences that had moulded our parents' lives and which in turn had shaped us and the way we brought up our children – that started us on this journey. Making explicit a child's genealogical inheritance is not the norm in European culture, but in talking about *our project* with people brought up elsewhere in the world, we were surprised how many described the way family descent was passed to the new generations in their home place. For instance a man from the *Suludnon* tribal group in the Philippines told of an epic poem – the *Suguidanon* – that gives the names of the forebears and their deeds. It takes 48 hours to recite but every few years the young people are gathered to hear their clan story. If Alexander and Felix read this book in less than a day they can be thankful to get off so lightly!

The research has taken three years. Through written records we have got to know many long-dead people, but it has also provided the opportunity to meet and talk with brothers, sisters, cousins, aunts and uncles from all four sides of the family, and to hear stories and anecdotes that have seldom been recalled. Though we have known only a handful of the ancestors a strange thing happened as we discovered their names, their jobs, their spouses and children – they began to take on appearances and even personalities. We could almost believe that they were pleased that at last somebody was writing down their histories. At least a dozen are such strong characters that their stories jumped out from the records, while others were more discreet and looked on nervously as we burrowed and dug to reveal things they had been so careful to keep hidden.

Each family line has its patriarchs, a grandfather whose efforts took his family in a new direction. Sometimes this was quite literally a new geographical location, for others it was a path that led to wealth and upward social mobility. Thomas George (TG) Evers is perhaps the most exciting and successful of these patriarchs. It was he who went to India at the end of the nineteenth century, developed his gift for training and riding horses and won race after race at the Calcutta racetrack. He married into a rich Scottish merchant family and retired to England while still quite young to lead the life of a country gentleman in Wiltshire. Surgeon Vice Admiral Sir Alexander Ingleby-Mackenzie was another larger than-life-figure: a naval surgeon during both the world wars who became Medical Director General of the Royal Navy; an outstanding athlete who even in retirement kept his interest in sport and was a committee member of the All England Lawn Tennis and Croquet Club.

Yet there are other patriarchs who did not achieve such public recognition but had the drive and courage to lead their families along new routes. Manoah Peberdy began life as a farm boy and shepherd in the 1830s and died in 1918 aged 82 working as a cow keeper and with his own dairy business. In Manoah we see the agricultural and industrial revolutions being played out. His grandfather had been a prosperous yeoman farmer; his sons and grandsons were firmly established as city workers in Leicester. He was obviously a hard-working man and died proud of his business, his properties and his library of books – all carefully allocated in his last will and testament. James Garnett is the other patriarch who took his family from rural to urban. Born in 1846 in the isolated village of Cold Ashby in Northamptonshire, he worked as an agricultural labourer but then took the adventurous step of moving to Kent to take a job on the great invention of the age, the railway. Eventually he took his young family back to Northamptonshire and then made the move a few miles further north to Wigston. By the 1890s he had nine children and had begun the newspaper shop business that was to last 100 years and keep three generations of Garnetts in reasonable comfort.

Many others tugged at our coat sleeves as we scrolled the computer records or turned the pages of old directories. Jacob Unna for example, a great, great, great, great grandfather of Alexander and Felix and one of the German ancestors. An early memory of his as a young boy in 1813 was of the French troops besieging his home city of Hamburg; while a few years later in 1815 another gene provider, Admiral Sir George Rose Sartorius, was present on the *Bellerophon* and witnessed the surrender of Napoleon.

But it was not just the larger-than-life men who demanded to be noticed: though few women had careers until the mid twentieth century, we caught glimpses of some strong female characters. Family tradition recalled that Serine Solomon, who married Jacob Unna in 1836, had been the illegitimate daughter of a Danish courtier. Whether this was true or not she was certainly brought up among wealthy people, or how otherwise could she have had her portrait painted by the famous Winterhalter? The picture of her in a blue dress was passed down through the generations until it was inherited by one of Serine's great grand-daughters, Dame Peggy Ashcroft. Another of Serine's great granddaugh-ters, and Alexander and Felix's great, great grandmother, was Violetta Ingleby-Mackenzie (neé Longstaffe) who was articulate and amusing. During the Second World War she became the Commandant of the British Red Cross. She had huge ability and who knows what she might have achieved if she had been born 70 years later when opportunities for women to have jobs outside the home were the norm even in peacetime.

Other grandmothers may not have achieved public recognition but many had the grit to get on with rearing a family in the face of whatever hurdles life attempted to erect. Great, great, great grandmother Eleanor Billing continued to run the Alexandra Hotel in Caernarfon for many years after her husband had died. Great, great grandmother Annie Wall as a widowed 23 year old brought up her two daughters from the end of the 1914–18 war and through the years of the Depression and was still cycling to her cleaning jobs in her eighties. Great grandmother Ethel Garnett, like her mother Edith, was a determined woman and after going to university in the 1930s did run a home and have a teaching career when it really 'wasn't the done thing'.

Many of the 300 or so great uncles, aunts and cousins that we identified also beckoned us to give them a second look. Great, great uncle John Longstaffe could have featured as a hero in one of the action comics of the 1950s: an early aviator and the first pilot in Latin America to use a plane to carry guns to a revolutionary army. He became an exhibition flyer on Long Island and died in front of a crowd on the day that his wife arrived aboard ship from England. Six years later another great, great uncle, Keith Ingleby-Mackenzie, died in the Royal Flying Corps one April afternoon over the German trenches. He was just 18, a schoolboy in fact, who survived almost three months at the front. Not long, but longer than the average pilot in 1917, who would be dead within ten days. But others did survive and at least one became a famous sportsman; Colin Ingleby-Mackenzie (a great uncle) was a schoolboy champion at many sports but excelled at cricket. He went on to become captain of the Hampshire County Cricket team and President of the MCC; he was President at the time when women were first admitted into the hallowed club, so like John Longstaffe he was a supporter of a revolutionary movement! The longest living relative from among the extended family was great, great aunt Freda Billing, a schoolmistress trained in the old school who was strict but kind. She told good stories to her nieces and lived to within a few weeks of her 101st birthday.

For us the grandparents who researched the family history, it has been an exciting journey. At times we were like detectives, who reaching an impasse in the investigation are forced to think along alternative lines of enquiry; it is a fact that no *Times* crossword can produce the same level of frustration as the unreadable Victorian handwriting on a key marriage certificate. *Exciting* may seem a strong word to use about an activity that involved sitting for many hours in the British Library or the Society of Genealogists, but levels of adrenalin are relative to what a 60-year old normally does during the day. But often it was more than intellectual excitement; imagine the sensual pleasure of a great cardboard box brought up from the vaults of the British Library. After undoing the ribbon and lifting the lid the very perfume of history rises up from the 200-year old documents of the East India Company, and there, dated 1819, is the application of the young Charles Rebenack to join the army in Bombay. We couldn't hear the voice of this great, great, great, great grandfather but we could read his answers to the Company's questions and see something of his character in the swirls of his handwriting.

Part of the excitement has been to discover the differences and similarities in the lives of the forebears. Some were very rich, others extremely poor. The wealthiest was probably Leopold Lewis, a Bradford merchant who when he died in 1905 left an estate worth many millions of pounds by today's values. It is harder to rank the poor. There is no record of any of the ancestors spending time in a workhouse but in the poverty stakes it would be difficult to beat great, great, great, great grandmother Isabella Harper who lived on the Packington Hall estate in the 1870s with her husband and six children and died of tuberculosis – the disease of squalor – at the age of 41.

Among the ancestors there is a microcosm of British society in terms of wealth, education and class, with grandparents who went to the most

prestigious of public schools and those who could only sign their name
with an 'x'. At one end of the occupational spectrum are doctors, lawyers,
a judge, farmers, vicars, army and naval officers and prosperous
merchants, at the other end shopkeepers, factory workers and agricultural
labourers. In terms of religion the majority were mainstream Church of
England, a handful of Methodists, just a hint of a few coming over from
Rome and at least half a dozen Jewish grandparents whose children
converted to Christianity. In terms of national identity they have all been
British but with many looking north of the Border for their cultural
identity and others being born in Germany and becoming naturalised
British citizens.

Nature and nurture are the two older sisters responsible for a child's
development. Researching seven generations of four family lines has given
some understanding of how change in Britain during the last 200 years,
the big historical trends, nudged, pushed and encouraged our ancestor's
lives into certain channels. Without doubt the two biggest historical
forces were the pushes and pulls of the agricultural and industrial
revolutions from the middle of the eighteenth century through to the
end of the nineteenth. The modernisation of farming and the enclosure of
land resulted in the Evers, Peberdy and Garnett families leaving the
villages where they had been for many generations and moving to the city.
It was possible in the eighteenth century to have a reasonable standard of
living from farming – land could be rented, livestock grazed on the
common areas, and small craft businesses run within the village. But this
way of life changed with the Enclosures and the concentration of
resources in the hands of landowners and larger farmers. First-born
sons stood some chance of becoming farmers in their own right, but
for the younger ones the options were either becoming an employed
labourer or moving away. Within the first few decades of the nineteenth
century the workshops and factories in the towns and cities were pulling
rural workers towards them: Thomas Evers to Manchester in the 1850s,
James Garnett to Wigston in the 1880s and Manoah Peberdy at about the
same time to the edge of Leicester which crept out and absorbed him into
the city. The same was happening with the grandmothers. As young
women they were moving – from Derbyshire to Lancashire, from the
Dales to York, from Northamptonshire to Caernarfon.

The rapid building of the rail network made these movements possible
and gave rise to another revolution as no longer did young women have
little choice but to marry men from within their own locality; with better
communications they encountered potential partners from across the

country. Trains opened up many new options. In Thornton–le-Dale, for example, there had been only one stagecoach a week, but once the rail line was completed the young Thomas Evers was just one of the many villagers to go in search of employment elsewhere. The lives of the Billing family in Northamptonshire was even more directly affected, as Joseph and his son John became railway excavators helping to dig the cuttings and tunnels for the new lines in the Forest of Dean. Their eventual move to Caernarfon to run a hotel was in part due to the demand that the new rail and ferry route to Dublin was making in the area.

From the 1850s onwards our grandparents were mobile. Professional men like Dr John Ingleby-Mackenzie worked in Devon, then Rugby and finally London; George Evers made the momentous move from Manchester to Essex and a new job in the City. Of course family relocations had happened before the railways – the Mackenzies had 'come down from the North' in the 17th century – but trains enabled ordinary rural people to have social networks outside their previous known world. An image that captures this revolution is of the little 14 year-old Annie Wall (great, great grandmother Annie Green) standing on the Leicester platform wearing her mother's over-sized hat and being met by Auntie Bertha to start a new life in domestic service. Her rural childhood was over and 70 years of work, marriage, daughters and widowhood began that day.

Hand in hand with Britain's industrialisation was trade, and hand in hand with trade was our expanding Empire. It was the entrepreneurship of the Glasgow and Liverpool merchants in India that gave the Everses their opportunity to prosper. The factories of Scotland and northern England needed markets for their goods, and where better than the sub-continent. After the Indian Mutiny in 1857 and the winding up of the East India Company and its replacement as ruler of India by the British government, the way was open for trading companies to export manufactured goods and import commodities such as tea, coffee, jute and indigo. The new steamships, the opening of the Suez Canal and inventions like the telegraph meant it was now quite possible to work in India but retain regular links and communication with family back home. Just as Jacob Unna and Leopold Lewis had traded English cloth across Europe, now the families of Walker, Liddell, Johnson and Sim opened up trading houses and banks in Bombay, Madras and Calcutta. There are many things that with hindsight we know were wrong about how the Raj behaved towards the Indian population, but the way they acted was a reflection of the certainty and self-confidence of the Victorians and

Edwardians. They had few doubts that they were 'doing good'; they became prosperous but also believed they were establishing good administration and civilising values. These men worked hard, played hard and did both with a great sense of duty and a certainty about how things should be done. We are the beneficiaries, a century and more on, of the wealth they brought back, so it would be hypocritical not to acknowledge how much of our well-being we owe to them.

It was not just the Evers family that benefited from trade with India; in one sense all British people experienced a standard of living that in part was maintained by the food and products that came from the colonies. But for the Peberdy and Garnett lines other historical changes had greater direct impact on how they lived. The improvements in public health and sanitation from the mid nineteenth century may not be a wildly exciting subject, but in conjunction with the various factory and workplace acts it dramatically improved the conditions for people living in cities like Leicester. Probably the most significant of Victorian legislation for our families was in education; it became compulsory for children to attend school up to their early teens. Each decade of the twentieth century saw the introduction of new reforms that gave the men and women of the 1900s a level of security and well-being that their own grandparents would hardly have comprehended: old age pensions, higher school leaving ages, the National Health Service, and for bright working-class children access to tertiary education. Within 100 years the families had progressed from making an 'x' on their wedding certificates to receiving a higher degree from the hands of a university Vice-Chancellor.

The Britain of the seventh generation and the Britain of Alexander and Felix are also different in a more profound way than the observable levels of prosperity and education. There were just 9.1 million people in 1801. This had grown fourfold by 1911 to 36 million, while today it is almost 60 million and heading for a forecasted 70 million. But not only are there more of us; the diversity of people is far greater. Few of the ancestors who lived all their lives in Britain would ever have met a person with a non-white skin, and other than seeing a few black American GIs during the Second World War this was the case up to the 1960s. The range of cultures and languages that we experience as part of everyday life was something unknown. For our grandparents it was class and class differences that distinguished people. Rarely did this lead to angst or conflict because the grandparents 'knew their place'. It is amusing to read in the early baptismal records that the parents of the newborn child would have this place identified – the father's position in society was allocated to either 'Quality, Trade or Profession'. When Thomas George Evers arrived in Calcutta in the 1890s he would have known where he fitted in the social pecking order, but if he were in any doubt he had only to open his copy of the Thackeray's Directory and refer to the Orders of Precedence; there it would be specified with absolute clarity who his host would sit him next to at dinner. Similarly the Peberdys and Garnetts who worked as agricultural labourers in the nineteenth century knew how they should relate to their employer, and like George Dewsbury, the retired country-man, would not have entered the farmhouse, even if invited by the farmer's wife, if the *master* was not at home.

War and the fear of war were not just things that the grandparents read about in newspapers or talked about with neighbours, they were directly and often tragically affected by conflicts. In the nineteenth century the casualties were soldiers and sailors, or if civilians then civilians in other countries. Midshipman Sartorius fought at the Battle of Trafalgar, one of his sons in the First Afghan War and another in the Ashanti Wars in West Africa. But in 1914 everything about war changed. This was the first conflict when the entire population was affected, not just the young men who fought but their families back home. The unprecedented scale of the deaths meant that no family escaped the mourning of a relative. By 1918 there were three million widows and six million orphans. Parents like Dr Kenneth Ingleby-Mackenzie and his wife lost their son. Annie Green with the loss of her husband was faced with bringing up her two infant daughters on a small war pension. The effect of the Great War did not end when the grieving ceased. It had a profound effect on society as a whole, and led to old certainties and relationships being challenged in a way that no one could have imagined at the turn of the century. For those left to cope in the aftermath it led to certain attitudes and responses; attitudes that were passed on to the next generations. Grandma Annie Green struggled during the 1920s and 30s to keep her family together. It was work and making do that was the centre of her life, not consuming or seeking pleasure; not taking risk and not getting into debt were her guiding principles. These were the values she passed on to her girls, one of whom in turn passed them on to her son.

Civilians in the 1939–45 war became targets in a way that had hardly happened in the 1914–18 conflict. Cities like Leicester were deliberately bombed in an attempt to destroy factories and demoralise the population. None of the grandparents died in the Second World War but like everybody else for five years the war determined how they led their lives. The men wore uniforms: Kenneth Evers was a young army officer in North Africa and then Northern Europe; Naval Surgeon Alexander Ingleby-Mackenzie was treating injured sailors; Ernest Garnett was a military policeman; Ernest Peberdy a district fire officer and Walter Peberdy a police constable. Few of the women wore uniforms but they *did their bit* – they worked in factories or volunteered to provide the drinks and food to keep the street wardens going; they ran their homes on frugal budgets and managed the family ration cards, and if they had a garden or allotment they dug for victory. And at times they were in the very thick of the war for when the German bombers blitzed the cities they were the ones organising the long nights in the Anderson shelters.

As had happened after the Great War, society changed after 1945. At one level people were optimistic that the bad old days of the 1930s were passed and that the new peacetime government would build a better and more equitable country. The creation of the National Health Service epitomised this hope, and by and large it did deliver. When Ernest Peberdy was dying of lung cancer in 1949 his medical treatment was free, and the old fears that the family would not be able to find the money for medicines was no longer an anxiety. Yet at another level Britain was in a period of post-traumatic shock; the war had turned upside down so much of the familiar. Many husbands had been absent for years and were strangers to their children; many children had been evacuated to safer rural areas and on their return were strangers themselves in their own homes; women had worked in jobs with levels of responsibility they had not known before but were now expected to fall back into their traditional roles. From the end of the war to the mid 1950s there was a retreat to the safe familiar things – familiar ways, familiar relationships and familiar rituals. All this was taking place in the context of austerity when shortages were often even greater than they had been during the war itself. But slowly things did become easier, and rationing finally ended in the 1950s. This was the world that grandparents Kenneth, Felicity, Max and Alyson knew so well. This was also the start of the Cold War and the very real fear of a nuclear and totally destructive Third World War. When President Kennedy confronted the Soviet Union over their siting of missiles on Cuba, ordinary people knew that the world was very close to conflict. Schoolboy Max sat and ate his lunchtime sandwiches listening to the radio news bulletin updating the country on whether Soviet ships were still heading for Cuba or whether they had changed course and were sailing away from the island. No one could have guessed that by the early

1990s the Berlin Wall would have tumbled and the Soviet Union been consigned to the history books. Countries once hidden behind the Iron Curtain became holiday destinations for the grandparents.

Most of the stories in this book are about men. For at least five of the seven generations it was the men who held the power, both in the workplace and as head of the family. The status and well-being of a woman was almost entirely determined by that of her husband. Scrolling through hundreds of pages of household census returns between 1841 and 1911 it is only rarely that any married woman has an entry under 'occupation'. Only unmarried daughters or widowed mothers are recorded as having a job. Of course many of those married to agricultural labourers would have earned extra money helping out with seasonal tasks on the farm, and in fact some farmers made it a condition of employment that family members all helped out at harvest. But for most women, if they married rich men their role was to manage the servants and household expenditure; if they married poor men they washed the dirty clothes on Monday, dried them on Tuesday, ironed them on Wednesday, cleaned on Thursday, baked on Friday or Saturday and ensured that the family dressed smartly for Church on Sunday.

It was during war that some middle-class women had roles outside the home – like great, great grandmother Edith Billing who was a nursing auxiliary in Caernarfon in 1914, and great grandmother Violetta in the Red Cross in the Second World War. Today it is taken for granted (well, almost) that women fulfil the same responsibilities in society as men, so we can imagine the frustration of strong, talented women constrained by the narrow norms of the day. Great, great grandmother Edith and her sister Alice did have 'independent means' in their later teenage years after their parents had died, and Alice used her freedom to do what she wanted; she ran away to London with her music teacher.

Unfortunately there is no evidence that any of the female ancestors was a suffragette, and we have to wait until the 1980s before grandmother Alyson chained herself to the perimeter fence at a US air base in Oxfordshire to protest at the siting of cruise missiles on British soil. She later turned her attention to the injustice of women not being able to be priests in the Church of England and became the Vice-Moderator of the Movement for the Ordination of Women. But generally we have to admit that our females have not been at the forefront of social reform.

Children and their histories are also in short supply. We have the account of Jacob Unna's 12 year old grandson who wrote about his grandfather's 80th birthday party, and we know about the walk that young Freda and Ethel Billing took which nearly led to the premature death of the future Lord Cledwyn, but there are no direct words from children until the accounts of the four grandparents. The reality for many born in to the eighteenth and nineteenth centuries was that they never became adults and did not live long enough to have stories to tell. The death of a young son or daughter was commonplace and some historians believe that this in part explains why parents were much more aloof and emotionally distant from their children, a self protection in the knowledge that the child could quite easily die; they were for example loath to show physical affection in the way that today's parents do without a second thought. Certainly all the parents up to the mid twentieth century would have related very differently to their children from how Alexander and Felix experience their parents; and the concept of childhood is also very different today. Children for much of history were treated as *small adults* who needed to be taught how to behave as small adults. It is only relatively recently that the development needs of children have been understood, while the concept of *teenagers,* an age group with their own aspirations, purchasing power and culture, did not appear till the 1950s.

Fathers were distant figures. In middle-class families children would be sent off to boarding school from the age of seven, while families like the Everses in India said goodbye to their sons at five when they took ship back to England. John and Charles Rebenack would hardly have known their parents as they attended school in Kent, and only months after the event learned of their mother's death in Bombay, followed a few years later by their father. Parents a hundred years ago had the same emotions as parents today; it was just not the done thing to express them to the outside world, so we can imagine their pain when they sent their children away. They believed it was the right thing to do, and certainly within middle-class culture it was what everybody did and not to have done the same would have led to criticism and ridicule. Poorer families were not faced with such decisions; their children were at home until they married, or if the house was too crowded, then living close by with a relative. But even with this proximity parents did not *play* with their children; a family walk on Sundays, a day trip to the seaside or music in the front parlour, these things were possible, but children were expected to take part in such activities as well behaved young adults, not with the excitement of a child.

Researching and writing this book has taken three years, and given that we have very full and busy lives such a commitment had the potential to become a task to get finished rather than the very enjoyable process that it became. We have been fortunate in this as not all experience the publication of a book as such a labour of love. Uncovering the early career of Admiral Sir George Rose Sartorius led us a naval dictionary written by William O'Byne in 1849. His opening paragraph, words from his heart, ensured that we placed a strict time boundary around our efforts:

At length, after six years of unremitting toil, mental and physical, I have succeeded, to the entire exclusion of every other pursuit, in accomplishing an undertaking deemed by most as arduous, to many impractical, disheartening truly in the perpetual, but in retrospect a source to me of some gratification and, I hope I may add, of honourable pride. (William R. O'Byrne. *A Naval Biography Dictionary*, 1849.)

Three years we gave ourselves and three years later we are finishing. Of course there is no end to researching family history, for as one wit once said, 'the trouble with history is that it is just one thing after another'. But it does mean that when Alexander and Felix approach the age of 60, in about the year 2055, and wish to research further there is lots left for them to do. By then genetic analysis may be so advanced that they will be able to identify their maternal grandmother to the 80th generation living in a Roman villa in Derbyshire, and the first man with the Evers family name to a twelfth century farmer in Yorkshire. We have left plenty of loose ends for grandsons to tidy up: why did the Mackenzies move south of the Border? Is HMS *Effingham's* bell with Felicity's name inscribed lying on the seabed off Norway or was it salvaged? Can we trace the Inglebys back to Frances Ingleby who was hung, drawn and quartered in 1586 and thus claim a martyr and a saint in the family? Why was Manoah Peberdy given such a distinctive name? And what did happen to the portrait of Serine after it was inherited by Dame Peggy Ashcroft?

If there is any sense of disappointment on our part it is the frustration of not knowing more about how they all thought and how they behaved to each other. We know their jobs, where they lived and how many children they had, and for a few their personalities were so strong that they did call out to us, but for the majority we can only guess at their character. Were they grumpy or nice people? Mean or generous? And the real test, would we have enjoyed their company on a two-week holiday to Greece?

Perhaps the closest we can get to knowing them in this sense is to look at the photographs that have survived. Most are the classic formal photographs taken at weddings or on the eve of departures but others show their happiness on holidays and when playing sport. Alexander and Felix may be able to spot the origins of some of their own features, the chin, the eyes, the forehead, and catch a glimpse of the man or woman behind the expression, more often friendly than distant.

Men in military caps and topees
Modest women wearing wedding veils,
Victorian sons stand stiffly for the camera,
Edwardian daughters attempt a pose.

Like treasures from a Pharaoh's tomb
These photographs lay in long neglected places,
Dug out and shown when would-be brides paid call
Then buried again in the sands of the everyday.

Do we see ourselves? Well yes . . .
The forehead that is Jessie as a child,
The Mackenzie chin once shaped from Seaforth land,
And Evers' eyes searching for Indian hills.

More vulnerable than mites in amber,
These photographs survived.
The rest have long since gone,
Lost in the tidiness of life.

Soon this book will also find its way
To landfill site or council burner,
So take a look at those who went before
And keep them safely in your smile.

APPENDICES

APPENDIX A
The Methodology

The simplest way to summarise how we did the research is to describe the process chronologically:

Step 1. **The start**: we began with the relatives still alive and recorded what they could remember of parents and grandparents, and the things they had been told about great grandparents. This was an obvious starting point and though it yielded some good material we were surprised by how little families knew about those who had gone before.

Step 2. **Searching through existing family documents and photographs:** certificates of birth, marriage and death helped us to identify forenames and key dates. This was vital because we needed to identify relatives living before 1901. The date was important because it was the latest year that the ten yearly household census data was available (during the research the 1911 material was released). Four family documents were especially helpful: Violetta Ingleby-Mackenzie's hand-written family tree; Robert Peberdy's research on the Peberdys of Saddington; Freda Owen's (Billing) written account of her childhood in Wales, and Angus Mackenzie-Charrington's history of his father, Alexander Ingleby-Mackenzie.

Step 3. **Using the web:** Family research is like field archaeology in that you start with the top layers and carefully work downwards. We started with the great grandparents and eventually got back to the seventh generation. We used the family website ancestry.co.uk as a main tool to trace BMDs and the household census records back to the 1840s. Other collections on this site enabled us to look at passenger ship lists and convict records for those transported to Australia. A range of other websites provided historical information about geographical locations. Once we had dates for births, marriages and death we applied online to GRO for copies of BMD certificates; this then gave us maiden names, and more information about occupations.

Step 4. **Getting back before the 1840s:** Official registration began in 1837 so before that date the main source of information for our ancestors (predominantly Church of England and living in England or Scotland) are the parish church records now held at County Record Offices. We visited these offices, or commissioned specialist ancestry researchers, to explore these records. The Leicestershire County Records Office was relevant to the Peberdy family, while the specialist researchers looked at the county offices: Sara Scargill in Staffordshire for the Inglebys; Vanessa Morgan in Warwickshire for the ancestors living on the Packington Hall estate; and Ruth Simpson in Yorkshire for the Evers. The Yorkshire researcher also explored the Bradford records for the Unna and Lewis families.

Step 5. **War records:** The military record of Kenneth Evers was obtained from the Army Personnel Centre (Historical Disclosures Section), and the military records of Keith Ingleby-Mackenzie, T. G. Evers and Alexander Ingleby-Mackenzie were identified by Geoff Dewing, a specialist military researcher, from the material held at the National Archives in Kew. War-grave websites gave information about Herbert Green and Keith Ingleby-Mackenzie.

Step 6. **British Library:** Many, many visits to the India Room of the British Library identified BMDs of the Walkers, Simms, Liddells, and Johnsons. The East India Company archive gave the career records of the Rebenacks, and various reference books described the Sartorius family. Directories and Calcutta newspapers had references to T. G. Evers and his sporting success in Calcutta.

Step 7. **Society of Genealogists:** their library provided information about the careers of ancestors in the professions (doctors, dentists and clergy), school histories gave information about Kenneth's time at Winchester; and trade directories identified grandparent's businesses in Manchester and London. Other sources gave background information about occupations like ore smelting and malt making, and local history books described the village locations during the period. The Society also holds parish records on microfilm that enabled us to explore early BMDs.

Step 8. **Putting the data together:** As information was collected the four family lines were drawn on four large boards (each three feet x two feet).

This allowed the seven generations to be constructed in the traditional family tree format with the names of siblings (where known) included.

Step 9. **Historical context:** To understand the time in which the grandparents lived we read more than 40 books relating to specific periods or events. The Frameworkers Museum in Wigston provided a physical link to some of the ancestors who had worked in this occupation less than half a mile away. Two Leicester historians were also helpful in describing the Leicester fire service and police force in the early twentieth century.

Step 10. **Drafting the book:** Notes were written throughout the information collection and these formed the basis of the first four chapters. Family members and others read early drafts to check for accuracy. Each of the three grandparent authors wrote their life stories and drafts shared for comment. Material for Kenneth's Story was provided by Felicity, Tim, Bruce and Angus Evers, with extra information from his war record and regimental history.

Step 11. **Photographs:** Once a first draft had been completed photographs were selected to illustrate people and places.

Step 12. **Finally:** The final format of the book was put together by a professional copy editor, a typographer and a designer.

From start (Step 1) to finish (Step 12) was three years.

Family Trees

Going back seven generations, the study identified 203 of the grand-parents, and a further 39 in generations 8, 9, and 10. For the grandfathers to be classed as *identified* both forenames and family name had to be known (and ideally at least the date of birth); in addition, for grand-mothers their name before marriage had to be known.

Given this large number of ancestors a representation in the traditional family tree format would be hugely complex and very difficult to understand. As an alternative the four family lines of the genetic contributors to Alexander and Felix, ie the direct ancestors but not the siblings, is shown in two tables. Appendix B Table 1 shows the ancestors of Angus Evers, and Table 2 those of Morag Peberdy.

It is interesting to see the different family surnames that appear in the 200 hundred years or so: to take the analogy described in the introduction these families are the streams and brooks that joined the four main surname rivers of the grandparents. In total 88 different family lines were identified.

EVERS: Walker, Woodhead, Kidd, Sim, Cockerill, Kendrew, Thackeray, Liddell, Johnson, Spenley, Lindley, Bagshaw, Craven, Jepson, Armsden, Greig and Turner.

INGLEBY-MACKENZIE: Taylor, Longstaffe, Mackenzie, Rebenack, Poole, Sale, Lawrence, Lewis, Unna, Ingleby, Richards, Bowzer, Gray, Glass, Heineman, Sartorius, Solomon, Weston, Smith, Walker, Gilliat, Stein, Arthur, Adam and Davis.

PEBERDY: Green, Duffin, Wall, Storer, Adkin, Hutchinson, Wright, Fulford, Holmes, Cook, Downes, Harper, Wood, Gamble, Noon, Swale, Copeland, Smith, Layne, Barker, Simson, Shuttleworth, Swain, Norman, Tauveley, Shirley and Goode.

GARNETT: Billing, Hackett, Betteley, Arthur, Mason, Goode, Cock-shoot, Colesworthy, Waterhouse, Holmes, Cleaver, Leonard, Eldred, Cooke and Cowley.

The two tables list the grandparents by generation.

Table 1: The Evers and Ingleby-Mackenzie family lines
Angus Evers b. 1918 (father of Alexander and Felix Evers)

Grandparents:	Kenneth Evers b. 1918	Felicity Ingleby-Mackenzie b. 1930
Great grandparents	Thomas George Evers b. 1877 and Dorothy Jean Lamond Walker b. 1886	Alexander Ingleby-Mackenzie b. 1892 and Violetta Longstaffe b. 1902
Great, great grandparents	George Evers b. 1855 and Hannah Woodhead b. 1858 William Walker b. 1850 and Beatrice Sim b. 1860	Kenneth Ingleby Mackenzie b. 1864 and Florence Sale b. 1862 Amyas Longstaffe b. 1859 and Alice Lewis b. 1861
Great, great, great grandparents	Thomas Evers b. 1824 and Mary Kendrew b. 1827 George Woodhead b. 1803 and Sarah Kidd b. 1818 George Walker b. 1819 and Susan Gertrude Liddell b. 1828 William Sim b. about 1828 and Elizabeth Jane Johnson b. 1829	John Ingleby Mackenzie b. 1834 and Emily Elisa Rebenack b. 1840 Richard Sale b. 1826 and Mary Poole b. 1831 John Longstaffe b. 1835 and Clara Taylor b. 1836 Leopold Lewis b. 1832 and Violetta Unna b. 1840
Great, great, great, great grandparents	George Evers b. 1778 and Eleanor Cockerill b. 1792 William Kendrew b. 1801 and Ann Thackeray b. 1806 John Jepson b. 1776 and Clarissa Woodhead b. 1778 Thomas Kidd b. about 1795 and Ellen ? William Walker b. about 1780 and Jean Lamond b. 1781 William Liddell b. about 1780 and Susanna Armsden b. about 1790 Joshua Sim b. about 1800 and ? George William Johnson b. 1801 and Jane Jepson b. 1805	John Andrew Mackenzie b. 1810 and Ellen Ingleby b. 1811 Charles Rebenack b. 1800 and Elizabeth Turville Bowzer b. 1806 William Longstaffe b. about 1804 and Sarah Paine Lawrence b. about 1808 Henry Lemon Taylor b. ? and Emma Ann? Alexander Poole b. 1801 and Mary ? b. 1801 Richard Sale b. 1802 and Emma ? b. 1802 William Longstaffe b. about 1775 and Ann Gilliat b. about 1777 Lazarus Levy Lewis b? and ? Jacob Arnold Unna b. 1801 and Serine Solomon b. 1813

Great, great, great, great, great grandparents	John Evers b. 1745 and Ann Spenley b. 1737 William Kendrew b. about 1775 and Mary Thackeray b. about 1777 Henry Woodhead b. 1749 and Elizabeth Lindley b. ? Alexander Lamond b. about 1760 and Jane Greig b. about 1760 William Johnson b. about 1780 and ?	Andrew Mackenzie b. 1769 and Helen Gray b. ? John Ingleby b. 1781 and Sarah Richards b. 1790 Johannes Rebenack b. 1775 and Caroline Heineman b. ? William Sale b. 1772 and ?
Great, great, great, great, great, great grandparents	John Woodhead b. 1722 and Elizabeth Bagshaw b. ? William Spenley b. 1688 and Ursula Craven b. about 1690	John Lawrence b. about 1765 and Elizabeth Smith b. about 1767 John Mackenzie b. 1742 and Janet Glass b. ? Andreas Rebenack b. about 1750 and Sophia Carolina Sartorius b. ? John Ingleby b. 1749 and Christian Weston b. 1746 Abraham Longstaffe b. about 1750 and ?
Great, great, great, great, great, great, great grandparents	John Woodhead b. 1688 and Ann Turner b. ?	John Mackenzie b. about 1704 and Alison Stein b. ? Hugh Ingleby b. 1723 and Anne Davis b. about 1725
Great, great, great, great, great, great, great, great grandparents	John Woodhead b. about 1660 and Ellen b. ?	Andrew Mackenzie b. 1676 and Helen Arthur b. ? Richard Ingleby b. about 1685 and Sarah b. ?
Great, great, great, great, great, great, great, great grandparents		John Mackenzie b. about 1650 and Christian Adam b. ?

Table 2: The Peberdy and Garnett family lines
Morag Peberdy (mother of Alexander and Felix Evers)

	Max Peberdy b. 1947	Alyson Garnett b. 1948
Grandparents		
Great grandparents	Walter Peberdy b. 1913 and Jessie Green b. 1914	Ernest Garnett b. 1908 and Ethel Billing b. 1906
Great, great grandparents	Ernest Peberdy b. 1889 and Emma Duffin b. 1888 Herbert Green b. 1890 and Annie Isabelle Wall b. 1894	Jesse Garnett b. 1886 and Martha Hackett b. 1888 Frederick Billing b. 1873 and Edith Betteley b. 1881
Great, great, great grandparents	Tom Peberdy b. 1864 and Ann Storer b. 1863 George Duffin b. 1862 and Elizabeth Noon b. 1863 Edwin Green b. 1849 and Eliza Holmes b. 1854 William Wall b. 1864 and Emily Cook b. 1871	James Garnett b. 1845 and Jane Arthur b. 1846 Benjaman Hackett b. 1862 and Elizabeth Mason b. 1862 John Billing b. 1848 and Anne Goode b. 1848 Stephen Betteley b. 1842 and Elizabeth Cockshoot b. 1858
Great, great, great, great grandparents	Manaoh Peberdy b. 1836 and Jane Wood b. 1836 Thomas Storer b. 1833 and Elizabeth Noon b. 1831 Charles Duffin b. 1835 and Elizabeth Ann Copeland b. 1841 William Adkin b. 1839 and Elizabeth Smith b. 1842 George Green b. 1828 and Mary Downes b. 1829 James Holmes b. 1828 and Elizabeth Hutchinson b. 1827 Richard Wall b. 1825 and Eliza Fulford b. 1828 James Cook b. 1842 and Isabella Harper b. 1844	Thomas Garnett b. 1804 and Mary Colesworthy b. 1805 James Arthur b. 1821 and Mary Cleaver b. 1823 William Hackett b. 1820 and Sarah Leonard b. 1822 James Mason b. 1831 and Ann ? b. 1832 Joseph Billing b. 1818 and Eleanor Eldred b. 1822 Samuel Goode b. 1827 and Elizabeth Billing b. 1823 Stephen Betteley b. 1799 and Mary Ann Cooke b. 1813 Edward Cockshoot b. 1824 and Mary Ann Waterhouse b. 1830

Great, great, great, great, great grandparents	William Peberdy b. 1795 and Elizabeth Layne b. 1799 Richard Wood b. 1796 and Catherine ? b. 1796 William Storer b. 1798 and Mary Gamble b. 1793 John Noon b. 1796 and Ann Swale b. 1794 William Duffin b. 1801 and Sarah Barker b. 1796 William Copeland b. 1811 and Ann Simson b. 1812 William Adkin b. 1816 and ? Edmund Smith b. 1811 and Elizabeth ? b. 1816 William Green b. 1801 and Charlotte ? b. 1796 ? Downes b. about 1809 and Elinner ? b. 1793 John Hutchinson b. 1803 and Mary Wright b. 1803 Richard Wall b. about 1805? Samuel Fulford b. 1786 and Sarah Wall b. 1800 Charles Cook b. 1800 and Prudence Shuttleworth b. 1798 William Harper b. 1791 and Sarah Swain b. 1811	William Garnett b. 1778 and Elizabeth Cowley b. 1782 Colesworthy b. about 1780 and ? James Arthur b. 1776 and ? Thomas Cleaver b. 1791 and ? John Hackett b. 1801 and Mary ? b. 1796 Henry Leonard b. about 1795 and Ann ? b. 1796 Samuel Goode b. 1807 and ? John Billing b. 1791 and Elizabeth ? b. 1795 Edward Cockshoot b. ? and ? Robert Waterhouse b. 1805 and Ann Holmes b. 1814
Great, great, great, great, great, great grandparents	James Swain b. about 1760 and Elizabeth Shirley b. 1760 John Peberdy b. 1771 and Ann Norman b. about 1770 William Wall b. 1781 and Elizabeth ? b. 1796 William Copeland b. 1781 and Ann ? b. 1781 John Layne b. 1768 and Sarah Goode b. 1762	James Cowley b. about 1754 and Sarah? b. about 1755
Great, great, great, great, great,great, great grandparents	Thomas Peberdy b. 1719 and Hannah Tauveley b. about 1720 John Lane b. about 1740 and Anne ? Thomas Goode b. about 1735 and Catherine ?	John Holmes b. 1789 and ?
Great, great, great, great, great, great,great great grandparents	John Peberdy b. about 1678 and Elizabeth ?	Robert Holmes b. about 1769 and Ann ?

APPENDIX C

Table 1: Age at Marriage*

	Average for all grandparent ancestors	Evers and their genetic network	Ingleby-Mackenzie and their genetic network	Peberdy and their genetic network	Garnett and their genetic network
MALES Total = 87	28 years	30 years	26 years	25 years	27 years
FEMALES Total = 77	23 years	25 years	23 years	23 years	23 years

* for those ancestors for whom the information is available.

Table 2: Age at Death*

	Average age at death	Evers and their genetic network	Ingleby-Mackenzie and their genetic network	Peberdy and their genetic network	Garnett and their genetic network
MALES Total =50	68 years	79 years	64 years	66 years	77 years
FEMALES Total =36	71 years	73 years	70 years	72 years	65 years

By century of birth

MALES	born before 1800	Total 16	77 years
MALES	born 1800 or after	Total 34	67 years
FEMALES	born before 1800	Total 10	69 years
FEMALES	born 1800 or after	Total 26	71 years

* for those ancestors for whom information is available.

BIBLIOGRAPHY

Aitkin, W. F. (1912) *The Family Friend,* Annual for 1913, Partridge and Co., London.

Allan, J. and Dodwell H. H. (1964), *The Cambridge Shorter History of India,* Chand, India.

Allen, C. (2008) *Plain Tales from the British Empire,* Abacus, London.

Beazley, B. (2001), *Peelers to Panda: An illustrated history of the Leicester City Police,* Breedon Books, Derby.

Beazley, B. (2004), *Wartime Leicester,* Sutton Publishing, Glos.

Best, G. (1979), *Mid Victorian Britain 1851–75,* Fontana.

Blatchford, R (2002), 6th edn, *Family and Local History Handbook,* The Genealogical Services Directory.

Briggs, A. (1979),*Victorian Cities,* Pelican.

Cabell, C. and Richards, A. (2005), *VE Day: A Day to Remember,* Pen and Sword Military, Barnsley.

Chinnery, G. A. (1974), *Records of the Borough of Leicester,* Leicester University Press.

Christian, P. (2005),*The Genealogist's Internet,* 3rd edn, The National Archives, London.

Clarke, J. (1977), *The Price of Progress: Cobbett's England 1780–1835,* Granda Publishing, UK.

Cobbett, W. (no date), *Rural Rides,* Volume Two, Dent, London.

Cobbett, W. (1926 edn), *Cottage Economy.*

Craven, E., as quoted in *The Four Graces and other Prayers to Celebrate Radnor 2000 AD,* Bourdillon, P. and Gibson-Watt, M. (1999), 1st edn, Bluestone Books, Pembrokeshire.

Creash and Humphries (1920), *The Victoria Cross 1856–1920.* London.

Delafore, P. (2008), *Monty's Marauders,* Pen and Sword Military, Barnsley.

Fielden, P. (1991), *Swings and Roundabouts,* privately published.

Fussell, G. E. and K. R. (1985), *The English Countrywoman,* 2nd edn, Bloomsbury Books, London.

Gilbert, W. (1828), Personal diary held in Leicestershire County Records Office, Wigston, Leicestershire.

Gordon, Colin (1980), *By Gaslight in Winter: A Victorian Family History through the Magic Lantern,* Elm Tree Books.

Gretton, R. H. (1930), *A Modern History of the English People 1880–1922*, Martin Secker, London.

Herber, M. (2005), 2nd edn, *Ancestral Trails*, Sutton Publishing, Society of Genealogists, London.

Hollowell, S. (2000), *Enclosure Records for Historians*, Phillimore, West Sussex.

Hoskins, W. G. (1957), *The Midland Peasant*, Macmillan, London.

Inder, Pam and Aldis, Marion (2002), *Finding Susanna*, Churnet Valley Books.

Jeffrey, D. (1931), *Thornton le Dale*, West Yorkshire Printing.

Judd, D. (1997), *Empire: The British Imperial Experience from 1765 to the Present*, Fontana.

Kynaston, D. (2009), *Family Britain,* Bloomsbury Books, London.

Lucas, O. D. (1993), *One Man's Wigston*, Leicestershire Museums, Arts and Records Service Publications no. 24.

O'Byrne, W. R. (1849), *A Naval Biography Dictionary*, British Library Collection.

Pitt-Rivers, J. A. (no date), *The Story of the Royal Dragoons 1938–1945*, William Clowes and Sons, London.

Pomery, C. (2007), *Family History in the Genes*, The National Archives Publications.

Sainsbury, K. (1976), *The North African Landings*, 1942, Davis Poyntor, London.

Snell, J. B. (1972), *Early Railways*, Octopus Books, London.

Somerville, D. (2008), *The Ultimate Illustrated History of World War II*, Anness Publishing, Hermes House, London.

Stevenson, J. (1984), *British Society 1914–1918*, Pelican.

Thompson, E. P. (1963),*The Making of the English Working Class*, Penguin, London.

Thomson, D. (1950), *England in the Nineteenth Century (1815–1914)*, Penguin.

Waugh, E. (1945), *Brideshead revisited,* Penguin Books.

Wigston Framework Knitters Museum (1999), *Notes on Framework Knitting*, Wigston, Leicestershire.

Williams, A. (1978), *Trains and Railways*, Purnell and Sons.

Young, G. M. (1953), 2nd edn, *Victorian England: Portrait of an Age*, Oxford University Press.

INDEX